Praise for
Keeping Your Head After Losing Your Job

Losing a job is like losing a piece of yourself. It can cause real damage to your self-image, your mental health and your physical health. Robert Leahy's *Keeping Your Head After Losing Your Job* is a practical guide to picking yourself up, restoring your health and wellbeing, and getting the motivation and confidence to move forward with your life. This invaluable resource also has tips for family members who want to help, but don't know how. Leahy is an international expert in teaching people how to recover from setbacks and live healthier, productive lives.
~ **Dr. Susan Nolen-Hoeksema**, author of the bestselling *Women Who Think Too Much*

Tough economic times bring tough psychological challenges -and that's where *Keeping Your Head After Losing Your Job* comes in. It's based on the best research for what really helps people cope - changing your thinking. You might not be able to avoid losing your job, but you can try to avoid the depression that comes along with it. The book also has invaluable practical advice on money management, job searches, and venting without wallowing in victimhood.
~ **Jean M. Twenge, Ph.D.**, Associate Professor of Psychology (San Diego State University) and author of *The Narcissism Epidemic* and *Generation Me*

A great self-esteem book
~ *Healthy Magazine*

Leahy provides psychological tools to help you handle your unemployment, with simple strategies that can be used immediately
~ *Money Magazine*

Every unemployed person and their family members will want to read internationally renowned psychologist, Dr. Robert L. Leahy's book, *Keeping Your Head After Losing Your Job*. Being unemployed is not simply about losing a job, but it also can involve losing hope, feeling ashamed, becoming isolated, financial worries, losing a sense of who you are and increased family conflicts. With powerful self-help tools for the many difficulties that you face, Dr. Leahy gives wise, compassionate, and empowering advice.

~ **Aaron T. Beck, MD,** Professor Of Psychiatry, University Of Pennsylvania

KEEPING YOUR HEAD AFTER losing your job

HOW TO SURVIVE UNEMPLOYMENT

ROBERT L. LEAHY, PH.D

Author of *The Worry Cure*

Behler™
PUBLICATIONS

USA

Behler Publications

Keeping Your Head After Losing Your Job
A Behler Publications Book

Copyright © 2014 by Robert L. Leahy, PhD.
Cover design by Yvonne Parks -www.pearcreative.ca.

Library of Congress Cataloging-in-Publication Data

Leahy, Robert L.
  Keeping your head after losing your job : how to survive unemployment /
Robert L. Leahy.
      pages cm
    ISBN-13: 978-1-933016-62-7 (pbk.)
    ISBN-13: (invalid) 978-1-933016-61-0 (ebk)
    ISBN-10: 1-933016-62-0 (paperback)
   1.   Unemployment--Psychological aspects. 2.   Self-esteem. 3.
Self-actualization (Psychology) 4.   Stress management.   I. Title.
    HD5708.L3943 2013
    158.7--dc23

                                              2013026416

FIRST PRINTING
ISBN 13: 9781933016-62-7
e-book ISBN 9781933016-61-0

Published by Behler Publications, LLC
North Fayette, PA
 www.behlerpublications.com

Manufactured in the United States of America

To my brother Jim, who is always there

Table of Contents

ACKNOWLEDGEMENTS

It is always a challenge to do justice to the many people to whom I owe a debt of gratitude. But I will try.

Let me begin by thanking my many clients, friends, family members and neighbors who have shared their stories about coping with unemployment. It is their voice and experience that I wished to convey in writing this book. Often the unemployed person feels marginalized, forgotten and desperately helpless, but their stories and their examples of courage and perseverance can give hope to others.

Once again I recognize how invaluable my colleagues at the American Institute for Cognitive Therapy in New York City (www.cognitivetherapynyc.com) have been. They have been gracious enough to allow me to share my ideas about this book and their insight and experience are reflected in whatever is of value. Thanks, especially, to Dennis Tirch and Laura Oliff, who continue to educate me and support our mutual work together. My research and editorial assistant, Poonam Melwani, has been tireless in her detailed devotion to the many projects that we work on.

In North America I am grateful to the many colleagues and mentors that I have had, including Brad Alford, Aaron Beck, Judy Beck, David Burns, Tom Borkovec, David A. Clark, Frank Dattilio, Allison Harvey, Steve Hayes, Stefan Hoffman, Steve Holland, Steve Hollon, Sheri Johnson, Thomas Joiner, Marsha Linehan, Chris Martell, Lynn McFarr, Lata McGinn, Dean McKay, Cory Newman, Art Nezu, Christine Nezu, Susan Nolen-Hoeksema, Christine Purdon, John Riskind, Kelly Wilson, Terry Wilson and many others. Writing is a lonely enterprise that, ironically, reflects the voices of a multitude. Thank you to all.

Thanks, also to my many British colleagues over the years whose work continues to inform and inspire: David M. Clark,

Christopher Fairburn, Melanie Fennell, Paul Gilbert, Emily Holmes, Warren Mansell, Costas Papageorgeo, Roz Shafran, Adrian Wells, Mark Williams and, of course, my good friend Philip Tata. I have been honored over many years to participate in the conferences held by the British Association for Behavioral and Cognitive Psychotherapies as well as the European and world conferences where I have been fortunate to get to know my international colleagues.

My editor at Behler Publications, Lynn Price, has been immensely supportive. Bob Diforio has been my dedicated, skilled, wise and wonderful agent for many years. His dedication to this work and to the message it represents has been far beyond the call of duty. Thank you, once again, Bob, for your friendship and support. And, to my brother, Jim, I am forever grateful for always being there, always generous, always wise. This book is dedicated to him. Finally, I once again realize that words are not enough to express the gratitude I have for my wife, Helen, who is the wind beneath my wings.

INTRODUCTION

There is no doubt that we are currently in a time of economic crisis. This creates a sense of added urgency for you if you are one of those who are unemployed — and it brings the threat of unemployment closer for many who are currently in work; however, it is important to remember that we always have had, and always will have, a substantial proportion of people who are unemployed. Indeed, many of those who are employed right now may well have been unemployed in the past — or will lose their jobs in the future.

Unemployment is a fact of life. I realize that will be of little consolation to you if you are unemployed, but it is vital to understand that you are not alone. I have seen how unemployment can demoralize and humiliate the very best of people — how unemployment becomes a life experience that people often experience in isolation. But it needn't be that way. You can survive unemployment and, although it may seem unlikely at present, even turn it into a positive period in your life.

How is that possible? Because you may not have a choice about what happened to you, but you do have a choice about how you handle your period of unemployment. And let's not underestimate the importance of taking care of yourself during this difficult time. Unsurprisingly, if you are unemployed, you are more likely to suffer a reduction in mental health, life satisfaction and objective physical well-being — and that equates to a greater risk of binge drinking, depression, anxiety and suicide.

Uncomfortable reading, I know, but it highlights how important it is to use all the skills you have — and some new ones — to adjust to your new situation. This book is designed to help you do that. Its purpose is to outline the psychological tools that I believe will help you to cope better with your period of unemployment. It is not a book on how to get a job, succeed at interviews or write a CV. It is far more important. It is a book that will help you — and your family members — cope more effectively during a period that may be the most difficult one you will ever face. Over the years I have worked with many unemployed people and have family members and friends who have faced unemployment, therefore a lot of what is in this book is based on what my clients, friends and family members have taught me about what works—and what doesn't work—during this time. It may be a difficult period, but there are things that you can learn that will help you deal with this time more productively, and indeed help you to live your life more effectively once you get a job. You can think of this time as "this is happening to me" or you can think of this as "I am going to make things happen." You can be passive or active; you can wait for the next job or take control of your life today and make your life your job. How you handle the "job" of being in between your last job and the next will be up to you. I have spent many years working as a cognitive behavior therapist and have found that a lot of the ideas that are used in cognitive-behavioral therapy, or CBT, have been helpful to clients of mine who had to cope with unemployment. Throughout this book I rely on the power of CBT. Quite simply, it is a form of psychotherapy that emphasizes changing the way you think ("cognition") and the way you behave. It isn't a long, drawn-out process (I won't ask you to examine your childhood, for example). Yes, it can take a little time to perfect some of the techniques, but rest assured that each self-help chapter will have simple techniques that can be used immediately to help you feel better and to act better. In the book you will find exercises to help you work through the suggestions and techniques that I have described. You may choose to complete some of these in the charts provided or you could use a notebook instead. There is no doubt that unemployment is an unfortunate and difficult time—and for a large number it is the most difficult time that they have ever faced—but by keeping your head and learning how to deal with this time well you can also learn how to live your life more effectively once you get a job. Unemployment is a time for new priorities and new meanings. It can also be a time when you rediscover what truly matters to you.

1
LOOKING DIFFERENTLY AT
WHERE YOU ARE NOW

You have lost your job and find yourself sinking into the depths of painful and confusing feelings. You may feel that this is one of the worst times in your life. Going home to tell your family that you are out of work is the most difficult experience that you have ever had. You feel embarrassed, you feel you have let them down, you feel that your world is crashing down on you. No longer leaving home to go to work, you sit alone, the hours drag on, then the days, and then the endless weeks out of work. You have nowhere to go.

You find yourself dwelling on your situation and think, "I never thought this would ever happen to me." Often you find yourself alone with your thoughts and feelings, not knowing when you will get out of this, not knowing if you will ever get a job that you would like. You worry about your finances and what your friends and family think, and you feel embarrassed telling people that you are not working. You are angry, confused, anxious, and depressed. At times, you even wonder if this could really be true. If you are unemployed, you are not alone.

I would suggest that you think of this time as "in between"—that is, the time in your life between the last job and the next.

You are not alone

To understand how others cope with this experience, let's look at a few people who have gone through what you are going through now.

Claire had been working in her marketing job for the last six years and she thought she was doing a good job. But business had been falling off, people were spending less on marketing, and business people were afraid of the condition in the economy. For a while things were not looking good, and then the "axe fell": Clare got laid off. Unemployed for four months, living alone, worried about finances, feeling like she had failed, and angry that she was in this predicament, Claire felt more and more discouraged.

Ed has three children and had worked at the company for over 15 years, but with new competition in the field, the company no longer needed him. Without a university degree and without a lot of savings, he took "a package" to leave, but he actually had no alternative. With income for a couple of years, he had to work out what to do to take care of his family. A lot of other friends and family over the years had also lost their jobs, so he knew it wasn't just him. Some had taken to isolating themselves, whereas others had taken to drinking. Ed decided that he would do whatever it took to make things work. Today he has several part-time jobs, none of which pays very well, but all of which add up to enough to live on and enough to support his family. He cuts grass, drives a local school bus and repairs computers. At 60, he looks in better physical shape than most people who are 30. He said to me, "I am working all the time. I have to."

Tom had been working at his company for over twenty-five years. They were downsizing and laid him off. Prone to depression in the past, he came back into therapy to see me, to get some support and some ideas on how to cope. For two months before coming in he had been sitting at home dwelling on how unfair this was, how he felt ashamed, and how he worried about taking care of his family. He was feeling sad and inclined to isolate himself, but we started working together to turn things around.

I said, "Let's consider this the time in-between your last job and your next job. Let's not waste this opportunity to make things better. Let's develop a plan and follow it through."

These are three people with three stories and you will meet others in this book. Your story might be similar, but perhaps it's different. There are tens of millions of stories about people who have been unemployed—or who are now unemployed. Each person copes with it in their own way, often approaching their time of unemployment with some of the same problematic or adaptive styles that they might use with other negative life events. Ironically, even though the chances are quite good that someone will experience unemployment at some point in their work history—or that their spouse will—no one has ever trained us in how to cope with this normal and difficult life event. There is no university course that you can take called "Unemployment Basics"—even though many people with degrees will have a period of unemployment. It may feel like you are a "different kind of person" because you are unemployed, but you are the same as you were before—and what has happened to you can happen to anyone.

Let's take a look at how widespread unemployment is, so that you will know that you are not alone. And then we will look at the downside of being unemployed, so that you will know that you need to take action to cope with this difficult time. Unemployment can affect your health, your self-esteem, your family relationships, and your risk of depression. It's important that you do all you can to cope the best you can.

It's bad enough to be out of work, but you have a choice about how you deal with your repetitive negative thoughts, how you act and how you relate to the people in your life.

Unemployment is everywhere

When I started writing this book the unemployment rate was 9.1% in the US and over 8% in the UK, with the expectation that unemployment would remain historically quite high for a long period of time. As disturbing as these figures are, it is even worse in many other countries, with Spain having a chronically high level of unemployment over the last three decades (averaging

14.2%), France averaging unemployment of 9.5% for the same period, and some countries showing astronomically high levels of unemployment: Zimbabwe reported in 2009 that its unemployment rate was 97%; many African countries are affected—such as South Africa (25%), Kenya (40%); and countries with political conflict report high rates—such as Kosovo (40%), Tajikistan (60%), Iraq (18%).

In many countries—including the US and the UK—the official unemployment figures often underestimate the actual number of people who are "really" unemployed, since many people have stopped looking for jobs (and are therefore not included in these figures), many others are under-employed (working part time) and many others fail to try to enter the workforce because they are discouraged about their prospects.

Another way of looking at employment is the "labor-force participation rate," which is the percentage of people of working age (16–64) who are actually employed. In the US this had dropped from 68% to 64% between 2008 and late 2011. That means that about 36% of people who are in the employment age range are not working for a salary (Bureau of Labor Statistics, US Department of Labor, 2011, October 7).

The figures were very similar in the United Kingdom. In 2011 the Labor Participation Rate was 62% (World Bank, June 2012).

Many of these people are homemakers, students or people on disability allowance, some are earlier retirees or people not looking for jobs. It's interesting, I think, that in the early 1950s the labor participation rate was about 55%—lower than it is today—primarily because a very high percentage of women were full-time homemakers and, therefore, were not counted as employed. Of course, if you had to pay a mother or wife for all the work she is actually doing, it might bankrupt most families. In my view, they have one of the hardest jobs, 24 hours per day, 365 days a year.

Whatever the current unemployment rate is, it will feel too high for those either unemployed or worried about losing their jobs. Adult men are more likely to be unemployed than adult women, and teenagers and blacks show the highest rates of unemployment. In 2010 the rates of unemployment varied considerably depending on ethnic group (Whites= 4.4%; Asian= 7.4%; Black= 12.1%) (Office for National Statistics, UK, July 2012). But unemployment hits all ethnic groups, all levels of income and educational level and, whoever you are, is difficult to cope with.

What are the costs of unemployment?

As widespread as the problem is, the facts about the effects of unemployment on quality of life are even more distressing. Unemployment is not simply a statistical figure, a number or a political point to make. It is about human beings, their families and their future. And the facts are not comforting.

The first fact to consider is that unemployment actually eventually kills some people. Long-term mortality rates are higher for people who have been previously unemployed. In a study in Finland by Pekka Martikainen of the University of Helsinki, mortality for the previously unemployed was 2.5 times higher than for people not previously unemployed.[1] Even when considering initial health differences and other demographics for the unemployed, the increased mortality is 47%. Margaretha Voss and her colleagues at the Karolinska Institute in Stockholm followed 20,632 twins in Sweden from 1973 to 1996. They found that unemployment increased mortality over this period of time, with significant increases in suicides, injuries and accidents, and with higher mortality rates among the less educated in this group.[2]

Secondly, unemployment leaves a scar for many. That is, the effects seem to continue even when people get a job. This lingering problem includes an increased likelihood of future unemployment,[3] decreased life-time earnings (even when discounting the period of lost earnings during the jobless period) and continued worries about losing the next job.[4] Research by

Paul Gregg and Emma Tominey of the London School of Economics indicates that youths who suffer periods of unemployment have a 13–21% decrease in earnings by the age of 41.[5] If you have been unemployed as a young person, you may be at risk of lower lifetime earnings. Unemployment, for many, may continue to affect life chances.

Thirdly, people who are unemployed have greater risks of a wide range of medical and psychiatric problems including depression, insomnia, anxiety, worry, suicide, feelings of helplessness, low self-esteem, malnutrition, cardiovascular conditions (especially heart attacks), alcoholism, increased smoking and generally poor physical health.[6] The threat of unemployment leads to increases in cholesterol — that is, thinking that you may become unemployed affects your cholesterol level.[7] According to the Pew Research Center and research by others, the unemployed are also at a greater risk of drug abuse and of engaging in crimes, especially burglary.[8] Relationship conflicts, marital distress and the loss of friends are not uncommon among the unemployed.

Fourthly, many of the unemployed delay important life decisions, such as marriage and having children in both the US and UK.[9] The unemployed, fearing the depletion of their financial resources and the uncertainty of future financial security, often experience this "lost time" during their period of joblessness. Life for many seems delayed. The opportunities and freedoms available to the rest of us are lost — some may have a difficult time recovering.

How you may be thinking today

If you are like a lot of other people who are out of work you know that your mind can be a dangerous place to spend time in. You may have had any or all of the following negative thoughts:

- I will never get a job.
- I failed.
- I am a failure.

- Nothing I do works out.
- Everyone will think I'm a loser.
- This is the worst thing that could happen to me.
- I have nothing to do with my time.
- Why me?

These negative thoughts seem to keep coming back; you dwell on them and you think that you will never feel better, never get a job and never get out from where you are. You may also think that "because I am unemployed I have to be unhappy." We are going to work together to change your mind about your mind — just because you are thinking these negative thoughts over and over doesn't make them true. Just because you are out of work for now doesn't mean you can't make your life better. You don't have to believe everything that you think.

You can change the way you think

We are going to look at a number of ways that your mind is working, how to change it, and how to act in your interests rather than passively focusing on the negative. Let's consider the following:

Your feelings matter

If you are unemployed, you are likely to experience a range of feelings — many of which are painful, disturbing and difficult for you. You may experience anger, confusion, frustration, humiliation, anxiety, sadness, hopelessness, helplessness — and even, on occasion, relief that you are no longer working at that job or waiting for the axe to fall. People may have told you to snap out of it, stop feeling sorry for yourself or to think positively. Of course, none of that works, which only makes you feel more alone and more misunderstood. You sometimes feel stuck in the feelings that you have at the moment.

How do you deal with these feelings? Do they make sense? Do you think that your feelings will last forever and do you think anyone understands or cares? Do you isolate yourself, drink, overeat, seek out reassurance or spend endless time surfing the internet to escape these feelings? Are you able to be compassionate and caring towards yourself or do you criticize yourself for the way you feel? Your feelings are important, and the first thing we will deal with in this book is your right to have the feelings you have. You are not a robot.

You need a plan and you need to take action

Have you become passive and isolated without any direction to your daily life? Like many people who lose their job, you wonder what you are going to do with all this time on your hands. You may not have a plan for the day, sitting passively, watching television, worrying, dwelling on the negative. But I am going to suggest that you now have two jobs — the first is looking for a job and the second is taking care of yourself. You have a lot to do, and you need to have a plan. That's where this book comes in.

You are stuck in your repeated negative thoughts

You sit at home, dwelling on the position you are in. Your repetitive negative thoughts—which we call "ruminations"—keep coming back, over and over: "Why me? I can't believe that I am in this position. I feel so bad, so alone, so much like a failure. Will this ever get better?" You sit with these thoughts, hour after hour, day after day, isolated in your head, alone, getting more and more depressed. You keep "looking for an answer," you keep trying to make sense of it, you keep repeating the most negative thoughts, images and feelings. And you get more depressed.

You need to turn your self-criticism into self-correction

Many people who are unemployed complain about a sense of failure, they believe that they are to blame for losing their job. Even though businesses have their ups and downs, and even though many lay-offs are part of national trends in the economy, it's not unusual to blame yourself. Your self-critical thinking only adds to your risk of depression and robs you of the possibility of living your life today. We will look at what you are saying to yourself and how to be more constructive and compassionate. But you might also say, "I actually lost my job because of my own behavior." That does happen; you are not the only one who "got herself fired" — if that is what really happened. If that is true, you have a choice now: either to spend your time blaming yourself or to work out what you have learned to make things better in the future. You have a choice between self-criticism or self-correction.

You need to stop hiding from the world

Some people feel ashamed of their position, often avoiding other people and embarrassed to tell others that they no longer have their job. They believe that other people look down on them and consider them inferior, and they believe that they need to avoid contact with anyone who might think less of them. Some "hide" from the reality of not having a job — one man got dressed in his suit every day, left his home, sat in a park, and came back later in the day, to make others think that he was still working.

You are more than a job

In our society, many people equate their sense of identity with their job and feel that without the job they have no sense of who they are — they have no role in the world in which they live. "Who am I if I don't have a job?" one man said to himself. Others worry about how they will take care of themselves. One woman thought that she would not be able to survive, even though she had savings and had skills that the marketplace demanded.

Being unemployed is often a lonely experience; you feel that the entire world is going to work today — except for you. Hidden in your home, embarrassed to tell friends, the unemployed person often believes that she is an outcast. Afraid to connect with friends and colleagues, embarrassed to contact people, your social support is cut off — often because you are cutting the ties. You may feel, "Who wants to hear me complain? Who wants to deal with someone like me with no job?" Not realizing that almost everyone that you know has either been out of work at some time or has a family member or friend who has been out of work, you often believe that no one could understand, much less have any compassion for you. You think of yourself as a burden to others, "If I call my friend, she won't want to hear about my plight." You think, "How can I take care of my family," as if the only thing that your family ever needed from you was your salary.

Your hopelessness may be temporary

You project into the future, "I will never get a job." Your predictions, for you, have become "facts." Because you repeat these negative predictions over and over you now believe that they must be true. You have been unemployed for some time — weeks, months, perhaps even years — and you are now convinced that you will never get a job. It seems hopeless. You are cursed, stuck, trapped and helpless. You may ask yourself, "Why go on?"

You find yourself arguing with your partner, embarrassed around your children, wanting to withdraw into yourself. You may feel blamed for losing your job or blamed for not trying hard enough to get a new one. You withdraw, thinking that your partner must feel that you are a burden. You become defensive and your partner begins to withdraw from you. You think, "I not only lost my job, but I am losing my marriage and my kids." You get more depressed and angrier. It all seems so hopeless to you.

You are not alone.

How thinking differently can help you

Even though there are always millions of people who are unemployed — and even though millions of others will eventually experience some period of unemployment — the unemployed individual often thinks that he or she is alone, a solitary figure who has failed, that no one could understand and no one could help.

During the economic crisis after October 2008 I was approached by people in the media to discuss how to cope with unemployment. Because I had written popular books on worry (*The Worry Cure: Seven Steps to Stop Worry from Stopping You*) and depression (*Beat the Blues before they Beat You: How to Overcome Depression*), and because I was writing regular blogs on the *Huffington Post* and *Psychology Today*, there was a sense that a therapist like myself could be helpful. People from the *New York Times, Wall Street Journal, The Early Show* on CBS, National Public Radio and many others wanted to hear what a psychologist had to say. As explained in the Introduction, in CBT we focus on what is going on today, not what happened to you when you were a child. It's not that your childhood isn't important, it's just that moving on to make your life better today means thinking, acting and relating in more productive ways.

Your negative thoughts can be transformed

In CBT we help people identify their negative thoughts, we identify short-term and long-term goals and we help you develop powerful tools to challenge and change these negative thoughts into realistic thoughts; we ask you to consider experimenting with changing your behavior and we give you self-help assignments to take what you learn in a session and practice it outside of the sessions. There is more research supporting CBT as an effective treatment for depression and anxiety than there is for all other forms of psychotherapy combined. It works, it's practical, and you can learn some of it by reading this book, and by doing things that I am going to recommend.

Taking care of yourself now

This book is about how you take care of yourself during the time between the last job and the next. I am going to lay out a plan of action for you that you can use every single day that you are unemployed. It will be a plan of setting goals every day, following habits that build on your strengths, helping you turn away from passive rumination on the negative to positive action and problem solving. I will urge you to rethink your self-criticism and your shame, try to treat yourself more compassionately, and learn to communicate more effectively with the people in your life that you need. It will be important for you to treat this period as one of self-care, rather than one of passivity, isolation and self-criticism. Since unemployment is often associated with increased health risks, as previously mentioned — often due to increased smoking or drinking, or to over-eating or lack of exercise, and increased physical stress — I am going to urge you to take this time "in-between" to get into much better physical condition. Self-care includes working on your health every day. You no longer have the excuse that you don't have time to exercise.

Expand your definition of yourself

We are also going to look at how you have defined yourself in terms of your job. One man said that he realized after being unemployed he wasn't really defined by his job; he was also the father of his children, the husband to his wife, and the brother to his brother. Your self-definition may need to be expanded. You are more than a job title, more than an employee. This time can be one of rediscovery of those other roles — the many ways that you fit into the world. I am going to ask you to think about volunteer work, as a way of turning around the isolation that has added to your depression and shame, and to think about helping others. Yes, you have something to offer other people — people who may be worse off than you. By joining a larger community you expand your sense of belonging to the world. And, who knows, you may develop contacts, skills or ideas that can lead to the next job.

I will also want you to think about the role of material things in your life. Many people complain that they will not have enough money to provide for the kind of life that they want. Certainly, financial limitations are real and important. But I have found that we can often re-evaluate what these material things mean to you. I truly believe that most of the "things" that we have — and things that we think we need — are just that: "things." They get their excess meaning because we actually believe that we "need" them. This time between jobs can be an opportunity to examine your drive for things — your "need" for things.

Rediscover time

Like many people going through this time, you and your family may find it difficult occasionally to cope with one another. But what I have found quite interesting is that some people actually find it can be an opportunity to find that their partner is really their best friend and that their kids are a source of joy and meaning. We will look at how you and your family can pull together, rather than pulling apart, and, if possible, become stronger in the process. It all depends on how you handle it. There are better ways to express your frustrations and better ways to solve problems together.

Finally, I want you to think about time. If you are like most people I know who are unemployed, you have a sense that you need the answer right now: "When will I get a job?" This urgent need for THE ANSWER may drive your repeated negative thoughts and your constant rumination (I'll be explaining rumination in detail in Chapter Five). If possible, perhaps you might consider stretching time, to give yourself more space to breathe, and learn how to get the very best out of the present moment. If you have time between jobs you can use it — or lose it.

It's up to you: you can choose how you cope with unemployment

Let's look at the problematic ways of responding to the reality of being unemployed. The illustration below depicts how you might be responding and how all these feelings generate from "The Reality" of unemployment.

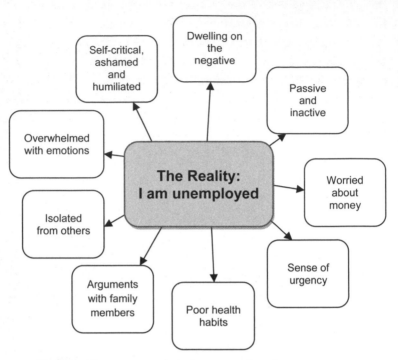

Problematic responses to being unemployed

These feelings are:

- You feel overwhelmed with emotions and you think that no one really understands.
- You criticize yourself and feel ashamed.
- You spend hours dwelling on repetitive negative thoughts.
- You are passive and inactive, doing less and less that is productive or rewarding.
- You are worried about money.
- You have a sense of urgency that you need the answer now.
- You have poor health habits—poor nutrition, overdrinking, not getting into better shape.
- You have more arguments with your family members.
- You have less contact with people and isolate yourself. Sometimes you feel that you are hiding from reality.

In the illustration below I suggest ways to change these problematic ways of coping, creating a different "Reality" at its core. You can see that each one of them addresses a problem in how you might be living your life right now. Perhaps you don't have all the problems in the first illustration, but I am willing to bet that you have a lot of them. The good news is that each of these problems can be addressed with the powerful techniques of cognitive behavioral therapy. These are techniques that you can begin learning and practicing today.

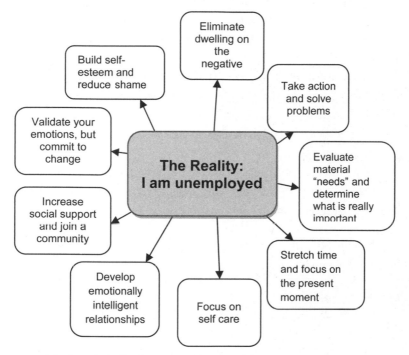

Adaptive strategies for coping with unemployment

What does this have to do with getting that job that you want? Well, as I said, this is not a book on how to "find that job." It's a book on how to cope better so that you will be the best *you* that you can be while you are looking for that job. And it will also give you tools to use once you have that next job.

As disturbing as the facts are about the human costs of unemployment, these dire outcomes do not have to be your destiny. It's important to take this time—in-between your last job and your next job—to take charge of your life. This is a transition period; it does not have to be a time of depression, worry, physical deterioration or relationship problems. In fact, I hope that if you use the ideas, techniques and strategies that I outline in this book, your life will be better over the coming weeks or months, and that you will continue to practice your program of self-help once you get that new job.

As one of my clients said when we went through the basic points in this book, "These are good ideas not only while I am unemployed but as things I should do for the rest of my life. These ideas apply to anyone."

I only ask that you apply them to yourself—*now*.

Just because you are currently unemployed does not mean that life has stopped for you. After all, *you have to live every day of your life*. Why not make every day a better day? You may be unemployed, but I am going to ask you to get to work on yourself—and on your life. You have a lot to do. This is now your full-time job: the job of living your life in-between and getting the most out of it. Let's turn this into a time to grow.

2

YOU HAVE A RIGHT TO YOUR FEELINGS AND THE ABILITY TO CHANGE THEM

What is the worst thing to say to someone who is unemployed? "Snap out of it and get on with things." If you have heard that, you probably felt similar to a lot of people who are going through this time. You may have felt angry, frustrated, infuriated, humiliated, ashamed, alone, hopeless, anxious and confused—or all of those feelings. You probably thought, "They just don't understand. They don't get it. This is really a miserable time for me."

We will deal with all of these completely human feelings throughout this book. But the first thing I want you to think about is that you have every right to every feeling that you have. You have just lost your job. You may feel that it was unfair, so you feel angry. You may think that you have been trying hard to get another job, so you feel frustrated. You may think that other people don't treat you with respect, so you feel infuriated and humiliated. Or you may think that others look down on you, so you feel ashamed and alone. You may dwell for hours on how this could have happened to you, so you feel confused. And you may think that no matter what you do, nothing will work out—it will always be as bad as it is now, so you feel hopeless.

Finding the strategies for moving on

One way to think about your feelings is that there are millions of other people who have felt the same way during their time of being unemployed. You are a human being coping with a difficult situation. It's hard, at times, to cope with this, and it takes some real effort to work out how to make things better when you are feeling so down. But I want you to work with me in this book to try some ways of coping that might really make a difference. It won't be easy; you may say to yourself, "I can't do this" or "I shouldn't have to do this—I should just get a job" or "What does he know? He has a job." All of these thoughts make sense, but they won't help you. This is an important time in your life where you need yourself to be on your side all the time.

You may feel that no one really understands what you're going through, and you may even think that no one really cares, but you don't know that these thoughts are true unless you try connecting with people. You might find that some people actually want to be supportive. I often think that it is a hallmark of my friendship when I can be supportive to someone I care about. It's a chance for me to be a friend, a chance to get closer, a chance to matter. I want to matter. Don't you?

It's hard to have feelings that are painful, that you feel alone with, and that you think others would never care about or understand. A lot of times people are ashamed of their feelings when they are out of work, thinking that other people are going to judge them or want to avoid them. They keep their feelings inside, isolate themselves, and hide from the people in their lives.

I have learned that the most important thing in a relationship is to show that you really want to understand how the other person feels and that you really care. The one person you can start this with is yourself. You can validate yourself, understand yourself and give yourself the right to feel the way you feel.

Let's try to work out how you can live with your feelings now.

1: Validate your feelings

What does it mean to "validate" your feelings? It means a number of things. First, it means that you recognize what your feelings are. For example, you might feel sad, anxious, hopeless and angry, So identifying your feelings is part of validating them. Sometimes you might focus on only one feeling—for example, sadness—and not realize that you also have a lot of other feelings about being unemployed. For example, you might also feel anxious and worried about the future. You could certainly feel angry that it was unfair. Or you might feel confused, not knowing what to do or why this has happened. If you feel anxious, you might worry about the future, predicting terrible outcomes and treating your predictions as if they are facts. You might find yourself thinking that you will end up homeless. Or if you are angry about being unemployed, you might find yourself directing this anger towards your husband or wife or towards your kids. Try to be honest with yourself about these feelings so that you know where you are coming from.

EXERCISE: WHAT ARE YOU FEELING?

Write out all the different feelings that you have been having. The more you can identify, the more you can understand—and the more feelings you can change.

You can understand that your feelings are related to what you are going through and how you are thinking about it. If you lost your job and you think that you will never get another job or that you will never feel good again, then it makes sense that you feel down. You can validate your sad and anxious feelings by saying to yourself, "Of course I am feeling this way. I've lost my job. I tried to do a good job, but now I am out of work. I think I won't get a job for a long time, I am having all these negative thoughts about myself and I feel isolated and helpless. So it makes sense that I feel this way right now."

Discovering what's really true

Realizing that your negative thoughts lead to your negative feelings does not mean that your thoughts are true. For example, you might feel sad and hopeless because you believe you will never get a job, but that is just a thought—it's not a fact. You can't know what the facts are until you get the facts. And the future, right now, is not known. You don't have a crystal ball.

Validating feelings doesn't mean that there isn't another way to feel—or to respond to your situation—it simply means, "I understand what I am experiencing. I can see how it makes sense." Ask yourself, "What am I saying to myself that is making me feel so bad?" How you feel is often based on what you think about things. Your feelings are related to a long stream of negative thoughts that you believe at the present moment. These thoughts are driving your misery.

Of course, there is always another way to look at what is happening and lots of different ways to cope with it. For example, if you believe it's all your fault and that you are a failure, then you are likely to feel bad. But what if there is another way to look at it? What if you are not a failure, and what if you could get another job, would you feel differently? Probably so. Validating the way you feel doesn't mean that you will have to feel the way you feel forever. It's only the way you are feeling now.

EXERCISE: MAKING SENSE OF YOUR FEELINGS

Ask yourself these questions now:
- What are the different feelings that I am having?
- Don't I have a right to those feelings?
- Aren't there other people who would feel the same way?
- What am I saying to myself that makes me feel the way I do?
- Could there be another way of looking at things?
- How would I feel if I took a different point of view?

2: Relate your feelings to your values

When you feel down because you think, "I won't be able to take care of my family now," your sad and hopeless feelings reflect important values. You care about other people. You want to be responsible and to do the right thing. So it makes sense that you would feel badly right now. Of course, we might examine whether there are ways of taking care of your family that don't include your job. For example, perhaps taking care of your family might involve loving them, being affectionate, doing things with them and helping out with the chores. You don't need a job to do those things. But if you believe that you won't be able to take care of them, it makes sense that your values will be affected; however, we can examine if that is *really* true — although it feels true for you right now.

Another important value is being conscientious and doing a good job. Your period of being unemployed might mean to you that you are not doing anything — because you have no job, so you feel down. As you will remember from Chapter One, though, I am going to argue in this book that you have a number of new jobs to do now that you don't have that old job. For one, your job is looking for a job — and that is a big job. But you have other jobs, including taking care of yourself, connecting with the people in your life, perhaps engaging in volunteer work, getting into better physical shape and preparing for the next job with the right attitude, the right way to cope and the right skills. Being conscientious doesn't require the old job, but it's understandable that you will feel down if you aren't living up to your values.

You may feel that you are not living up to your values of taking care of your family or that you are not being conscientious because you don't have a job right now. Your values are important — they are part of who you are. Even though it's hard at the moment, it would be harder if you gave up on your values. Perhaps there are ways of being supportive and loving without having that job, or of being conscientious. For example, you could be conscientious by focusing on self-care — such as exercise, proper nutrition, reduced drinking and eliminating smoking. You could be conscientious in searching for a job, and in helping out with chores in the home and being there for your family. You could acquire new skills, and network with people to reach out and broaden your possibilities. There are lots of ways of pursuing the right values.

Values and identity are greater than any job

It's possible to love and support your family—even more—now that you have more time to do it. It's possible to be conscientious: working at finding a job, working at taking care of yourself, and even volunteering to help others. You might even have more work to do right now, simply because you don't have that other job. You don't want to give up your values simply because you lost your job. In fact, you might want to double-up on those values, by really focusing on the right thing to do, and then to do it.

EXERCISE: THINK DIFFERENTLY ABOUT YOUR VALUES

Consider the following:
- What are the values that you feel are affected by being unemployed right now?
- Are there other ways of aiming towards those values?
- What could you do today to move towards those values?

3: Notice that your feelings change with what you are doing

Over the last 30 years of seeing people who are anxious and depressed, one comment always strikes me as intriguing because it is never really true: "I am always depressed." Even the most depressed clients that I have seen—people who have recently come out of the hospital, or people who report years of treatment for depression—have changes in their moods every day. I often like to reflect with them, "I noticed that you said that you are always depressed, but I noticed that you laughed a few times in our session today. How is this consistent with the idea of always feeling sad?" If your feelings can change in the next ten minutes, then it may be possible that we can work out how to change them every day.

This is important: your feelings change during the course of the day. For example, let's say that you are feeling sad and I ask, "From 0 to 10, how sad do you feel?" and you say, "10." That's really sad, but I am willing to bet that if I asked you to keep track of your sadness every hour of the week you might find that your sadness increases and decreases depending on what you are doing. For example, Claire, who we met in Chapter One, found that she was a lot less sad—actually feeling pretty good -when she was out to dinner with friends. One client, Dave, felt much less sad when he was working out at the health club. Another, Karen, felt a lot less sad curling up with her dog and listening to music. Feelings are not permanent—however painful they may be at the time.

So what are you doing when you feel the most sadness? Here are some examples of activities commonly related to feeling down: sitting at home alone dwelling on your negative thoughts, watching television for hours, lying in bed doing nothing, or hiding from other people because you don't want them to know that you don't have a job. Changing your activity may help you change the way you feel—at least, today—at least, for now.

EXERCISE: KEEP TRACK OF PLEASURE AND EFFECTIVENESS

Keep track of your activities every hour of the week. Then, rate your feelings for each hour and each activity using two different categories: pleasure ("How good did I feel doing this?") and effectiveness ("How competent did I feel doing this?").

Use a scale from 0 to 10 with 0 representing no feelings of pleasure (or effectiveness) and 10 representing the most pleasure or effectiveness that you could imagine. For example, taking a bath might be "8" in pleasure for you, but only a "3" in feeling effective, so your response here would be 8/3.

Putting together a list of people to contact about jobs might be a "2" in pleasure but a "7" in effectiveness, so your response here would be P=2/E=7. Sitting around dwelling on how bad you feel might be a "0" in both pleasure and effectiveness, so your response here would be 0. Below is an example of the sort of thing that you might write. However, don't forget you need to write down and rate your activities from when you rise until bedtime

	Monday	Tuesday	Wednesday	Thursday	Friday	Saturday	Sunday
10 am.	Sitting watching television P=2/E=0	Went for a jog P=6/E=6	Talking to my friend Carol on the phone P=6/E=4				

Once you have filled in a few days of activities, and at regular intervals, look back at what you have written and think about these questions:

- Which activities were you engaged in when you felt worse? What were you doing?
- What were you doing when you felt better?
- If your feelings change depending on what you are doing, what does that mean to you?

4: Your feelings depend on what you are thinking

Like a lot of people who are unemployed, you believe that you have too much time on your hands. You may be sitting at home, dwelling on lots of negative thoughts that you just automatically believe. Try to see if your feelings are related to what you are thinking. For example, "I will never get a job," "I must be a failure," "I have let everyone down," and "I will never be happy again." When these thoughts come to you, you might treat them as if they are proven facts—indisputable. The more you dwell on them, the truer they seem to you.

What if your thoughts are not true? Or, what if they are only 20% true? Your feelings might then have been based on thoughts that were lies you are telling yourself. Imagine if you were employed and you were sitting at home and someone was yelling at you every minute, for hours: "You are a failure" or "You will never be happy." How do you think you would feel?

You don't have to believe everything you think. You can look into what you *think* and change it.

You can treat these thoughts as annoying, pestering bugs that keep biting at you. The way to defeat them is to recognize them for what they are — just thoughts.

EXERCISE: CHALLENGE YOUR THOUGHTS

Write your thoughts down, then keep a tally, and plan your attack. For example, you can challenge each of these thoughts with the following:

- What am I saying to myself? If I didn't believe this thought, how would my feelings change?
- What is the evidence for and against this thought?
- What advice would I give my best friend if they were out of work and they had these thoughts?

For example, Claire was saying to herself, "I must be a loser. I don't have a job." This made her feel sad, hopeless and ashamed. She realized that if she didn't believe this thought she would feel a lot better — more hopeful, more accepting, more able to enjoy her life right now. She realized that the only "evidence" that she was a "loser" was that she didn't have a job at this moment in time, but there was a lot of evidence that she was not a loser — she had graduated from university, she was a good person, she had worked well at her job and on other jobs that she had held in the past, and she had a number of good friends. She said, "If I had a friend who thought this I would be supportive and tell her that unemployment happens to millions of people — good people — and it doesn't say anything about you as a person."

EXERCISE: CHALLENGE YOUR NEGATIVE

Write down some of your negative thoughts and then alongside this, list the evidence in favor of the thought and against the thought. Here's an example of how to do this

Negative thoughts	Evidence in favor of thought	Evidence against thought
I am a failure	I don't have a job	I graduated from university. I had a job for several years. I did well in my job. I have a wife and two children and I am a good father. I have friends.

When you look at the evidence in favor and the evidence against your thoughts, what do you conclude? Take the thought, "I will never get a job again," for example. What is the evidence in favor of this thought? You might say, "I don't have a job, I have been looking for a while and the job market is pretty bad." The evidence against the thought might be, "Almost everyone eventually gets a job, there are always changes in the job market; I am willing work, I have skills that other people might need." How does this affect how much you believe the thought about never getting a job? Do you believe it any less than before? Why or why not?

EXERCISE: WHAT ADVICE WOULD I GIVE A FRIEND WHO IS OUT OF WORK?

Write out your negative thoughts about being unemployed and your life right now and then list all the advice you would give a good friend who was thinking in this way. Are you more supportive to your friend than you are to yourself? Why or why not? Here's an example of how to do this.

My negative thoughts	Advice I would give a friend
I failed	You didn't fail. There are millions of people out of work through no fault of their own. It can happen to anyone. Look at all the good qualities that you have, all the things that you have done that are good. You are a good friend and a good family member. I still care for you and respect you.

A lot of times we are much more objective, realistic and kind to a friend—or even a stranger. Are you being unnecessarily tough on yourself during this difficult time? If you were as supportive to yourself as you would be to a friend, how would your painful feelings change? Try "The Best Advice to a Friend" for the next few weeks and see how you feel.

5: Observe your feelings without getting hijacked by them

Sometimes you might start feeling anxious about not having a job and you get revved up, more and more anxious, and you even find yourself getting anxious about the fact that you are anxious. You are getting hijacked by your emotions. If this has happened to you—and it probably has—you are more and more afraid of what you feel. You might even try to suppress those feelings only to find that they keep coming back. And this makes you even more afraid of your feelings.

When you are unemployed you are likely to have a lot of painful feelings. But you can develop a different way of experiencing them. One way that is helpful is the "mindful way." Let's take the example of being mindful of your breathing. When you are mindful of your breathing you are simply standing back, noticing your breathing and keeping your mind on the fact that your breath goes in and out. You are not judging your breathing, you are not controlling it—you are observing it. You are standing back, watching the moment come and go.

By standing back and observing your breath without controlling or judging, you gain a distance from your thoughts, you learn that your breath—like your thoughts and feelings—can come and go. By practicing mindful breathing you will be able to observe your negative thoughts without getting hijacked by them. You can notice them, then let them go. Breath to breath, thought to thought—each is one moment that passes. Practicing mindfulness can help you address the

root causes of your worry: your fear, your tension, your mis-
taken belief that you are in continual danger. It will help you
to stay in the present, where anxiety does not exist. Anxiety is
built on thoughts of what has happened in the past and fears
or expectations about what will happen in the future. When we
are anxious we have left the present moment to worry about a
future that may or may not ever happen. By staying in the
present you let go of that worry, let go of the future, and live
your life in this moment. The same is true about your
rumination and anxiety about the past. Let it go, let it stay in
the past, and live in this moment now. Mindfulness will calm
your mind and relax your body. If you keep at it, you may find
the strength of your anxiety diminishing considerably.

Try this exercise every day:

EXERCISE: MINDFUL AWARENSS OF YOUR BREATH

1. Begin by sitting in a comfortable position. It doesn't have to be cross-legged, it can be kneeling on a cushion or sitting in a chair. It's helpful if your spine is erect. Close your eyes.
2. Start by bringing your attention to your breath. Notice how it goes in and out, rises and falls. It does this by itself: you don't have to "do" anything to make it happen. Continue observing the breath, moment by moment, as it flows onward.
3. What you will notice next (probably within seconds) will be the mind wandering away from the breath into the world of thought. Perhaps you will be distracted by some worry of yours, perhaps apprehension around how you will "perform," perhaps a feeling that you need to be doing something instead of just sitting here.
4. Or, hearing certain sounds, you may start wondering what's causing them or what they mean. You may begin to think about tonight's dinner, yesterday's football match, or how things are going at work. It doesn't matter what the content of the thought is. The key is this: as soon as you become aware that the attention has wandered, bring it gently but firmly back to the breath, back to the moment. Do this without comment or judgment; just bring it back.

5. As many times as the mind drifts off, simply notice this and restore your attention to the breath. Do this for as long as you like.

As you practice mindfulness, you'll probably be both able and motivated to do it for longer periods.

Why mindfulness is helpful

None of this may seem at first to have much to do with the major "issues" of your life—but it does. That's because the practice of mindfulness is connected in a very deep way with our thoughts—or rather with the relationship we have with our thoughts. Being in the present moment means being attuned to whatever is going on: our breath, the sound of a clock ticking, a pain in the back. But what's happening in the moment also includes our thoughts. Thoughts are events to which we can direct our attention. Like the sensations of our breath, thoughts arise in the mind and pass away, coming in and out of existence with no apparent effort on our part.

We don't often treat our thoughts accordingly. We treat them as though they were reality or, rather, pictures that infallibly describe reality. If we think something is So it is so. We form an abstract concept like "This traffic is unbearable," or "My life is a mess," and accept it as truth. If we think of someone as a good or a bad person, then that's what they are. Conceptual thinking drives us—never more completely and powerfully than when we are anxious. We worry that something terrible is going to happen, and presto, the threat is real. We assume that our anxiety is informing us of all the things "out there" in the world that we need to be concerned about. Anxiety, more than almost any other human feeling, depends on the belief that our thoughts are accurate descriptions of reality.

Recognizing that our thoughts are not reality

We can view our thoughts in a different way, however. We can see a thought as just a thought—an event in the mind, with no necessary connection to what goes on in the world at all. Rather than getting caught up in the content of our thoughts, we can simply notice them in the moment—just as we did with our out breath. It's possible, in short, to be mindful of our thoughts. This changes our entire relationship with them. When we see our thoughts as part of the flow of consciousness, when they're simply phenomena passing through the mind rather than descriptions of reality, their power over us suddenly looks a lot smaller. Instead of reacting with "This is awful," or "I've got to do something right away," we can say "Ah yes, there's that thought again." Watching our thoughts come and go, we realize how ephemeral they are, how tenuously connected to anything important. We don't have to "obey" them anymore.

The same thing can be done with those feelings that you have. You can observe your feeling at the moment. You can say to yourself, "I notice that at this moment I am feeling sad." You don't have to judge it, you don't have to control it, you don't have to get rid of it right now. Instead, you can simply say: "At this very moment I notice sad feelings."

Your attention will be drawn to sensations in your body when you are feeling anxious or sad. Perhaps you notice your heart beating rapidly, or the tension in your shoulders, the tingling in your fingers. Perhaps you perceive your sadness when you are feeling a heaviness in your chest, your face feeling tired and droopy, your eyes closing. What are the sensations that go along with your emotions of sadness: anxiety, anger? Where are you feeling it? Try this exercise.

EXERCISE: BREATHE THE SADNESS AWAY

When you have those sensations, watch them in the same way that you have been watching your breath:

1. Observe them and describe them to yourself. For example, "I notice that my shoulders feel tense right now."

2. You can then stand back, aware, observing and not judging, just for now—not trying to change it. You might say, "I notice that I am having a heavy feeling in my chest at the moment."

And then return your attention to your breath for a few minutes, and with each out-breath say to yourself, "Letting go."

3. Moment to moment the breath, the sensations, even the thoughts, are coming in and then going out. Letting go for a moment. Just for a moment.

4. You can imagine your sadness is the breath—it comes in, you notice it, and you let it go—for this moment in time. Coming and going, taking in and letting go. Like all feelings, all sensations, all breathing in and out—it is temporary, it returns, then it is gone.

Use the list below to guide you through your mindfulness practice:

- Stand back and notice what you are feeling.
- Are there physical sensations that are part of the feeling?
- Don't judge or control the feeling, just watch it.
- Practice Mindful Breathing every day.
- Imagine that you are breathing in and out, and with each out breath the feeling goes away.

6: Improve the moment

When you are sitting at home feeling down about not having your job, you might feel stuck in that feeling. It's as if the thoughts and feelings show up and take you prisoner. You have nowhere to go—but down. Whatever the down moment is, though, there is always something else to do. You need to have a plan for improving the moment—something to take your mind off things, something else to do.

Let's start with a reward menu. I think of this as a list of things to do that will continue to get longer and longer each day that you engage in activities and think about rewarding things to do. You can start your reward menu with recalling what you have enjoyed doing in the past: listening to music, watching a movie, connecting with people online, exercising, taking a walk, playing with your pet, reading, talking with your family members, calling up a friend, taking a warm bath, cooking a delicious treat. The possibilities could go on and on. The essential thing to realize is that there are other things to do rather than getting hijacked by your thoughts and feelings. If you make up your reward menu before the difficult moments, you will be ready to change the moment when it arises. You will have rewarding things to do.

Bad moments and painful feelings may come and go. You can avoid being hijacked by them if you can realize that they are temporary, they will not destroy you, you don't have to escalate them, you can observe them, and you can distract yourself with other activities rather than getting pulled away by what you are feeling.

EXERCISE: USING REWARDING ACTIVIES—YOUR REWARD MENU

Improving the moment is a big step in improving your life. Here's how to work through achieving that:

- Make a list of rewarding activities that you might want to do.
- Add to this list every day, if you can.
- Notice when you are having a bad moment that you could do one of these rewarding activities.
- Spend some time improving the moment.
- Notice that moments come and go.

7: Accept the reality as it is given

Before you can move on to the next stage—before you can move from validating your feelings—you will have to accept the reality that is given. These are the cards that you have been dealt. In order to get to where you want to go, you have to start from where you are. The "given" right now is that you don't have that job. It is a hard given for you, but we have to start somewhere. Accepting it as the given for now, means that you can give up—for now—protesting, blaming yourself, or waiting for things to change. Accepting it as the given for now means that you are going to turn it into a problem to solve, a place that is your starting point, a place that you will eventually leave behind.

There are a lot of things that we have learned to accept in life—traffic, unfairness, getting older, disappointments and losses. Accepting reality simply means that you recognize that it is what it is, without protesting or ruminating about it. For example, one client, Ted, found that his company was downsizing and he was laid off. He finally recognized that he had to live with what was given—however unfair and unpleasant it was. It was hard to accept, but there really wasn't any better alternative. At least accepting it gave him a starting point: "Where do I go from here?"

Change begins with acceptance

Accepting reality doesn't mean it is fair, it doesn't mean it is good and it doesn't mean that you are giving up. It simply means that you recognize you have a real thing to cope with and you need to take real action. In fact, accepting it as it is right now means that you are beginning to make progress on how to change it—and how to change your life.

When Ted was complaining about how unfair it was that he got fired, he only felt angry, sad, hopeless and helpless. Those feelings made sense. He's human. But my thought for him was, "Even if all these feelings make absolute sense, how long do you want to feel this way? How long do you want to be stuck at this point?" This doesn't mean that he doesn't have a right to his feelings. It only means that he has a right to make his life better. Even given what happened, he still has power to change the way he lives his life. You always have a choice—no matter what you are feeling right at this moment.

EXERCISE: ACCEPT AND MOVE ON

Change doesn't mean that your feelings don't matter. Change means that your feelings matter so much that you want to aim for something better. Use the list below to help you.

- Describe the reality that you are facing.
- What are the advantages of accepting it as a "given" for right now?
- Imagine that you stopped protesting how bad it was and started to plan how to make your life better. What would change?
- Complete this sentence: "It is what it is and now I can . . ."

8: Commit to making things better

There is no question that unemployment usually brings a lot of painful thoughts and feelings, and many people isolate themselves, criticize themselves and feel hopeless. Those are your feelings. You can look at coping with unemployment as a series of stages in moving forward. The first stage is the shock, disbelief and the pain of losing your job. Perhaps you could not believe that this was happening to you. The second stage might be all the painful feelings that you are having now—sadness, anxiety, hopelessness, anger. In this stage, you may be coping with the unhelpful behaviors we've already looked at: such as isolating yourself, remaining passive and inactive, staying in bed for long hours, sitting watching television endlessly, ruminating, drinking, over-eating, smoking, or complaining.

While you are in the second stage you can ask yourself if you want to stay there for more time—and you can recognize that you have the right and the freedom to do what you choose to do. But I am going to suggest you move on to a third stage: the stage of committing to change. In the third stage you recognize that you are unemployed and you are going to do everything you can to make your life better during this time between your last job and your next job. This is going to require a lot of work. It will be a challenge. It will mean doing things that you don't want to do. You may be uncomfortable facing your fears, overcoming your shame, taking the initiative to reach out, trying new things, and perhaps acquiring new skills.

I know that it is hard for you being unemployed, but I am going to ask you to meet a challenge, beginning right now. Here is the challenge: "Are you willing to do things that are hard to do?" I am not asking you to simply relax and wait until you find a job. I am asking you to take on a new job. This job involves taking care of yourself. It means that you are going to have to do things, such as identifying what you are thinking, challenging your own negativity, changing the activities that you do, confronting your fears and anxieties, setting goals every day, every week and every month. It means that you are going to have to do things that you might find unpleasant to do.

Will you accept the challenge?

Here is the challenge: "Are you willing to do some things that you don't want to do in order to make your life better?" In fact, I am going to suggest that unless you are doing things every day that might be a little hard or a little challenging, then you are not doing enough to take care of yourself. Do what is hard now so that it will be easier in the future.

Throughout this book I want you to realize that ultimately coping with losing your job is about two things: how you can feel better and how you can feel empowered. Losing your job does not mean that you have lost yourself. You are still the man or woman you were before. But this may be a hard time to cope and a lot of this will be up to you. I am going to ask you to consider taking on the new job of coping with unemployment by thinking and acting in ways that could be helpful for the rest of your life.

Think about this time between jobs as your "basic training" in the fight for your life. Think about it as an opportunity to develop the ability to change the way you think, focus on values that can empower your work and your relationships, and develop the ability to do what you don't want to do, but that you know will be important for you to do. This time of losing your job may be the end of one experience but the beginning of a new way to live life.

EXERCISE: PREPARE TO MAKE CHANGES

Committing to change does not mean that your feelings are unimportant. It means that they are important enough that you are willing to do something about them. Answer the following questions:
- Are you stuck in feeling down, isolated, passive and feeling trapped?
- Would you be willing to do some new things to make a change?

- Would you be willing to be uncomfortable, set aside the past for now, and try to make a better life today?
- Are you willing to be flexible and creative in living a better life?

SUMMARY

You have a lot of painful feelings and a right to each and every one of them. Write them out, list the thoughts that go with them, validate that you have a right to be human, and recognize that this is where you are starting from. Try to do each of the following every day:

Keep a diary for **My Time Between Jobs**. Each day, write out examples of what you are doing to help yourself, using the suggestions throughout this book. You can start with the following entries.

- Validate your feelings.
- Relate your feelings to your values.
- Realize that your feelings change with what you are doing.
- Realize that your feelings depend on what you are thinking.
- Observe your feelings without getting hijacked by them.
- Improve the moment.
- Accept the reality as it is given.
- Commit to making things better.

Your new job is to take care of yourself. You now have a lot of work to do.

3

TAKE ACTION

You will remember from the second chapter that your feelings change depending on what you are doing. If you are isolating yourself in your house or apartment, lying around on the sofa, eating junk food, watching television and dwelling on your negative thoughts, then you are almost guaranteed to feel worse. Ken, who had been out of work a few years before I interviewed him, told me that the absolutely worst time of the day was when he got up in the morning: "I had nothing to do. I had all this time on my hands. I had nowhere to go." Having nothing to do, nowhere to go, and feeling helpless about doing anything productive guaranteed that each day was a day in hell. Ken isolated himself because he felt ashamed of being unemployed. He just sat around, watching television and dwelling on the negative, until he felt "free" to leave his apartment at five in the afternoon; he believed others would not assume he was unemployed since people who worked would be out and about after five. He was a prisoner of his inactivity, his forced self-isolation and his shame.

One way of looking at depression is that your sad and painful feelings depend on how you respond to them. You can respond to negativity with more negativity or you can respond in more adaptive ways. You actually have a choice. You can either make things better or you can make things worse.

For example, let's say that you feel sad. You respond to this by thinking, "No matter what I do, it won't get better." You then isolate yourself, do nothing but sit around by yourself, and engage in activities that are not rewarding—such as watching television and dwelling on the negative. You avoid facing the situation and close down. You feel worse, and then you just start the same pattern of isolation, passivity and avoidance, as a way of dealing with your new—and probably more intense—sad and painful feelings. The ironic thing is that you are maintaining your worst feelings because you think that doing anything new will make you feel even worse, so you trap yourself.

Let's contrast this with a different strategy to deal with your sad feelings. This involves GETTING OUT, LIVING YOUR LIFE, and DOING SOMETHING. So let's take this new approach to your sad feelings. Rather than isolating yourself, you GET OUT. Rather than shutting down living, you LIVE YOUR LIFE. And, rather than remaining passive and doing nothing, you DO SOMETHING. Keep in mind that if you feel sad and you avoid facing the situation and remain passive, you are likely to feel worse and worse. As explained earlier, when you are unemployed you are at great risk of depression, worry, anxiety, hopelessness, anger and feelings of helplessness. Your tendency might be to avoid facing the situation and isolate yourself.

First we have to find out what could be rewarding to do. In the previous chapter you kept track of your activities for every hour of the week and this is an important step before you can move on to the exercises in this chapter.

1: Review your activity schedule

In Chapter Two I asked you to keep track of what you did every hour of the week to see how this was related to your feelings of pleasure and effectiveness (see page 25). If you are like a lot of people who are unemployed, you might notice that a lot of your time is wasted dwelling on the negative, engaged in passive activities (such as watching television or surfing the internet for useless information), or complaining to people about how bad you feel or how unfair things are. (Although things can be bad and unfair, complaining might simply make you feel worse about them.) Your passivity might also involve lying in bed until later in the day, half-asleep, half-awake, ruminating and dwelling on negative thoughts and images. This passivity might also manifest itself in your lack of response to people who reach out to you. Passivity maintains your negative feelings.

On the other hand, your activity schedule might also contain information about those things you do that bring you some pleasure and some effectiveness. For example, one client, Bill, found that he felt really good when he took his son to school. Not only did it feel pleasurable, but it also made him feel effective. He was doing something. He loved his son and being involved with him—now even more than before when Bill was working—and it was making him feel good for that hour. Bill also noticed that when he went out for a walk near to his home, he felt better putting on his iPod and listening to music. He also felt better when he got some chores done around the house, painting the outside, and feeling like he was making a difference. Doing something leads to feeling better.

EXERCISE: LOW- AND HIGH-PLEASURE ACTIVITIES

List all the activities you associate with feeling down (low pleasure) and all the activities associated with feeling better (higher pleasure). The example below shows the sort of activities people list. (You can make a similar list for activities that are associated with feeling effective or not effective. For example, filling out a job application may not be as pleasurable as playing basketball or talking with your friends, but it might be associated with feeling more effective.)

Low pleasure	High pleasure
Sitting at home thinking about not working	Going for a bike ride in the park. Playing with my daughter. Talking with my best friend

Now, let's think beyond your current situation and try to remember the kinds of activities that you used to enjoy in the past. Did you exercise, have hobbies, hang out with friends, spend time with family members, or do anything that might be relatively simple—activities you found gave you pleasure or a sense of effectiveness or "mastery"? For example, Bill remembered that he used to work out, enjoyed reading and listening to music, enjoyed talking with friends, playing catch with his son, and preparing dinner with his wife. We can call these the "Past Rewarding Activities."

Now, to add to your possibilities of rewarding activities, think about things that you thought of doing but didn't really follow up on. These could be possible "Future Rewarding Activities." For Bill, this included practicing the guitar (he used to play when he was a kid, but put it down for the past 15 years), increasing his exercise (by jogging, rather than only walking), learning more about his heritage (he was Italian), learning how to cook some new cuisine, reading more about political affairs and getting in contact with people he knew from university. These were possible new activities.

EXERCISE: PAST AND POSSIBLE REWARDING ACTIVITIES

Now list your past rewarding activities and the possible new rewarding activities—see the example below.

Past rewarding activities	Possible rewarding activities
Taking a drawing class. Playing with my children	Seeing my friends. Listening to music. Going to the museum

You are concentrating on two things:
- List the activities that you have enjoyed in the past.
- List the activities that you might enjoy doing in the future.

Looking at what you have written:
- List the activities that make you feel worse.
- Keep track of what you do and how you feel when you are doing these things.
- Is there a pattern to what you are doing when you feel better and what you are doing when you feel worse?

2: Plan rewarding activities for yourself

Taking care of yourself during this difficult time means that you need to do some things for yourself. Lying around, waiting for a job offer is no way to take care of yourself. Now that you have a list of your current, past, and possible future activities, your challenge is to schedule some things for you to do. You can assign yourself positive activities for each hour, each day, and each week. Don't wait until you wake up in the morning to decide what you are going to do. Have the next day planned in advance — the day before.

You can start with your list of past, present, and future pleasurable and effective activities. (Part of your list will be the job search activities, but that comes later in this chapter.) I tend to think that getting up at a set time, getting started with a good breakfast (a healthy breakfast), getting out and exercising (take a walk, go to the gym, get active) is a great way to start the day. But it's up to you. There may be people to contact, things to learn, courses to take, relaxation exercises, food to prepare, kids to attend to, plans to make. The more active you are, the better you will feel.

Part of your down mood—and your tendency to avoid facing the situation and be passive—is that you think that none of these activities will be helpful. These are your predictions and, like any other thought, they could prove to be true or false—or more or less accurate. You can list some activities that you are going to do today and then write in how much pleasure and how much of a feeling of effectiveness you think you will get. We call this "Pleasure Predicting," and what you will find out is whether your expectations are overly negative. Try this exercise.

EXERCISE: PREDICTING PLEASURE AND EFFECTIVENESS

Assign some activities that you think might be associated with pleasure or effectiveness. Write down how much pleasure and effectiveness you expect to get for the activities you are going to do today, using the 0 to 10 scale. Then, after the activity, write out the actual pleasure and effectiveness. Here's an example to help you.

Day: Monday	Activity	Expected Pleasure	Expected Effectiveness	Actual Pleasure	Actual Effective- ness
10 am	Going for a run	4	4	6	7

Is there any pattern to your expectations? Are they overly negative, overly positive, accurate?

Fill out a different sheet for each day of the week, including weekends, showing the predicted pleasure and effectiveness. Try to note if your expectations are accurate or not.

More activity = more reward

Some people find they often predict certain activities will not yield any pleasure or effectiveness, so they don't engage in them and don't find out if they are wrong. You might find that exercise, spending time with friends or family, or learning new skills or other activities might be rewarding, so that you can assign these to yourself, again allowing yourself to build up a menu of rewarding and positive things to do. Sometimes an activity might help you to feel effective, such as contacting some former colleagues and exploring the possibility of new contacts for a new job. This kind of activity could or might not be pleasurable. It could be the kind of thing that you might do to feel more effective and to move yourself forward. Also, it may be that you may have to do an activity many times before the pleasure and effectiveness "kicks in." At first, it may be harder to do, and perhaps even not very pleasant. But more activity tends to produce more reward and may help you to get out of those negative thoughts and painful feelings that you have when you respond to your sadness by avoidance and passivity.

EXERCISE: BUILD UP AN ACTIVITY MENU

Rather than avoiding taking part in activities because you worry that they will not be pleasurable, find activities to do and then discover how you feel about them once you have tried them.

- Start to assign some positive activities to yourself.
- List your predictions of how you will feel when you do these things.
- Carry out the experiment—by doing these activities—and then rate them for pleasure and effectiveness.
- Are you predicting that behavior won't be that rewarding, but you find out that sometimes it's more rewarding than you anticipated?
- What is the consequence of predicting that really rewarding behavior won't work for you?
- If it's not that rewarding when you do it, are you willing to continue to try to do these things until the "reward" kicks in? Perhaps it takes a while.

3: Challenge your negative thinking about taking action

You might find yourself thinking, "How can these activities help me get a job? How will exercise, or listening to music, or hanging out with friends, get me the job I need? My problem is that I don't have a job and everything else is useless. Who are you kidding with this nonsense? I have a real problem; I don't have a job." Well, it may be true that exercise and doing fun things or seeing people you like might not get you a job, but it might get you out of your doldrums. After all, you still have to live your life every day. You still have to fill those hours with something.

And, who knows, perhaps if you are in better shape—mentally and physically—you might do better in a job interview. If you are depressed and anxious, and you aren't enjoying your life, it may make it more difficult for you to take part in the interview well. Your depression and helplessness may make it less likely that you will search as effectively for a new job. Your passivity and isolation may spill over to your job search and trap you even more.

Is there any downside in filling your day with some pleasurable, challenging and meaningful activities? Will anyone be worse off if you are feeling better?

You may also have other thoughts that lead you to negate or discount doing positive things to help yourself feel better. For example, you might have thoughts like "This used to feel better when I had a job." For example, going for a nice long walk in the countryside or riding a bike might have been more fun when you weren't feeling down. I would imagine that a lot of the things that you could do for pleasure and effectiveness are not as rewarding as they were when you felt better. Let's assume this is true. So what? *You have to start somewhere.* Why not start from where you are and build from this point on? It's like getting into shape. If you are out of shape, it's more difficult to exercise. So what would you do? Would you wait until you were in shape and then begin to exercise? *Do the hard things now until they become easier.*

The fear of negative thoughts can stop you

Another reason that you might think that these rewarding activities will not be as pleasurable is that when you do them you are thinking all kinds of negative thoughts. For example, you might go for a long walk to get some exercise but find yourself dwelling on negative thoughts such as, "It's pathetic that I am reduced to this—walking around. I used to have a good job." Or you might be thinking, "I am walking but getting nowhere. It's the story of my life." It's natural when you are feeling down to carry a lot of these negative thoughts around with you. But you have a choice of what to do with them. You can dwell on them or you can challenge them.

It's not pathetic, for example, to exercise to feel better. It's adaptive. It's taking care of yourself. It's being responsible to yourself. Exercise can increase those chemicals that make you feel better—they're called endorphins. It's like taking a pep pill. It's also good for your health. So what's maladaptive or pathetic about that?

Your thought that you are getting nowhere is also irrational.

You don't have to be getting somewhere when you are taking care of yourself. You are doing something right now to make your life better. And, by the way, that is *somewhere*. IT'S HERE AND NOW!

Negative thoughts diminish the power of positive actions

Keep in mind that when you take notice of these negative thoughts when you are doing positive things, you are taking away the power of your actions. One way of diffusing these thoughts is to imagine them as a funny little character in a clown outfit that is walking a few feet behind you chattering away. It's like a radio station with static and the words are hard to make out. Perhaps it's a bit annoying, perhaps it occasionally interferes with enjoying the moment. But you don't have to have a conversation with a radio station that's not playing your kind of music. If you can, imagine reaching over, turning down the volume and saying, "I know the chatter is there, but I don't have to engage in it, I don't have to dance to that music. I am taking care of myself."

Keep track of these negative thoughts every day. Challenge them. In the table below you can see how Ken challenged some of these thoughts when he found himself discounting positive things that he was doing. Keep in mind that it all depends on how you respond to your negative moods. If you just sink into them, dwell on them, remain passive, and isolate yourself, you will feel worse. If you take action, connect with people, carry out your plans and challenge these self-defeating thoughts you will feel better. You do have a choice. Look at Ken's responses below.

Ken's Responses to His Negative Thoughts

Negative thoughts	Adaptive thoughts
None of this will help me get a job. I used to be someone with a job.	My job right now is to take care of myself. Doing positive things, including exercise, is a great way for me to take care of myself. I have to live my life, don't I? And, if I am feeling better and looking better, I might do better on a job interview.
These activities are pathetic.	Taking care of myself is not pathetic; it's adaptive. What is the alternative? Should I just sit around and dwell on the negative. I am being adaptive and proactive. I am actually doing something. I am still someone even if I don't have a job right now. I am someone doing adaptive things every day.
I used to enjoy these things more when I felt better.	Well, that's not a surprise. When you feel down you don't enjoy things as much. I need to do these things so that I can improve my mood and keep myself active. Feeling better depends on acting better.

EXERCISE: NEGATIVE THOUGHTS ABOUT HELPING MYSELF

Following Ken's example, keep track of your negative thoughts about your self-help activities and then challenge these thoughts. Is there a pattern to these negative thoughts? Are you constantly saying, "It doesn't matter if I don't have a job" or "This is pathetic"? Keep in mind that you always have a choice to help yourself or defeat yourself. During this time between one job and the next you need to have yourself on your side.

Here's another example to help you.

Negative thoughts	Adaptive thoughts
"What good will this do me? Nothing can help me if I don't have a job"	Taking care of myself is a job I have right now. I can work at getting a job, but having plans every day, doing things that are rewarding, and giving myself credit are all useful and important things to do to help myself.

Now work through the following questions:
- When you do potentially rewarding things, do you have a lot of negative thoughts?
- What are these thoughts? Write them down.
- How would you challenge these negative thoughts?
- Would you be willing to experiment with doing the opposite of what your negative thoughts say? For example, if you are saying, "This won't work," are you willing to keep up the potentially positive behavior for a while? Act *against* what you think and feel.

4: Your current job is looking for a job

Just because your prior job ended, it doesn't mean that you don't have a current job. Your current job is looking for a job. Dedicate some time each day to your job search. This can include looking at ads, contacting people who are potential leads in a network of people in your field, and asking for more leads to contact. You can expect that there will be lots of dead-ends, but—like working in sales—looking for a job takes persistence. You never know when a job will open up and you happen to be the person they are looking for.

As I said at the beginning of the book, this is not a book about how to get a job. It's a book on how to take care of yourself in between the last job and the next. But one way of taking care of yourself is to keep busy looking for a job. You could devote several hours a day, or less than an hour a day—it depends on what there is to do that would be productive. I have found that people who take a "problem-solving approach" when looking for a job tend to do better. So what would this look like?

The problem-solving approach

First, identify what a solution would look like. For example, if you think that the only option you would consider is a job exactly like your prior job, then you are limiting yourself. This might be OK, but it has trade-offs. It might be that there is less demand in the economy for that kind of job. On the other hand, you would have an easier time qualifying for that job and doing it. So always keep in mind a range of options that you could consider. Rank them in order from the most to the least desirable.

Second, get your CV in order. Update your CV so that it reflects all the skills and experiences that you have obtained. Keep in mind that you are selling your labor in the market, so you want to compete as effectively as you can.

Third, make a list of contacts of people you know—or even people you have heard about who know people you know. Categorize these people in terms of how relevant they might be in helping you to find work. For example, someone who works in a company that does the same kind of work that you used to do could be categorized as "A" for most relevant. On the other hand, your brother-in-law who works in an entirely different line of work might be a "C." My view is that everyone knows someone else, so when you contact people always look for more leads—especially relevant leads. A lot of people get their jobs through networks of people who know people. If each person you list as a possible contact knows more people, your contact list will expand with every contact.

Fourth, search for jobs on the internet, through ads and other published sources. The job market is always fluid. People are always leaving jobs, new jobs become available because of expansion and new businesses move into town. Even if the general economy is in a bad shape, there are always some jobs on the market. The key thing is to be willing to search in that market.

Fifth, know the company before you apply. The best way to get that job is to know what the company does. Get as much information about the company as you can and then craft your message about yourself to the needs of that company. I know that when I interview people to work at our Institute in New York City, the worst interviews are with people who don't seem to know anything about our group. It's often easy to find out about a company. You should go to their website, ask colleagues in the business, and research as much as you can. And, then, think about how you can sell them the idea that you can add something to their company that they need. Don't go into the interview with the message "This job would be good for me." No one has set up a business so that it is going to be good for you. You are selling; they are buying. So sell them what they need by knowing what they need, and make yourself the best match for them.

Sixth, be ready to handle rejection. It's often difficult to go to interviews and get rejected. It may add to your feelings of hopelessness. But interviews and the job search is a matter of numbers. The more you search and the more interviews you have, the closer you get to being accepted. It may be difficult, but it is the best way to move yourself forward. Don't take rejection personally. Take it as part of the market. People who work in sales will say to themselves, "With each rejection I am getting close to my number. I am getting close to making the sale." It's a useful approach to apply to going for interviews—giving up is not a workable strategy.

Seventh, use each interview to make the next interview a better one. Think about how your last interview went and then go into "self-correction mode." What this means is that you do a realistic assessment and ask yourself, "What went well and what didn't go well?" For example, you want to avoid complaining about your previous employer or sounding as if you don't know how your skills will fit this job. One woman went on "information interviews" to find out what was out there, what people were looking for. These were actually people working in companies that did not have current openings. She simply asked friends to give her leads for people working in an industry that she wanted to get into. These information interviews helped her to learn more about the field and more about how she needed to present herself, and they helped her develop a strategy for a real interview. Make yourself into someone who is constantly getting better at job interviews. The better you get, the more likely you are to get a job.

EXERCISE: BE METHODICAL ABOUT LOOKING FOR A JOB

Use this list to help you create structure in your search for a job.
- Your current job is looking for a job. Go to work every day.
- Identify what kinds of jobs would be OK for you. Could you consider being more flexible? Why or why not?
- List your contacts, potential contacts, and resources for looking for a job.
- Have a schedule each day, every week, for what you are doing towards looking for a job.

- Research companies before you consider an interview. Know what they do and what they need.
- Think of each interview as a step towards the next interview, which is a step towards a job.

5: Schedule some fun for yourself

Although you are unemployed, you don't have to be morose. Keep yourself busy by scheduling daily activities that are interesting, fun or even challenging. Get out your old hobbies or start a new one. Get more exercise. Have lunch with friends, read a book, or travel. I suggest to people that you think of this time as a kind of sabbatical from your previous job. You may as well make use of the time now, because when you are back to work you will kick yourself for not having had some fun while you had the time.

Having fun is—well, a lot of fun. Some people I have counseled use this time to get more involved in a sport: tennis, golf, biking, hiking, running, or just plain exercise. One man who was out of work thought this would be a good time to get into better shape, so he started taking three-mile walks every day. He had to build up to it, but he was out there most days with his mp3 player in his ear, enjoying being outside. (Incidentally, some people have "seasonal affective disorder," which means they feel worse in overcast weather, so getting more sunlight early in the day is very helpful. Perhaps you could start each day by taking a walk or jogging. The more sunlight, the better.) Having fun is one of the best protectors against depression.

Spending time with the ones you love

Having fun can also include time with your kids, your partner, or your pet. One of my clients, who was a very serious person and seemed to have been wrapped up in his work when he had a job, had previously not taken time to have much fun with his eight-year-old son. I asked him how his son saw the world.

"Well, he loves soccer, and he loves kicking the ball around, and making believe that he is a famous soccer player," he said. He agreed that his son knew how to have fun. I suggested that he spend some time each day trying to learn from his son how to have fun. Playing was the answer. Make-believe could work. So he began playing with his son, getting into the make-believe world, announcing what they were doing like they were on television. He learned that he could get a lot out of being a kid for an hour. And his son got a lot more out of his dad.

Marie had a dog that she adored. I suggested that having fun might include taking really nice long walks with "Jill" and enjoying Jill's enjoyment of the city. There were lots of other dogs out there—and, in New York City, you are known as the father or mother of your dog. Getting out with your dog is a way to meet other people—and other dogs. Your dog will love you more. Not only does your dog not care that you don't have a job but he also might think that taking him out for a walk is the best thing in the world that you could possibly do.

Creative play—it's part of your day

Try to be creative with fun things to do. Perhaps there are some films you want to see, or museums, exhibitions to visit or music that you want to listen to. You might think, "I can't afford to do anything." Certainly, financial concerns and limitations are real, but do you really mean "anything"? The challenge may be to find activities that are free—or at very low cost. For example, riding your bike, going to a free museum, taking a walk, visiting the library—all can be free and valuable. (Also, in Chapter Seven I look at some of the things that you can do that don't cost you anything.)

Since you have a lot of time right now—and you won't have this free time when you get back to work—try to have more fun doing what you wanted to do in the past but never had the time. One man who followed this advice began having so much fun keeping himself busy that, when he finally got a job, he said to me, "I wonder if this means I won't have as much fun anymore."

Some people—including the partners or spouses of the unemployed—will say that you don't deserve to have fun if you are out of work. You should be looking for a job. Well, you *should* be looking for a job—but you can't do that 24 hours a day. As I said earlier, looking for a job *is* your current job, but you also have another job: taking care of yourself. This will involve keeping busy, having daily plans, doing pleasurable and rewarding activities and having fun. Of course, you and your partner may need to discuss how money is spent, but being unemployed does not mean that you should deprive yourself of pleasure and fun activities. I would suggest that taking care of yourself—by doing rewarding activities—is a great investment that can pay off.

Having fun doesn't mean that you neglect looking for a job. If you balance your job search with self-care, you will probably be more upbeat and in better physical and mental shape when you go for an interview. Having fun will improve your outlook and your ability to do a good interview. But it's good to have fun no matter what. Just ask your kids.

Use the table below to list some fun things every day, every week. Plan fun things a day and a week in advance. If possible, allow yourself some "silly time," just as if you are a kid for a few minutes each day. Having fun isn't going to hurt anyone—there is nothing bad about pursuing happiness.

EXERCISE: HAVING FUN

Keep track of what you actually do and what you felt and thought while you did these things. Here's an example.

Fun things to do	When did you do this?	What you thought and felt while doing these things
Going for a bike ride	Tuesday morning	This is beautiful being out in nature, moving along the pavement, feeling the wind. Even if it rains, it's great to be riding my bike. I used to enjoy this so much when I was a kid

Use this list of points to help you plan for more fun in your life:
- What are some things that you used to do that were fun?
- Schedule some fun every day.
- Give yourself permission to live a good life. If you can laugh every day, you are making progress.
- Look at people or animals who have fun—who know how to play—and learn from them. Look at the world from the innocence and awe of a child. Then, play.

SUMMARY

Getting active and staying active is one of the best ways of taking care of yourself during this time between jobs. You don't have to sit around passively waiting for a job to show up. Every day you actually have two jobs: looking for a job and taking care of yourself. Realistically, you may need to spend more time on the second job—taking care of yourself. It's important to have an active, coping strategy every day—rather than waiting to get a job so that you can "move on." You have to live your life every day. People who plan their days get more done and find that they have something to wake up for.

Being passive is a guarantee for getting depressed. In this chapter we have examined some specific, concrete and simple things to do today—and each day—to make your life better. Now let's review some of the main points.

Have a daily plan, and a plan for every week so that you have rewarding and effective activities in your schedule. Be strategic in looking for a job. Take a problem-solving approach rather than dwelling on negatives, complaining or isolating yourself. Think of everyone as a potential lead, as part of a larger network of people who might be able to connect you to that job. And be sure to have some fun—you deserve it.

Keep in mind that your mood depends on how you respond to your mood. Remember what I said at the beginning of this chapter. If you respond to your sad feelings with avoidance and passivity, you will feel more sad and hopeless. But if you respond to these feelings by getting out, living your life, and doing rewarding and effective things, you will feel better. Feeling better is about acting better.

What is your strategy when that sad mood arises—because it will? Making your job looking for a job and taking care of yourself puts you in charge of your life. And, when those negative thoughts try to rob you of your happiness, you can act against them, do positive things anyway and prove to yourself that these thoughts are distorted and unrealistic. You are in charge—if you are willing to do the work.

4

BUILD YOUR SELF-ESTEEM

In a recent article in the *Wall Street Journal* 26% of those currently working had some period of unemployment during the past 30 months. Nevertheless, many people who are unemployed feel a sense of shame. "I feel like a loser," one man said. "People will look down on me."

The irony of these shameful thoughts is that they don't seem to reflect the fact that unemployment is highly likely for millions of people in the workforce. Market conditions—changes in financial stability, declining demand, over-supply, and pessimism about business—have lead companies to lay workers off. The central and local government cuts mean that, at times, there is no alternative other than to lay off highly qualified workers. Private companies also suffer in difficult economic times. People have less money to spend, they are more cautious, there is less demand and companies lay off workers because there is less work needed. It's a vicious cycle. Unemployment is part of a larger system of uncertainty, change and lack of control. It is often beyond the control of those who are laid off.

Let's look at how you can handle your self-critical thoughts and your sense of shame. What can you do?

1: Normalize the problem

When you watch the news, you recognize that you are not alone. Millions of people are in the same boat. That doesn't mean the boat is sinking, it only means that market economies like ours go through ups and downs. If you are out of work, join the crowd.

As I mentioned in Chapter One, about 36–38% of the adult population is not working at any given time. (This is the "labor participation rate.") Unemployment is so widespread that there isn't a family or a friend that doesn't know someone who is out of work or who has once been out of work.

Think about all the people you know who have been out of work at some point. It could be your father or mother, brother or sister, your friends, your neighbors, or your former colleagues. Whenever I discuss the issue of unemployment, people tell me their personal stories or the stories about people close to them. It's an unfortunate but widely experienced problem—I can't imagine anyone not knowing someone who has gone through a period of being unemployed.

Danny lost his job in the construction business during one of the economic downturns. He knew construction work was cyclical, and when the economy was booming, there was plenty of work to go around. But when the economy stalled, lots of people were laid off. For Danny, normalizing the problem was recognizing that a lot of people he knew—and people he did not know—lost their jobs. I asked him if he knew other people over the years who had been out of work. He thought for a moment and began to smile—that smile of recognition that says, *I am not alone.* "Yes, my brother was out of work two years ago. So was my neighbor, and some of my other friends. Come to think of it—so was my cousin." As he began realizing it was "normal" to be out of work, he began feeling less different from other people.

I asked him what he thought about these people. "I actually seldom think about them. It's funny, but I am sure that they probably were going through a lot of the experiences and feelings I am having right now. But if I were to think about them I suppose I would think, 'It must have been a hard time for you.'" He realized that he would not be critical of them, he would try to be supportive, and he would realize that they are human just like him.

EXERCISE: LOOKING AT OTHERS WHO ARE OUT OF WORK

Spend a few moments thinking about people who have had periods without work.

- What do you think about the fact that there are always millions of people out of work?
- Do you know any people who have lost their jobs in the past? Or now?
- How do you feel about them?
- Are you more understanding and accepting of them than you are of yourself?
- If So why?

2: Think of it as a "situation" rather than as "you"

People who are unemployed are not "different people;" they just find themselves in a temporary situation with which they must cope. Perhaps market conditions changed, perhaps there is a "downsizing" in the company, perhaps a new "team" is being brought in, perhaps it has nothing to do with you—except that you are the one who lost his or her job. Is it the situation or is it the person ("you")?

There are four ways of thinking about something not working out:

1: Simply bad luck. Sometimes you are the unlucky person who is working for a company that is having a downturn. Danny had the bad luck of working in construction when the economy hit a recession. Or perhaps you have the bad luck that your boss didn't like you. Bad luck can change.

2: It was just too difficult. For example, Karen was trying to sell software that could not compete with the new software available. It was simply too difficult. Laura, another of my clients, was working in a literary agency that couldn't get publishers to buy the books. It was simply too hard. No matter how hard she tried, the market wasn't there. When things are too hard, it's important to do a "realistic diagnosis" and recognize that if the rewards aren't there, it becomes too difficult a task. That doesn't mean there aren't lots of other things that you could do. It just means this one was too difficult.

3: A lack of effort. It could be that you lost your job because you didn't try hard enough. Perhaps you didn't get to work on time, perhaps you took time off or didn't work hard enough, perhaps you didn't follow tasks through. For example, Wendy was fired from her job because she was wasting time Googling and using the internet rather than doing her job, and not getting things done that her boss required. The good news is that she learned from that experience and moved on to the next job where she was far more focused on getting things done at work rather than wasting time with things that had nothing to do with work. You can always change your effort the next time. You can learn from your mistakes rather than dwelling on them.

4: You didn't have the ability to do the job. For example, Paul dropped out of the university where he was studying law—his grades were abysmal. He realized, later, "I just wasn't cut out to be a lawyer. I found it so hard. I hated every minute."

Recognizing your strengths and weaknesses is important. Paul went on to find a career helping other people as a counselor. He is a lot happier working with his strengths.

The label makes a difference

If you think of this as a "situation" or "a problem to solve" rather than as a badge of failure, you can be more proactive in dealing with your temporary period of unemployment. If it is the "situation," you can think of it as something external to you, perhaps a result of bad luck, perhaps something that might be temporary (situations change). If it is the situation, then you need to find a better situation—a better alternative. If it is the situation, then thinking creatively, looking for other situations with better outcomes would make sense for you. Even if the "situation" was that you were going through a difficult time at work and you were laid off because of something you did, that is a situation you can change the next time.

Think about the reasons why you lost your job:

- Did you lose your job because of luck, the difficulty of the job, a lack of effort or a lack of ability?
- Do you think of being unemployed as a "situation," or is it a reflection of who you are as a person?
- If you thought of this as a time to solve problems rather than criticizing yourself, how would you feel?
- Are there different situations — different possibilities — that might be out there? If so, what are they and what can you do?

3: Do you have a maladaptive way of looking at this?

In cognitive therapy, we have found that people who are prone to depression, anxiety, or anger have problematic biases in their thinking. You may not have been depressed or anxious before you lost your job, but you may be prone to these feelings now that you are out of work. This may be related to how you are thinking about what has happened — and what it means.

Let's look at some problematic ways of thinking that you might be using right now.

RECOGNIZING NEGATIVE THINKING

Look at the table below and see if you have a tendency to use these thinking biases. We all do, at times, but you might be more prone to do this now than in the past. Note down the ones you are prone to: is there any pattern to your thinking—and how it is related to your feelings?

Typical biases in thinking	Definition	Examples
Mind reading	You think you know what people are thinking and feeling	People think I am a loser. Everyone knows I don't have a job
Fortune-telling	You are predicting the future without sufficient evidence	I will never get a job
Negative filter	You only focus on the negatives	I can't take that holiday that we planned because we have to watch our money
Discounting the positives	You don't see the positives as valid and you think they don't really count	Yes, I can do a lot of things even though I don't have a job, but they don't count because the only thing that counts is getting a new job
Catastrophizing	You view what is happening or what might happen as awful—as if the world is going to end	I just can't stand it that I don't have a job. It's the worst thing in the world. I will probably end up homeless
Personalizing	You take things personally, as if they are directed at you or as if you are to blame	It must be me. I failed. Even though there are a lot of people out of work, I must be at fault
Labelling	You label yourself in global terms	I am a failure, a loser
All-or-nothing thinking	You think in black-and-white terms and you don't see the shades of grey in your life	Nothing works out. There is nothing that I can do. I don't do well at anything

EXERCISE: CHALLENGING NEGATIVE THINKING

It's a good idea to write your thinking biases down as they occur. Below you can see how to challenge these negative thoughts.

Typical biases in thinking	Challenging your negative thinking
Mind reading	How do you know what other people are thinking or feeling? Could you be wrong? Maybe they aren't even thinking about you right now. You are not a mind-reader.
Fortune-telling	You can't predict the future. We don't know what could happen until it has happened. How many times have you been wrong in the past? What are some things that could happen that might lead to a good outcome? How can you increase the chances of positive outcomes?
Negative filter	Are you only focusing on the negative? What good will that do? Why not look at all the evidence –everything that is going on? Make a list of the positives and negatives. Try to "catch" positive things happening so that you have a more balanced view. This is not the "power of positive thinking"—this is the power of "realistic thinking."
Discounting the positives	Are you not counting positive things? Why? What is the consequence of this? Do you think you are being realistic? What would be the advantage of also counting the positives? Would it help motivate you, decrease your feeling of being discouraged? Are you thinking, 'This doesn't count because I don't have a job?' What is the justification for this narrow discounting way of thinking? Try to keep track of all the positives for a week and see if it helps you feel better.

Catastrophizing	Are you viewing life as awful? Does this mean that there is nothing positive, ever? It may be a difficult time for you, but viewing it as a catastrophe only makes it worse. Try a more balanced view and see if there are any pleasurable and effective things that you can do. What can you still do even if you don't have a job right now? Do those things and then give them credit.
Personalizing	Not everything is your fault. Companies often lay off people because of market conditions over which you have no control. Sometimes bosses are unrealistic and don't understand that workers are human. If there are millions of people out of work at any one time it must be that there is something about the economy that leads to this. There is never full employment.
Labeling	If you label yourself in such negative ways you are likely to feel worse. You can look at the different positives and negatives that you have and get a more balanced view of yourself. No one is perfect and no one is all bad. Look at the things that you have done in your life that are positive, and give yourself some credit. Try to be more compassionate and kind towards yourself.
All-or-nothing thinking	If you look at yourself in this black-and-white way you are not being realistic or fair. Take a look at degrees of positives and negatives. Look at how your behavior might vary or change across different situations. Perhaps there are some things that you have been better at and some that you are not so good at. You can use self-correction rather than self-criticism to continually think of how you can improve yourself.

Don't believe everything you say to yourself

You may remember that Ken used to isolate himself because he felt ashamed of being unemployed. Let's look at how he could use these challenges to his negative thoughts. Ken was mind-reading: "People think I am a loser because I don't have a job." But his challenge was, "My family seems 100% on my side and has been encouraging me. I also don't know what people think. If anything, my former colleagues might be thinking they are next." His personalizing included his thoughts that he had failed at the job, which is why he was laid off, but the facts were that the company was downsizing and laying off hundreds of people. He also realized that his position was being squeezed out because of changing priorities at the company. His labeling thought was, "I must be a failure," but his challenge to that was quite powerful: "I graduated from a university, I had done a good job for years, I am a good husband and father, and I am a good person." The more he challenged these negative thoughts, the better he felt. Just because he had a *thought* didn't make it a *fact*. We tell ourselves a lot of things that are just plain distorted and not true.

Let's take a closer look at how you put yourself down.

4: Examine your negative thoughts about yourself

What are you saying to yourself about you? Perhaps you are like some people who label themselves as a "failure": "I don't have a job, I must be a failure." Perhaps you even think of yourself as "unlovable": "Who would want me, if I don't have a job?" You are engaging in all-or-nothing thinking, and you are "labeling" yourself. It's as if everything about you is a failure if you don't have a job right now. Is that really true?

EXERCISE: ANALYZING A NEGATIVE THOUGHT

Let's start working on the thought "I am a failure." Answer the following questions:

- How much do you believe (from 0% to 100%) that you are a failure?
- What would count as successful behaviors in life for someone?
- Have you ever had successful experiences?
- If someone else lost their job, would you consider them a "failure"?
- If you were a failure and then got a job would you be a failure the

minute before you got the job and a success right at the very
second you accepted the job?

- Are there some behaviors that you can engage in now that are
rewarding and meaningful?

Now, looking at your answers to these questions, is it possible
this label you give yourself is unfair and inaccurate? Look at how
Claire, whom we met in Chapter One, dealt with these questions:

Q: How much do you believe (from 0 per cent to 100%) that you
     are a failure?
A: 90%

Q: What would count as successful behaviors in life for
     someone?
A: Accomplishing goals, getting an education, being a good
     friend, taking care of yourself, doing the right thing,
     working, getting good feedback from people.

Q: Have you ever had successful experiences?
A: Yes. I have had a lot of successful experiences, although I
     don't have a job right now.

Q: If someone else lost their, job would you consider them a
     "failure"?
A: Probably not. I have had a number of friends out of work in
     the past and I have tried to be supportive to them.

Q: If you were a failure and then got a job would you be a
     failure the minute before you got the job and a success right
     at the very second you accepted the job?
A: It makes no sense to think that you are a failure at one
     minute and a success at another. And, since I have had a
     number of successes in the past—and I still do many things
     well—it doesn't make sense to think of myself as a failure.

Q: Are there some behaviors that you can engage in now that
     are rewarding and meaningful?
A: Yes, I am a good daughter to my mother, who has had

medical problems. I am a good friend. I try to go to exercise class and I try to do the right thing.

Claire realized that her criticisms of herself were unfair and unrealistic. She was personalizing a job loss—blaming herself—and then discounting all the other behaviors, accomplishments, and qualities that she had. We tend to do that when we label ourselves as a "failure" because we fail to see the bigger picture of the multifaceted qualities that each of us has. A specific job at a specific time is one part of the many experiences in your life. *You are bigger than one job.*

5: Are there any advantages to criticizing yourself?

Some people think that they if they lose their job they have to feel bad about themselves, and they have to be depressed. But losing your job doesn't imply anything that is necessary about how you think about yourself. If 26% of people are out of work during a three-year period, why would they all have to feel bad about themselves? What good is that? Losing your job is a *situation*—something that happens—but how you think about yourself is up to you. And it's also up to you whether you use this time between jobs to be depressed or to be adaptive.

Sometimes we think we can motivate ourselves if we criticize ourselves. For example, you might think, "I lost my job, so if I don't put a lot of pressure on myself and criticize myself for being unemployed, I won't have any motivation to look for another one." It's true that you don't want to become complacent or lazy, but how will putting yourself down really help you look for a job? It's like saying, "If I get really depressed I will do a terrific job in finding that next job." The opposite is probably true.

Acceptance, not criticism, is helpful

You don't need to criticize yourself to solve problems and find a job. If you want to solve problems—like searching for a job, getting your CV together, networking with people, or developing new job skills—you are better off accepting your situation and taking care of yourself. You are likely to do better at interviews if you are feeling confident than if you are feeling depressed.

Or perhaps you think that self-criticism is "being realistic." First, you may have lost your job because of a situation external to you. One man lost his job in sales because the technical training he was selling had become somewhat obsolete.

Another woman lost her job in public relations because the company she was working for was getting less business. But even if you did do something that led you to get fired, being realistic is simply acknowledging and recognizing the mistake—and then working out how not to repeat it. First we will look at self-criticism and then, a little later, I will distinguish between self-correction and self-criticism.

EXERCISE: WHAT DOES SELF CRITICISM ACHIEVE?

Ask yourself these questions:
- Do you think that criticizing yourself has any advantages?
- Do you think that you will motivate yourself or that you are being realistic by criticizing yourself?
- What is the real evidence that criticizing yourself is helping?
- How is criticizing yourself hurting you?
- Is criticizing yourself really helping you solve problems?

6: What if I lost the job because of what I did?

Sometimes you lose your job because you are not doing your job properly. I doubt this accounts for the high rates of unemployment, but it's a point worth considering. Sometimes people lose their job for good reasons—and it's really their fault. How can you deal with this reality without sinking into rumination, guilt, and excessive self-criticism? One man lost his job because he became passive–aggressive when his boss did not give him priority.

When we are passive–aggressive we withhold from other people by purposefully not doing what they expect us to do. It's a way of being hostile without owning up to it. He was late getting work done, he complained to other colleagues (who, in reality, can never be trusted with your complaints), and he stopped acting like a team player. It was true that it was his fault. Another woman was sacked because she was continually asking for reassurance from her colleagues and her boss, and became too "high maintenance." Another man lost his job because he got into arguments with his boss. Perhaps the boss over-reacted, but in the real world you need to play along with the team or you won't play at all. So how can you handle this kind of situation that leads to "realistic" self-criticism?

Do a realistic assessment of your mistakes

All of us make mistakes. The people I described above truly did things that led to them getting fired. Let's face it, sometimes you can be your own worst enemy. Rather than ruminate (dwell and brood) on your mistakes, make up a list of what you did wrong and keep it handy. You want to learn from your mistakes rather than repeating them. One man listed the following: "Complaining about my boss or the job to other people at work; not getting work done on time; expecting and demanding fairness in everything." Now he has a list of mistakes not to make again.

Make a to-do list of how to improve
your future performance

Knowing your mistakes helps you avoid repeating them. It's called "learning." Criticizing yourself is not the same thing as learning. No one says, "I did well on the test the second time because I criticized myself." They are more likely to say, "I took it seriously. I studied this time." You may have made some really stupid mistakes, but why dwell on them? Use them for a to-do list for your future job. For example, make a list of objectives so that your mistakes can improve future performance: "Don't complain, don't avoid, get work done on time, don't argue with the boss." Move forward with a plan to make things different in the future.

Replace self-criticism with self-correction

Self-criticism involves all of those useless, depressing labels about you: "I screwed up, I'm a failure, I can't do anything right." Even if they are true, getting stuck on self-criticism keeps you trapped. If you play tennis and your coach tells you that you swung the wrong way, don't sit down and criticize yourself. Swing the right way. Self-correction is a plan of action that leads you forward, propelled by the learning involved in making mistakes: "In the future I commit to getting the work done and not complaining." Once you have moved the self-criticism into self-correction you have a plan of action. You can let it go, plan for the future and enjoy the present moment.

Why feel shame? When we are ashamed, we sink into a morass of self-negation, we become depressed, isolating ourselves, and refusing to get out and try again. Self-correction is the opposite. You are knocked down—perhaps because you tripped up—but you get back up and learn a new way to cope. Let's take a closer look at how to reduce your shame.

EXERCISE: TURNING CRITICISM INTO SELF-CORRECTION

Look at your past mistakes afresh by answering these questions:
- Do a realistic assessment of your mistakes.
- Make a to-do list of how to improve your future performance.
- Replace self-criticism with self-correction.

7: Reduce your shame

The consequence of your shame is that you may isolate yourself: "I don't want people to know I'm not working." As a result you stay home, don't return emails, and hide from the world. This leads to more rumination, more shame, and more isolation. In Japan, many businessmen who are unemployed get dressed in their suits and leave their apartments in the morning, take a train to a different part of the city and sit in the park all day. They don't want their neighbors to know they don't have a job.

If you have ever known anyone who lost a job, would you treat them like a pariah—an outcast who is a social leper? Or would you sympathize with them and try to think of how you could be supportive? As mentioned earlier, perhaps you are not giving your friends and family enough credit—perhaps they can be understanding, compassionate and supportive. Perhaps they have gone through the same thing that you are going through.

Talking to others can help you

Some of my clients who have been unemployed have found that there are some people out there who actually want to help. For example, one client, Phyllis, told her friends that she was out of work and looking for a job. One of them knew someone in another company who was looking for new employees and Phyllis was able to get an interview. Sometimes talking to people means that they might talk to other people on your behalf, and your network of connections grows. Isolating yourself only decreases your chances of finding a job.

It's true, though, that there are going to be some people who will avoid you (some former colleagues perhaps), or even judge you. There could be a lot of reasons why people avoid you. Some may be afraid of getting fired themselves and may view maintaining contact with you as a liability. Others may feel guilty that they have kept their job while you have lost yours. Still others may simply be self-centered and think that you can't help them anymore so they don't bother.

That says something negative about them, not about you. I've always thought that when someone I know is having a hard time, it's my turn to step in and support them. If there are people out there who are judgmental, then keep in mind that you never want to be like them. One day—when you have that job—someone else you know will be unemployed. And you can be a better friend than some fair-weather friends that you may have had.

Shame is not a way to cope, and being laid off is not a personal failure. It's a situation that needs to be addressed. I don't recall there being an eleventh commandment that says, "Thou shalt not lose thy job."

EXERCISE: UNDERSTANDING YOUR FEELINGS OF SHAME

Put your feelings into context by answering these questions:
- What do you avoid because you feel ashamed of being unemployed?
- Do you think that other people who don't have jobs should feel ashamed? Why or why not?
- Would you be supportive to someone who lost their job?
- Even if someone thought less of you, does that mean you have to think less of yourself?

8: Act against your shame

It's one thing to realize that your thoughts are unfair and inaccurate, but it's another to actually change your behavior and act against the way you are thinking. If you are ashamed and are isolating yourself—or avoiding certain situations or people—then you are still holding on to these shameful thoughts and feelings. Are you avoiding family members, neighbors, friends or former colleagues? You are probably doing a lot of mind-reading—that is, anticipating what other people might think without even knowing. For example, your mind-reading might be something like this: "My cousin will think I am a loser. She won't want to talk to me." How do you know? Perhaps your cousin is actually someone who could care about you. Perhaps they loved you before you had the job that you no longer have. Or you might think, "If someone I worked with thinks less about me, then I have to think less about myself." Does that make sense? Should you base your self-esteem on what someone else might think—someone who is unfeeling, uncaring, and judgmental?

Shame is something that you have to "buy into." No one can make you feel ashamed unless you actually believe the irrational thoughts that lead to shame. For example, imagine the following dialogue between your shame thoughts and your rational thoughts:

SHAME THOUGHTS: You should feel ashamed that people might know that you don't have a job.

RATIONAL THOUGHTS: Really, why should I feel ashamed? I haven't done anything immoral, illegal or malicious. Perhaps you can help me understand why I should feel ashamed of not having a job.

SHAME THOUGHTS: Well, because everyone will think you are a loser.

RATIONAL THOUGHTS: I doubt that everyone will think I am a loser. I am still the same person I was when I had a job. I lost a job—millions of people do. In fact, about one-third of the population will lose their jobs in a three-year period. I don't think of them as losers.

SHAME THOUGHTS: Well, it's terrible if even one person thinks less of you.

RATIONAL THOUGHTS: Why would it be terrible if someone thinks less of me? It only suggests that they don't really understand the nature of unemployment. It sounds like you are saying that I should base my feelings on what an irrational, intolerant, judgmental person thinks. That doesn't make much sense to me.

SHAME THOUGHTS: Well, I think less of you.

RATIONAL THOUGHTS: Yes, I know you do. You are judgmental and intolerant. You aren't my real friend. I have news for you: I don't care what you think of me!

Confront your shame

Are you ready to confront your shame and put it down? You have already looked at some ways to think differently — and you may be changing how you actually feel. But the real test is acting against your shame. Here are some things to consider actually doing:

1: Tell someone you are avoiding that you lost your job. But before you tell them, write down what you predict they will say. Ask yourself why you have been reluctant to contact them — then challenge your thinking. For example, you might have been thinking, "They will think less of me." Your challenges could be, "I don't really know what they might think. If they think less of me, it says something about them, not about me. Why should I care if someone else is not understanding? It may also be that they could be understanding and I have misjudged them. Perhaps I can give them a chance to see if they can be a good friend."

2: Go to places where people might see you. For example, if you are like some people, you may be barricading yourself in your home. Go out during the day and walk around. Let people see that you are not going to work. Treat yourself like you are free to go anywhere that you want to. Ask yourself if you have been imprisoning yourself because of your fear of what others might think. Then consider how much more important it is for you to be free to do what you want to do. You really don't know if other people are even thinking about you. If they are, it's up to them to be understanding and decent. Perhaps they will lose their jobs next week.

Keep increasing your anti-shame behavior each day and each week. If you are talking with someone, tell them that you are in-between jobs. Go out to stores, health clubs, restaurants, see friends, make contacts, talk to people. The more time you get out of your shame and start living your life again, the better you will feel.

EXERCISE: BE PROACTIVE ABOUT YOUR FEELINGS OF SHAME

Work through the following points:
- What would be the advantage of feeling less shame and going to places and meeting people that you have avoided?
- Identify your shame thoughts and challenge them. Put down your shame.
- Should you base your feelings about yourself on what an intolerant and unsupportive person might think of you?
- Tell someone you are avoiding that you lost your job.
- Go to places where people might see you.
- Take your life back.

9: Show some compassion towards yourself

You are going through one of the more difficult times in your life, and you will need all your energy and all your confidence. You will need to be the best that you can be in meeting this challenge. *You will need to have you on your side.*

What does that self-critical voice sound like? Can you form an imaginary visual image of that character that keeps putting you down? Perhaps it feels like a harsh, high-pitched, sharp, grating voice. Perhaps you can imagine it pointing at you, scolding you, telling you how bad you are. There is no compassion in that voice, it doesn't want to support you. It's not on your side.

If you have been criticizing yourself, you have been acting as your own worst enemy. Your self-criticism won't motivate you; it will demoralize you. It's not realistic—even if you have made mistakes—it's better to self-correct than to self-criticize. It's better to be kind to yourself and reward yourself every time you do something that is positive. I know it may sound frivolous to say this, but imagine you were training the dog to do something new. You would reward him every step of the way. I like to tell my clients that it's sometimes good to *be your own dog.* Be kind, reward, support and love. That's how I treat my dog. That's how I try to treat myself.

Being your own friend

Imagine if you were to become your best compassionate and loving friend. Every hour of every day this friend would be there, cheering you on, praising you for the steps you are taking to make your life better. This friend is filled with kindness: "Hey, I know you lost your job, but I am always your friend, I will be there even more for you during this time." This compassionate best friend is filled with warmth—her voice is soft, gentle, and soothing—she puts her arms around you and strokes your hair. She reminds you that you are loved. Perhaps your self-critical voice sounds louder in your mind, and may seem more forceful and convincing. But you will need some compassion for yourself, some kindness. Everything you do during this time between jobs should remind you that you are the one who has to take care of yourself—you are the one that you need, and you are the one who can direct loving kindness towards yourself, especially when you are feeling down, lost, and all alone. You are never all alone, if you have yourself on your side.

I asked Karen (who previously worked as a software salesperson) to tell me how she would treat her daughter if she had lost her job. "I would tell her that I love her, I am always here for her. I would tell her that she can count on me, that I want to help. I would give her a hug." I then asked Karen if she could imagine doing that for herself. "You know, I am a lot more compassionate towards other people than I have been towards myself." Directing compassion inwards is as important as directing it outwards. You are human, you also need and deserve loving kindness.

EXERCISE: PRACTICE SHOWING COMPASSION

Work through the following questions to establish the difference between a self-critical voice and one of compassion and the feelings it would evoke.

- What does that self-critical voice sound like?
- If you were to imagine it as a person, what would it look like?
- What would the most loving, warm and kind voice sound like to you? Who would it remind you of?
- What would it be saying to you?
- Imagine expressing this compassionate loving kindness towards someone you love who is going through unemployment.
- What would it feel like to express that towards yourself?

SUMMARY

Building your self-esteem is a great way to keep your head above water and to approach your next job. You can change your belief that "If I am out of work I have to feel bad about myself" to a new belief: "Since I am out of work I have to take care of myself." Follow these pointers every day to get your self-esteem back on track:

Normalize the problem: Recognize that millions of people are unemployed at any one time. It's part of the reality of having a job that sometimes you will find yourself in between jobs. Think of it as a "situation" rather than as "you." The situation right now is that you are unemployed—but that is not who you are.

Do you have a maladaptive way of looking at this? Examine what you are saying to yourself. Are you looking at this in entirely personal terms, labeling yourself, viewing it in all-or-nothing terms, and treating it as a catastrophe? Examine your negative thoughts about yourself by writing them down. Consider how often you find yourself putting yourself down.

Are there any advantages to criticizing yourself? Sometimes you might think that criticizing yourself will motivate you and make things better. It's OK to identify mistakes that you may have made—these are behaviors, not who you are as a person.

If you really believe that you lost your job because of something that you did, treat it as a *learning experience*. What can you learn to do differently in the future? How can you use this information to empower yourself in your next job? It's important to be realistic about mistakes that we make. That's how we grow. Have a plan of how you would do things differently. Criticizing yourself is not a good plan. Changing behavior is a good plan.

Make a to-do list of how to improve your future performance:
It's always useful to have "targets" to aim for—like the target of positive behavior that will help you in the future. Correcting yourself is empowering—it means you can realize that you have room to grow. When you find yourself criticizing yourself, decide to set aside the negative labels and replace them with a list of things to do differently. Then plan to do those things.

Reduce your shame: There is nothing unethical or immoral about losing a job. Recognize that this is a normal event for millions of people. Ask yourself if you could be supportive to a friend who lost his or her job. Then be supportive to yourself. Realize that you might be avoiding people and places because you are ashamed or embarrassed about being out of work. Then practice acting against your shame by talking to people, going places and acting against your shame. The more you normalize living life every day, the less ashamed you will feel.

Show some compassion towards yourself: The best friend that you really need is yourself. Be kind and gentle and compassionate towards yourself. Validate your feelings, encourage yourself, give yourself credit for trying. The great thing about supporting yourself is that you are always there to do it.

5

DON'T GET STUCK IN YOUR HEAD

You probably remember Ken from Chapter One, who complained that the worst time of the day was when he got up, because he had nothing to do. He would sit in his apartment going over all the bad things that seemed to have happened to him. He would wake up in the morning and lie in bed for an hour brooding over how terrible it was that he got fired. He would recall the image of being told that he had lost his job, recalling how bad it felt, and his thoughts would then take off: "Why me? Didn't I do a good job? It's not fair. I can't believe this happened to me." Getting up, having his coffee, he would distract himself with the morning news, but then, once alone again with his thoughts, he would continue with further over-thinking: "I feel like a loser. How can I face the day? I have nothing to do." His thoughts would turn to worries about the future: "Will I ever get a job?" and "How can I support my family?" Over and over again, his mind was off and running, making him feel worse and worse.

Ken was like many unemployed people who are facing the difficulty of what to do with all that "free time." You may be similar; you probably spend an inordinate amount of time "thinking about things." These repeated, negative thoughts are called "rumination" and you will remember that I mentioned them in passing in earlier chapters. Cows "ruminate" when they chew on their cud, continually chomping away for long periods of time. When you chew on your thoughts, going over the same ones and getting no answers and no solutions, you are also ruminating. It's not just having a single thought and then moving on; it's as if you are stuck in your head, spinning your wheels, getting deeper and deeper into negativity, digging yourself a deeper hole.

You sit at home, isolated, and keep playing out scenes in your head: "Why did this happen to me?", "I can't believe I don't have a job," or "This really is lousy." You dwell on it, chewing it over, repeating the same negative thoughts over and over. You keep focusing on questions that may have no answer, like "How could this happen to me?" or "Why me?", or focusing on how bad you feel, "I can't believe I'm so depressed." You may replay in your head the experience of getting fired: "I can't get it out of my head that she told me my contract was terminated." You may ruminate about the unfairness of it all, the sense that you are stuck, or the belief that everything is hopeless. Sometimes you ruminate about your physical aches and pains—which may be quite real—but you continue to focus on them, feeling worse and worse.

The reasons you might be ruminating

You may be ruminating so you can work out why this happened—as if repeating the negative thoughts will answer a question. But the fact that you don't have a job right now and that you need to find better ways to cope is the *reality* you must deal with. Rumination won't provide an answer that will solve your problems.

Rumination leads to depression and keeps you depressed.[10] People who ruminate withdraw from the real world, often isolating themselves from other people. When you ruminate you are almost always focused on something negative—what is going on in your head. Because you are focused on all the negative chatter in your head you are accessing negative content and emotions, which makes you feel even worse. In addition, you are less likely to engage in positive activities now. It adds to your sense of helplessness and makes you feel worse.

Why do we ruminate? People who ruminate actually think that they will work things out, solve a problem and avoid making the same mistake in the future.[11] Of course, there may be some truth that ruminating may "give you closure," or lead to solutions—but excessive rumination simply makes you more depressed. So what can you do if you are out of work and find yourself ruminating?

1: Catch yourself ruminating and keep track of it

It seems that many of my new clients are not aware they have been ruminating. It's as if their mind is always busy, always nagging them, but they are so used to it that they don't realize they are doing it. And, of course, they don't realize that they have a choice. It's like the white noise in the background; you don't realize it's there until it's not there.

Run through this check to see whether you are ruminating. Do these thoughts ring true?

- I find myself having repetitive thoughts.
- I seem to pay a lot of attention to what is on my mind.
- I have a hard time letting go of my thoughts.

One of my clients, Harry, who had a long history of more traditional talking therapy, didn't realize that he had been a chronic ruminator. "I think I have been ruminating since I was a kid," he said, adding, "I ruminate all the time." But the fact was that he was more likely to ruminate when he was not busy or when he noticed that someone was doing well and, therefore, "getting ahead of him." He was less likely to ruminate when he was playing with his son, talking with his wife, or reading something of interest. When he was not busy, however, the negative ruminations would pop into his head and he would dwell on them. It's as if he thought he had to spend a lot of time with whatever negative thought came around. It didn't occur to him that he had a choice about getting entangled with his negative thoughts. And when he heard about someone else doing well, it triggered his negative ruminations about himself doing poorly.

So, in our sessions, we identified that his "trouble time" was when he was by himself and hearing about someone else doing well. By narrowing down to these trouble times he was able to quickly catch his rumination and have a plan to carry out to turn it around. The pointers that I discuss in this chapter were extremely helpful to him.

Another of my clients ruminated about how being unemployed was not consistent with how he saw himself. Ken, however, was stuck in the unfairness of being unemployed. He said, "I don't understand. I have a good education, I did everything right, worked for a good company, but now I am out of work. This is not what I expected. I did everything right." He kept repeating these negative thoughts, making himself sadder and angrier.

The benefits of awareness

Simply being aware that "I am ruminating now" can be helpful. It's natural to have some rumination—most people who are out of work know that. But you may be hijacked by these thoughts and find yourself caught up in them to no avail. Another sign of your rumination is endless, repetitive complaining about the same thing: how bad it is, how unfair it is. You wonder why you are stuck and unable to move on.

You can keep track of your rumination by checking off the number of times you ruminate during the day, what the thoughts are, what your mood is, and what triggered the rumination. For example, Claire found that she ruminated more when she isolated herself in her apartment and began to think about looking for a job. Rather than taking positive action—either to look for a job or do something constructive for herself—she would begin to ruminate. She noticed that her rumination was associated with feeling sad, anxious, and angry. It was never associated with feeling good.

Another of my clients noticed that he was ruminating more when he sat down to pay his bills. This triggered negative thoughts about how unfair it was that his boss had fired him, reminding him that he didn't have the income he had in the past. His rumination thoughts were, "This is so unfair. I can't believe he did this to me. I feel so depressed. This is awful." His mood was always negative when he ruminated. When he began this rumination he would feel worse, pour himself a drink, ruminate more, have another drink, and then find himself feeling numb. His rumination about the unfairness just led to numbness. As he drank more, he became more depressed, had difficulty staying asleep, and felt hung over the next day. And then he would ruminate all over again, repeating the cycle.

Recognize the triggers
Use the table below to find out what triggers the rumination and what your feelings are. See if there is a pattern to the triggers, the things you are saying to yourself, and the mood that you have. Then ask yourself, "Is this really helping me?"

EXERCISE: KEEPING A DAILY RECORD OF RUMINATION

It is useful to keep track of your rumination—your repetitive negative thoughts. These are thoughts that you keep going over and over and can't seem to get out of your mind. They may also be complaints that you keep repeating. What events or situations trigger this rumination? What are you thinking when you are repeating these thoughts? What mood or feeling do you have when you do this? Are you feeling sad, angry, frustrated or helpless—or do you have any positive feelings? Here's an example of how to do it.

Day/time	Trigger	What I am thinking	Mood
Wednesday, 10 am	Watching television and hearing about all the unemployed people	I will never get job. Why has this happened to me? It's not fair. I can't stand it	Depressed, anxious, angry and bitter

2: Examine the costs and benefits of ruminating

I asked Harry what he hoped to get out of his rumination about being unemployed, and he said, "I suppose I am trying to make sense of what happened. I can't seem to work out how this could have happened to me. Did I do something wrong?" Claire thought she would be able to work out how to avoid this kind of thing in the future: "If I can work out what happened, then I won't get fired the next time." People ruminate because they often think this will help make sense of what has happened, it will help them avoid the problem, they can now solve the problem if they ruminate, and their rumination will help motivate them ("I don't just want to sit back and accept it the way it is. If I think about it, I can motivate myself to find a job."). Others think their rumination will eliminate uncertainty, which they think is a bad thing: "If I think about it, I will know for sure why things happened. Then I can rest."

But there are costs to ruminating about your situation. Certainly, you don't have a job, but rumination is not likely to help you find one. Rumination is not the same thing as solving a problem or taking action. For most people who ruminate, it results in more depression and anxiety. It sends you on a mission of misery where you hope to find answers to questions that don't have answers ("Why me?") or where the answers won't help you anyway. What you really may need is not *answers*; but a *plan to live your life* more effectively now, during this time between jobs — and a plan to find the next job.

A path to depression

Claire thought her rumination would help her work out why she was let go. She spent hours trying to "work it out," and found herself dwelling on her sadness and anxiety, overeating and isolating herself from her friends. As we talked about the costs and benefits of rumination, she began to realize that her rumination was actually perpetuating her depression about being unemployed. I said, "Could it be that your rumination, as a response to the situation, has now become almost as much a source of your depression as the fact that you are unemployed?" Although she knew that her unemployment was a real problem, her rumination was only compounding it.

What do you think you will get out of this rumination? Will it really help you to solve any problems? Will you get closure? What are the costs to you? Is it making you more depressed and angry?

EXERCISE: IDENTIFY THE COSTS AND BENEFITS OF RUMINATING

Once you have a daily list of how you ruminate, start to list all the costs and benefits that you think you will get from ruminating. Don't try to be rational and say, "There are no benefits." Everyone who ruminates believes there is some potential benefit. Here's an example of the sort of thing people write.

Costs	Benefit
Makes me miserable. I feel stuck	Maybe I will work out why this happened to me

When you start ruminating, you may believe that you will get something out of these repetitive negative thoughts. What do you think the benefits will be? Don't try to be rational. Just be honest. Do you think that rumination will motivate you, give you the answer, provide closure, eliminate uncertainty, solve your problems, avoid bad things in the future, or are there other potential benefits that you hope to gain? What are the costs to you of ruminating? Are there negative effects on your mood, your ability to live effectively now, or even on your relationships? How would you weigh out the costs and benefits? If you had to divide 100 points between the costs and the benefits, would the costs outweigh the benefits?

3: Explore the evidence that your rumination is helping you

Now that you have identified your beliefs about the advantages of rumination, let's examine if it is really working—are you really getting what you are aiming for by spending all this time with these repetitive thoughts?

For example, is your rumination really solving your problem? And what is the problem that you are trying to solve? Is it finding a new job? Enjoying your life today? Having a better relationship with your partner? Let's take the idea that your rumination is motivating you. Really? How? Or is it making you more depressed and less involved in real life?

What does the evidence show you?

Look at table and list some of the advantages that you think you might be getting from rumination (just refer to the previous table that you completed above). Now list the evidence that you are really getting that advantage and the evidence that you are not. For example, Ken thought that ruminating would motivate him to look for a job. The evidence that it *was* helping was that he did spend part of the day looking for a job. But the evidence that it *wasn't* helping is that he would have looked for a job even if he hadn't ruminated. The other evidence that it wasn't motivating him is that the rumination made him more depressed, angry, and helpless and this often led him to overdrink and overeat.

Claire recognized that her rumination was not helping her get the next job or plan a better strategy for moving forward. It was not motivating her, she wasn't learning anything through her rumination, and it was not solving any real problems. In fact, it was generating more problems and more worries. I asked Claire to think about rumination as a "tool" that she grabbed when she felt down: "Perhaps if I use this tool I will make progress." But this tool is like taking a hammer and hitting yourself over the head and then wondering why you have a headache.

EXERCISE: IS MY RUMINATION REALLY HELPING ME?

Go over the list of the advantages that you think you will get from ruminating about your situation. Then list the evidence that you are really getting those advantages and the evidence that you are not. For example, if you think that rumination will help you get clarity and certainty, list the evidence that it is working and the evidence that it is not working. What do you conclude? Here's an example.

What I hope to get out of my rumination	Evidence rumination has helped	Evidence it has not helped
I hope to work out why this happened to me	I can see that there are a lot of people who are unemployed through no fault of their own	I still feel stuck and I find I am unhappy when I ruminate. I can't enjoy anything

4: Will your rumination lead to any productive action?

If you think your rumination is really helping, then I want you to think of how you would answer the following simple question: "What productive action can I take today that will really solve my problem?" I think there is productive and unproductive rumination. Productive rumination will lead to a to-do list today. For example, if you had a job interview and you noticed you were complaining about your last employer—and you didn't get the job—make a note of that mistake and don't repeat it. The productive action is simply making a note—that took you one minute. All the rumination after that minute is a waste of your time. Another example of productive rumination is reflecting on whether your CV is up to date. Productive action: your to-do list today is to get out the CV and work on it. That is taking action. All the other excessive thinking about it is useless—and depressing.

Focus on what needs to be done, not on ruminating

The good news is that the answer is irrelevant. Even if you had the answer as to why this happened, or what it means, or what caused people to make decisions—you are still stuck with the same problems to solve today: finding a job and building a life. And rumination does not help with real problems in the real world. In fact, by focusing on rumination you take your eye off the ball. The ball to hit is getting a job and getting a life. Now, the good thing about those problems is that you can actually do something about them in the real world—not the world going on inside your head.

Is there any productive action *today* that you can take? If you lost your job, you can't reverse history. But perhaps you can engage in other productive behavior: exercise, socializing, looking for a job, acquiring new skills. If there is no productive action that your rumination suggests, then set it aside.

Claire realized there was some productive action that she could take; she could contact some people she knew in her field, meet with them, and talk with them. This was productive because it got her out of her rumination, it helped her feel she was making some effort to move forward, they might know of some leads, and they could also comfort her by normalizing the problem of being unemployed and supporting her in coping with this difficult time.

EXERCISE: IS THERE ANY PRODUCTIVE ACTION THAT I CAN TAKE?

List the content of your rumination down the left-hand side of a piece of paper. This could be thoughts like, "Why did this happen?" or "I can't believe it" or "It's not fair"—or whatever is going over and over in your mind. Then beside it list the productive action that will help you make progress in solving the problem. For example, finding the answer, getting closure, working out why it happened, and so on. Is there any productive action today? If not, why not? What keeps you from making progress on finding the answer, closure, and the other thoughts you are having? Write this down on the right-hand side. See the example below.

Content of rumination	What productive action can I take today?	Why is there no productive action to take today?
I can't believe I don't have a job	I could look for a job. I can do some positive things for myself	There is always productive action to take. I just tend to think it's not productive if it doesn't immediately lead to a job

Now work through the list below to help you move forward.
- What specific behavior would be productive now?
- What can you do that is rewarding for you?
- What are the goals that you need to achieve—and will rumination help?
- What will help you achieve these goals?

5: Set aside specific times to ruminate-and put it off until then

Ken felt that he was ruminating all the time; from the moment he woke up until the moment he went to bed, and he woke up ruminating during the night. He could never escape. I asked him why he had to pay attention to those negative thoughts, and he looked at me with a puzzled expression. "I don't understand.

They just come into my head." He thought he had to pay attention to them and find an answer to every thought that came into his mind.

Do you really have to follow your rumination when the first negative thought appears? Do you really have to keep spinning your wheels and digging yourself deeper into a rut? The answer is NO.

Book ahead to ruminate

You can make an "appointment" with your rumination. Catch it, write it down, and set it aside for later—say, at 4.30 in the afternoon. You can ruminate then. At all other times, write it down and set it aside.

You might say, "That's ridiculous." You think that the moment it pops into your head you have no choice than to follow the negative thoughts right down the drain. But you do have a choice. Here's how you can prove it to yourself:

Have you noticed that when you are ruminating, and the phone rings, you immediately stop ruminating? Or, if your partner starts talking to you, you stop ruminating?

Or, try this.

Look around the room that you are sitting in and describe all the objects that are blue. Then describe the objects that are white. Now, try black. As you have refocused your attention to other things in the room you will notice that you are not ruminating. This kind of distraction helps you realize that you can choose to redirect your attention somewhere else. You are in charge.

What do you think you will find if you put off your rumination until another time during the day? Most of my clients think they can't do it—until they do. Here's what most people find:

1.   They are able to put it off until later.

2. When they get to the time for their appointment with their rumination, they no longer care about most of the things they were ruminating about.
3. They realize they are ruminating about the same things over and over — so it's a lot less overwhelming.

CBT techniques to use at your rumination appointment

When you get round to rumination time you can then use some cognitive behavioral techniques to focus your thoughts:

1. What are the advantages and disadvantages of ruminating about this?
2. Is there any productive action to take today?
3. If it is unproductive worry, you can set it aside and start using some of the acceptance techniques described below.

Now that you have a strategy to get past the orders and the nagging of your rumination, you are in charge.

When you get to rumination time, you will find that a lot of the thoughts that bothered you earlier in the day are no longer problematic. They just don't seem important to you. What does that tell you? Perhaps you think a thought is important because it "intrudes" on you — like a burglar trying to break into your home. But it turns out that the thought is just a thought — nothing more. It's the wind against the blinds. It means nothing.

Or you may find that you are having the same repetitive thoughts — and nothing is really new. If that is the case — and these thoughts still bother you — at least you know it's only a few thoughts, not a million. Now you can use your cognitive therapy techniques listed above. Is there any advantage to ruminating about the thought? Is there any productive action you can take today? If so, then plan the action and do it. If there is no productive action about this thought, then perhaps you can accept that you don't have the answer right now and you can then focus on productive action about something else. For example, if there is no productive action to take right now about getting a job, go back to your reward menu (see page 34), then plan and do some rewarding things. There is always something else to do besides ruminating.

Plan ahead

Have the following plan in mind ready for when you start to ruminate:

- Set aside rumination time.
- When a negative thought pops into your head and you think you are going to get stuck on it, write it down and make an appointment to deal with it later.
- When you get to rumination time, are those thoughts really bothering you as much? Are you having a few thoughts — over and over?

If you are having thoughts that bother you earlier, but don't bother you later, perhaps you don't really need to pay attention to them. If they get weaker and less relevant as time passes, then let them go at the earlier time and get on with enjoying your life now. You don't need to solve a "problem" that goes away on its own.

Or, if you are having the same thoughts over and over, you are really having "one thought." If that is the case, you can recognize that you are repeating yourself ad nauseam to no avail. Just recognize, "Oh, it's the same thought that keeps coming up; I can just use the same cognitive therapy techniques on it. I don't have to keep nagging myself with the same thought." Those techniques are outlined below.

6: Accept that you can't always know why things happen

We humans are always looking for answers and meaning. You may be ruminating because you think you need to know why this has happened. Or you may ruminate because you think you need to know what will happen in the future. As I have said, rumination about your unemployment keeps you focused on the negative, and leads to more negativity, depression, and anxiety. You keep thinking that you will get the information and the insight so that everything will make sense. But is it really working? Are you really getting the insight and the answers? You may think that the advantage to rumination is finding the answer. But you may be chasing the air. You will never catch it. You can't know what other people were thinking or how the market forces or the company decisions were made. It's out of your control and probably unknowable.

Sometimes we need to accept uncertainty or the lack of answers. Sometimes accepting limitations actually empowers you. It allows you to give up on a lost cause and can help you move on to more productive and helpful behavior. If you over-think the situation you are in, you will find yourself trapped in inaction and passivity. Accepting, "I don't know and I don't need to know," may lead to, "Now I need to take productive action."

In the next chapter we will look at a specific focus of a lot of your rumination: your sense of the unfairness of what has happened to you and your feeling, at times, that you are an innocent victim. I want you to be clear that I am not saying that what has happened *is* fair or that you are *not* an innocent victim. But I want you to consider how you might get stuck in this way of thinking and that it only adds to the difficulties that you are having.

SUMMARY

Rumination is a key factor in a lot of your suffering—and your feeling of being stuck. We have looked at some simple and powerful ways of turning away from rumination and getting back to your life. Catching yourself ruminating, monitoring it, looking at the triggers and the moods associated with it, examining the costs and benefits of rumination and asking if it is really productive are simple, easy and powerful. Rumination won't get you a job and it won't improve your life today. Look at the tips below and start practicing them daily.

- Catch yourself ruminating and keep track of it.
- Examine the costs and benefits of ruminating.
- Is your rumination really helping you?
- Will your rumination lead to any productive action?
- Set aside specific times to ruminate-and put it off until then.
- Accept that you can't always know why things happen, and that you don't need to know.

6

WHY ME? FEELING LIKE A VICTIM OR BECOMING EMPOWERED?

We met Bill in Chapter Three and found that he had rediscovered being involved with his young son and also found a number of rewarding activities from the past to enjoy again. Previously, Bill had been working for a small company that he had tried to build up, but he and the boss had some run-ins. Bill felt that the boss didn't give him enough credit, that his pay wasn't what it should be, and that he was being ignored. He didn't feel appreciated. Angry and bitter, he began to drink more, get into arguments with his wife, and act grumpily around his children. Eventually he lost his job.

For weeks afterwards, Bill focused on how unfair everything was, complaining to his wife and to me that his boss really didn't give him a fair chance, and that he had been "squeezed out" of the company. He would fantasize about getting revenge — thinking of how he could ruin the reputation of the company by telling competitors what his boss was like. When he thought of looking for a new job he felt both discouraged and bitter. His bitterness was based on his view that he shouldn't be in this position — he shouldn't have to look for a job or, to make matters worse, settle for less than he was getting before. When his wife told him that he seemed angry all the time, Bill retorted, "What do you expect me to feel? I was screwed!"

1: Validate the unfairness

Yes, it really might have been unfair. After all, you had a job, you were trying to do your best, and then it was taken away from you. That wasn't the deal, that wasn't what you expected. You went to work and then you were "robbed" of your livelihood. Who wouldn't feel upset? If you hadn't lost your job—if they hadn't taken it away—you wouldn't have these problems. You wouldn't worry about money or the future, and you wouldn't feel ashamed or have these arguments with your partner. You wouldn't be ruminating, worrying, and complaining. It's not what you wanted. They did this to you.

These thoughts, I believe, are perfectly natural. You are human. When we feel someone has hurt us, we feel it's unfair, and we complain. I do think that really unfair and lousy things happen to good people—and I agree with you, it shouldn't be this way. If you do your job, you shouldn't have to lose it.

But you did.

So your feelings of anger and resentment, your desire for retaliation, and your complaining all make sense. But I want you to think about how long you want to stay in this frame of mind; angry, resentful, bitter. You have a right to it, but how long do you want to stay where you are?

2: Are you thinking like a victim?

I know if I mention this—that you feel like you are a victim—you will think, "He doesn't understand," and "He makes it sound so easy—it's not." I know you may think I am dismissing your feelings, minimizing the wrongs done to you, and even making you feel like a victim once again. You may be thinking as you read this, "This therapist is just putting me down, just like my boss did. He doesn't know what it's like to be in this position. I really was treated badly. I deserved better. Are you telling me to just lie down and be a doormat?"

I think that your thoughts and feelings on this make absolute sense. For a therapist, it's tricky to validate your right to have a feeling but also suggest there may be some new ways of coping. You think that by focusing on moving forward is like someone saying, "You are making too big a deal of this. Get over it." It's almost as if you think that we need to stay with witnessing and recognizing the injury done to you. We can't fix the problem. We have to fix the blame.

When we think about new ways of coping, you may remember all the things we discussed in Chapter Two—validating what has happened but committing to change. Validating the hurt doesn't necessarily mean that you don't commit to change. After all, why would you have to solve problems and make things better if you had not been hurt in some way?

Here's one way of thinking about this. Imagine you cross the street and you get hit by a car running a red light. You are lying there in the street, your legs are twisted, broken and bleeding, screaming out in pain, and you yell, "That bastard who hit me, I am going to sue him for all he's worth!!!" But then you notice that the greatest surgeon in the world, Dr. Wizard, has come over and she leans down with a magic wand and says, "I know you're in pain and you have a right to sue and be angry and complain. It's terrible. But with this magic wand I can fix your legs *and* make them stronger than ever before. You will be able to run and jump like you never did, your pain will be gone and your life will be better. Should I wave my magic wand?" You look up, happy for a moment, "Of course! At once!"

But then Dr. Wizard says, "Oh, but there's a catch. If I cure you, then you can't sue them, you can't complain, you have to get up and walk on into the rest of your life."

What do you want her to do? Do you want to give up on the complaints, or give up on the magic wand?

I don't have a magic wand, but I know that if you get too stuck on the unfairness, on being a victim, on seeking retaliation, and you keep complaining, it will be hard for you to accomplish your valued goals. It's a hard choice, but one that you need to think about.

We all have to deal with unfairness

Let's be honest with ourselves — we all think like victims sometimes. That's because we all get treated unfairly. People lie to us, cheat, betray us, stab us in the back, don't live up to their agreements, make promises they never intend to keep, take the side of people we detest, and violate our rights in a multitude of ways. When I asked a group I was lecturing if anyone had ever been treated unfairly, almost everyone raised their hand. It's part of life — an unfortunate, unpleasant, and unfair part of life — but it is what life gives us to deal with at times.

Let's take a tally of some common ways you might be looking at your unemployment experience when you get into the Victim Mode of thinking.

Past orientation: You focus on what happened to you in the past, rather than on what you can do to make things better now.

Express your feelings: You are continually talking about how bad you feel, sometimes openly complaining, sometimes pouting passively.

Resist solutions: You reject advice that might be helpful and refuse to solve the problem because you feel you didn't cause it, so why should you have to deal with it?

Blame others: You repeat your complaints that other people have put you in this situation and you blame them for everything that has gone wrong.

Complain about discomfort: You not only complain about "them" but you complain about your mental and physical discomfort. You complain about feeling sad, frustrated and angry, and then you complain about aches and pains.

Impatience: You have no patience about things and demand an immediate answer to the problems you face. Without an immediate answer, you conclude that it's all hopeless, so why try?

I should only do what I want to do: This is a central feeling of entitlement: thinking that you are entitled to your down feelings and entitled not to have to struggle to make progress. You think you should do things on your terms.

Now, complete the table below and ask yourself if there are some specific examples of how you are thinking like a victim.

EXERCISE: ARE YOU THINKING LIKE A VICTIM?

Write down the various ways that you might be thinking of your unemployment as part of Being a Victim. Some common types of victim thinking are given below—with a few examples to help you get started. Try to notice this way of thinking during the next week. How is it making you feel physically as well as mentally? Is it making you feel tense, tired, agitated. Do you lose sleep, have indigestion, complain of aches and pains? Feeling like a victim can affect your physical well-being, draw down your energy, make you feel both tense and tired. And it can make you angry, depressed, anxious, helpless, regretful, bitter and resentful. It can keep you stuck in your rumination and rob you of your chance to make your life better today. How is it affecting your relationships?

Victim thinking	Examples
Focus on the past	I can't believe that they fired me
Emphasis on expressing your feelings	I think I have to tell people how bad it is for me—I need them to understand
Resist solutions	

Blame others	
Complain about discomfort	
Impatience	
I should only do what I want to do	

The anger and resentfulness that accompanies feeling like a victim

Bill realized that he was doing a lot of victim-thinking. He was continually talking about what happened to him in the past, replaying in his mind the memories of getting fired and not being treated fairly at his previous job. He would express his feelings by complaining, shouting, and repeating the stories of how bad it was. When others would suggest some things he could do to move on, such as looking for a job, developing a plan, networking, or doing productive things for himself, he would often get angrier. He felt people were telling him he didn't have a right to feel angry and sad. He not only blamed his former boss, but he also began to blame his wife, and then he began to blame the businesses that were not offering him a job.

He would complain about how hard it was, sometimes complaining about aches and pains, feeling tired, having indigestion, and difficulty getting going. He was impatient with the job search, but also with his wife and kids, often feeling that talking to them was a burden, a source of friction, and that they were taking too long to "get to the point." When his wife or friends would suggest some proactive and productive things to do to assist his job search, he would say, "I don't want to do that," and "It's not fair that I am in this position. I worked hard. Why should I have to grovel for a job?"

The result of this way of thinking is that Bill felt angry, resentful, anxious, helpless, and alone. He felt misunderstood. He was stuck in the Victim Role.

I am not saying you don't have a right to respond this way. But be honest with yourself; look at the list in the exercise above and ask yourself if this actually describes you at times. If it does, you might be *stuck* in the Victim Mode.

3: Empowering yourself: thinking about means and ends

I think of the Victim Mode as the first step in recognizing that something bad and unfair has happened. It's like saying, "Ouch—that really hurt!! This shouldn't have happened!" It's your recognition that your needs and rights are violated and your realization that it was not fair, not right. But once you have recognized this, you can either stay in the Victim Mode or move on to Being Effective. Like the injured person lying in the street deciding if Dr. Wizard should wave her magic wand and fix the problem, you have a choice of whether you will stay with the injury or embrace the cure.

Means–Ends Thinking

So how would you think about things if you were focused on Being Effective? I suggest that you would identify positive goals and think about a plan of how to achieve them. This is what I call "Means–Ends Thinking." Here are some examples.

Future orientation: You focus on future events and goals rather than on what has happened in the past. You are more concerned with making the future better than on making sense of the past.

Goal orientation: In pursuit of the future, you identify goals that you want to achieve that are positive and productive rather than past injuries or justifications for why you feel down.

Problem solving: You think about problems in terms of possible solutions rather than as burdens that you don't deserve or cannot overcome. You focus on planning and carrying out plans, on actions that lead to solutions. You view rumination as a waste of time.

Personal responsibility: You believe that it is up to you to do what has to get done rather than blaming others for what has happened or expecting others to solve the problems for you.

Invest in discomfort: You are willing to do what is uncomfortable now so that life will be better in the future. You believe that discomfort can be constructive at times — as part of the means to reach your ends.

Delay of gratification: As part of your investment in discomfort, you are willing to wait for satisfaction and gratification, rather than demand immediate results. You take a longer-term approach. You are willing to persist, stay at it and increase your effort.

Staying in Victim Mode does not help you accomplish goals

As I've already said, there are two very important problems for you to solve during this time between jobs. The first problem is finding a job and the second problem is taking care of yourself. You can either be focused on feeling like a victim — and stay in Victim Mode — or you can focus on Being Effective and accomplish valued goals in your life. My experience tells me that when people are trapped in the Victim Mode they have a hard time being as effective as they could be.

Let's take an example. When we met Bill in Chapter Three, we learned that he found spending more time with his son to be pleasurable and also effective. He had every reason to feel like a victim, however, because he had been treated unfairly at work; his boss didn't honor his side of the bargain, Bill was marginalized within the company, and he got fired. It was unfair. He had every right to be angry. But that may not be the bigger picture for Bill. When Bill and I met, we discussed this idea that he could have a choice about staying in the Victim Role or Being Effective. But he couldn't do both.

We looked at the advantages of being in the Victim Role. Bill suggested the advantages were that he was right, that he was standing up for himself, and he couldn't just "accept" it because that would mean he was weak. He worried that accepting it was saying it was OK, and if he became weak, other people would think they could take advantage of him. These were strong advantages in his mind.

Bill also identified the disadvantages of the Victim Role. These included constant anger, frustration, depression, irritability around his family, complaining, feelings of helplessness, humiliation, rumination, and difficulty living his life day to day.

The dilemma for Bill was how to move on from the Victim Role without having to say "It's OK that I was treated badly." How could he do that?

I suggested that he could always believe he had been given a raw deal and that it was unfair, and that his boss was a pig. That was a belief that he could hold for the rest of his life. The issue was not the truth of the belief, or the right to hold it. The issue was *getting stuck* in the Victim Role. Yes, he *had* been a victim on the job and got fired, but he had a choice of whether he would wake up tomorrow and choose to look at the world as a victim. He could choose to look at the world in terms of valued goals, productive action, and being effective. The victim role could be in the past tense: "I was a victim." The present tense could be, "I am now being effective." Yes, there is a choice.

We began to discuss the idea of making a choice when he found himself ruminating about being treated unfairly, or complaining to his wife and feeling misunderstood. "Bill, you can choose which way you go when you have these thoughts about how unfair it is," I said. "You can decide to start ruminating, or you can decide if there are some useful goals for you to pursue." Bill thought about this, knowing this was exactly the problem he had to face. He had to decide if he was going to continue sinking into the role of being a victim, or choose to focus on useful behavior. He knew he couldn't do both.

Getting started on Being Effective

Looking back at our list of examples for Means–Ends Thinking on page 102, how could Bill put into use the different parts of Being Effective? The first thing was to think about the future and what he wanted it to be (*future orientation*). I asked him what specific goals he had. Bill wanted to get a job, but he also wanted to get into better physical condition, and he wanted to cut back on his drinking. He wanted to have a better relationship with his wife and kids—to end the arguing and the bickering and the crying (*goal orientation*). I asked him to think of these as problems to be solved—rather than problems to blame on someone else, or to blame on himself (*problem solving*). "OK," he said, "I suppose I really need to work on looking for a job, and research some of these companies, and network with people."

I suggested it would be helpful if he viewed himself as taking *personal responsibility* for these things—not to blame himself or burden himself with this—but to view this as requiring that he had to do something, that it was going to be up to him. "What obstacles have you overcome in your life?" I asked him. Bill recounted how he had worked in a bakery when he was a child, and had worked long hours in unpleasant conditions—but he had made his own money, and he didn't have to rely on his father for anything. He described how he and his wife started out with nothing, but eventually got a small house, then they had their first child, and he had worked long hours in his new job trying to get ahead. "You know, I'm really good at solving problems. I've overcome a lot in my life," he said.

I suggested that this was another time in his life when he might *invest in discomfort*—he might be willing to do the hard things now so it might be easier in the future (*delay of gratification*). "You're right. I really need to get more self-discipline, keep working hard to make it better. I've been feeling sorry for myself, and that's got me nowhere," he said.

"Well, you have a right to have sympathy for yourself and to recognize that things have been unfair and hard for you, but when you shift to thinking about Being Effective, I noticed that your mood changed."

"Yeah. I noticed, too. I felt like my old self again."

Seeing our goals ahead gives us strength to fight on

That's where we wanted to be — to get back to being empowered, energized — to keep your goals in front of you. If you have been knocked down, get up and fight even harder to win back your life. But it's up to you. Falling back down into the Victim Role actually re-victimizes you. You've been knocked down, but you don't want to keep yourself down when there is hard work that you can do to make it better.

EXERCISE: HOW TO THINK LIKE AN EMPOWERED PERSON

Look at the various ways that you might think in a more empowered way. For example, to focus on how you can get from where you are now to valued goals in the future. This is Means–Ends Thinking. Write out some examples of each of these and try to notice this way of thinking and acting during the week to come. How does it make you feel when you think and act in an empowered way? How is it affecting your relationships? Here are some areas to think about and a few examples to help you.

Thinking in an empowered way	Examples of how you can do this
Future orientation	I can continue looking more widely for a possible opening somewhere
Goal orientation	I can focus on positive goals every day
Problem solving	
Personal responsibility	
Invest in discomfort	
Delay of gratification	

Getting results from Means–Ends Thinking

Bill kept track of the more empowered ways of thinking over the next week. He began to develop a "business plan" for his life and for his job search. This involved cutting back on drinking and overeating, and increasing his exercise. His plan for the job search was getting his CV in order, identifying prospects to contact for networking, and making plans to set up informational interviews in the future. His goals were to exercise three times each week, monitor his drinking, and contact at least ten people. He had a plan. He began to think of the situation as a problem to solve—or, in his case, "problems" to solve. Since he realized that he had a long history of being good at solving real problems, this energized him and activated him to make decisions and do things, it also increased his hope about getting better and finding a job. He wavered a bit on "personal responsibility," and was still ruminating and complaining about the old boss, but now he realized what he was doing and that this way of thinking and behaving only added to his sense of helplessness.

Bill recalled being on the running team at school, and that "discomfort" was a sign of a good workout. He used the idea of "constructive discomfort"—that is, the willingness to do hard things in pursuit of valued goals. He actually felt more proud of the fact that he was doing some things that were uncomfortable—things that his negative mind thought, "I shouldn't have to do what I don't want to do." He was beginning to reframe this as, "I need to do what I don't want to do so I can get what I want to get."

His mood visibly changed in the next session. He was getting more fired up.

4: Turn off revenge

What's the most natural response to being humiliated, put down, rejected, and hurt? It's to seek revenge. We are hard-wired this way. Our ancestors who were attacked or humiliated knew there was an enemy who would not stop with just pushing you around. He would eventually kill you, kill your children, and take the women as slaves. The only response that made sense to our prehistoric ancestors was to kill before you got killed. But that was a long time ago and revenge has a price that you will not want to bear. It's just that your first feeling—your inclination at times—is to seek out revenge, to get back at the bastards who hurt you.

One client, Carol, described her recurring thoughts and fantasies of getting revenge against her former boss. She would replay in her mind images of going in and telling him what a horrible person he was. She fantasized about spreading the word to his competition that he was unethical and a liar. The more she held these fantasies, the angrier she became, which led her calming herself with a few drinks, but with a sly smile on her face as she recounted her fantasies of retaliation.

Recognize the role of revenge in the victim's mind

The desire for retaliation is a major part of the Victim Role—it almost completes it: you got fired; you have been miserable; get revenge and the score is even. But life may not be about evening the score. It may be about building a better life. If you focus on your enemy, you are not going to focus on other goals. Of course, Bill was the expert at these revenge fantasies. He would pour himself another drink and dream up another way to get back at his enemy—the former boss. It was like inviting the boss into the privacy of his home so that he could fantasize about miserable mental torture. Ruminating, escalating anger, living in a fantasy world that got him nowhere—it's all too human, unfortunately. That's how we are wired.

"So Bill, you can be enemy-focused, or you can focus on your goals. Which do you really want to do?" Now, Bill had every right to be angry—he had been treated unfairly—but he also knew that his revenge fantasies just magnified his feelings of humiliation and helplessness. After all, if he acted on these fantasies, he would destroy his credibility with the business community and everyone he knew. The revenge would really be on him.

Change the focus

The next week, Bill came back to therapy and said it was very helpful to think about this contrast between focusing on an enemy vs. focusing on positive goals. "I got a lot done this past week—and I also drank less. I worked on my job search, contacted some people, and even arranged a meeting. It's not a job interview, just an information meeting, but it's something. I actually felt I had made progress."

The great thing about practicing the skills of Being Effective is that you are no longer helpless. You actually have some real things to do in the real world. You can take action, make plans and accomplish goals. Perhaps the world won't change as quickly as you like, but when you are caught in the Victim Role you are trapped in the past and the only "action" is in your head, and it's all fantasy—it's useless.

EXERCISE: THE COSTS AND BENEFITS OF REVENGE

What are the costs and benefits of thinking about or seeking revenge? Look at the example below and write out your own version.

Costs	Benefits
Miserable, angry, feeling stuck	Perhaps if I get back at them I can move on

Now think about the following questions:
- How is this thinking affecting your mood, your choices and your relationships?
- What does it mean to you if you set aside revenge thinking and decide not to pursue it?

EXERCISE: THE COSTS AND BENEFITS OF EMPOWERED THINKING

If you set aside revenge thinking and focus on empowered thinking, what would be the costs and benefits of that? Again, look at the example below and think of your own costs and benefits.

Costs	Benefits
It's like saying that it didn't happen to me– that it's OK. It isn't!	I can take control of what I can and let go of past resentments. I can focus on positive goals

Now answer this question:
• What would you do differently?

The reasons why you may hold on to revenge fantasies

Let's now look at what you are saying to yourself that makes it hard for you to set aside revenge fantasies. Do any of the following make sense to you if you turn away from seeking and fantasizing about revenge?

- It means I am saying it's OK for people to treat me unfairly.
- It means I am not a "real man"/"real woman."
- It means I am weak or inferior.
- Other people will see I am weak and take advantage of me.
- It's not consistent with the way I see myself: someone who stands up for his/her rights.
- I could never respect myself unless I got back at them.
- I could never stop thinking about this if I didn't get revenge.
- I need to win—they need to lose.

These are powerful and ultimately destructive thoughts. But, as I said in the beginning, we are hard-wired to seek retaliation against those who have hurt us. You should try to identify your own, individual thoughts about seeking revenge—because this is a powerful emotion that you are facing.

Look at some of the common revenge thoughts above and ask yourself if they really are rational, reasonable and helpful. You can look at some possible ways of challenging these negative vengeful thoughts and ask yourself if there are additional ways of challenging them. Is there another way of looking at these thoughts so that the vengeful feelings don't come back to haunt you? Here are some answers to the statements made above:

Why not getting revenge is a problem for me	Challenges to these thoughts
It means I am saying it's OK for people to treat me unfairly	I can recognize that what happened is unfair but choose not to seek revenge. Rather than revenge, I can seek making my life better
It means I am not a "real man"/"real woman"	Being a grown-up is about pursuing productive and useful goals. In my case, getting a job and getting on with my life is not consistent with seeking revenge
It means I am weak or inferior	Being 'weak' is more about not being practical, effective and empowered in your life. Seeking revenge weakens me because it focuses on the past and on achieving a goal—revenge—that won't help me
Other people will see I am weak and take advantage of me	I don't really know what other people will think and they may not even be thinking of me at all. But if they think that I am focusing on revenge they will likely think I am not getting on with making my life better. They may think I am stuck in the past
It's not consistent with the way I see myself—someone who stands up for his/her rights	I also have a right to get on with my life and make it better. That may be the most productive and practical right

I could never respect myself unless I got back at them	I could learn to respect myself for being empowered, focusing on positive goals rather than fighting an enemy from my past
I could never stop thinking about this if I didn't get revenge	On the contrary, focusing on revenge keeps me from getting closure and moving on. It keeps me thinking and ruminating. Focusing on being empowered gives me constructive things to do every day
I need to win—they need to lose	If I think of life as winners and losers I am struggling with people who are no longer part of my life. I can think about getting my life back by doing constructive things for myself and giving up on this power struggle. I need to get on with my life

The past person is irrelevant

I have found that the ultimate resolution of the revenge trap is to make the past person irrelevant to your current and future goals. Once you get to the point of thinking and feeling, "They aren't relevant to my life anymore," you are freed from the past, freed from the anchor that will sink you in despair, and free to move on to a productive and empowered life where you make choices, you are in charge and you can make things happen.

SUMMARY

It's natural to feel like a victim when, in fact, you have been a victim. It's natural to want validation, to complain and even to want to seek revenge. This is part of being human. It's a most basic emotional response to personal attack, injury, or humiliation. The delicate balance is to validate your right to your feelings and your ability to change your life. I think of our responses as following stages: First, noticing that you have been fired is painful; second, feeling angry, resentful and realizing that you want to seek revenge; and, third, deciding whether you move on to the next stage in your life—to be empowered and to accomplish valued goals.

Validate the unfairness: It's important to treat yourself like a human being who has understandable emotions and expects to be treated unfairly. It does feel bad when we are treated unfairly and it's important to validate that for yourself. But it's also important to live your life after the event has happened—not to continue to get stuck in what happened to the exclusion of coping with the difficult realities that you need to confront today

Are you thinking like a victim? Be honest and recognize if you are overly dwelling on how you are a victim. Are you focused on the past, ruminating and repeating to yourself how unfair things are, blaming almost everything on the situation you are in and the people who put you in this predicament? Are you reluctant to change and cope because you think it's not your fault, so why should you have to change?

Empowering yourself: thinking about Means and Ends. It's natural at times to feel like a victim, but it's much more adaptive to take the next step: to empower yourself. Personal empowerment means that you focus on goals, purpose and plans, you carry out difficult behavior, you are willing to invest in discomfort and delay gratification to pursue your goals, and you are willing to be flexible and adaptive in coping with a realistic problem.

Turn off revenge: You are human and may have feelings that you want to seek revenge, but focusing on your enemy only deprives you of focusing on positive goals. Examine the costs and benefits of focusing on revenge and ask yourself if your primary goal is to fix the problem or fix the blame.

The empowered choice is to bounce back from unfairness and build your life as best you can. Unfairness is an unfortunate part of reality and some people suffer more than others. But you can gain more positives by building your life than on getting stuck with what has happened to you. It may be hard at times—and you may rightly think that you should not be in this situation. But building your life means coping with what is—not the way things should be.

Overcoming obstacles means that you eventually leave them behind. You have problems to solve, goals to achieve, plans to carry out, a present and future to live. If you look at life now as coping with problems and overcoming obstacles you will find that the past recedes as you engage more fully in your life now. The next step should carry you forward, not backward.

7

MIND OVER MONEY

"How am I going to take care of my family?" Brian said, worried that his life was falling apart now that he had lost his job. He did have a small amount of severance money. Kathy, his wife, worked part time, but that wasn't going to be much money for them to live on. They relied on his income. With two children and a credit card payment due, it looked pretty bleak. Money was a real issue for Brian and Kathy, and they both shared their worries about how they would get through this difficult time.

Most people who lose their jobs will suffer a financial setback. It's the rare person who has a large financial parachute that can provide a soft landing. For many, there is a small amount of severance pay — or just the final month's earnings — followed by reliance on benefits and savings. Many people will get into greater debt during this time between jobs. If you are the breadwinner, you will feel the added burden of this responsibility, often thinking that you won't be able to take care of your family and blaming yourself for letting them down. These are perfectly human sentiments and come from your honorable motives to be responsible and to help your family.

Our emotional connection to money

Money has emotional significance to us. It often represents success, status, responsibility, security and freedom. But we may tend to over-value money and equate ourselves with how much we have and how much we make. After all, people kill other people because of their desire for money. We will examine how you can change your relationship to money and the meaning of money in your life so that money becomes less a source of depression, anxiety, and helplessness while you expand the meaning of your life and recognize that there are many experiences, behaviors, and relationships that do not involve money. In fact, I have found that a lot of my clients who over-valued money learned during their time between jobs that they just were not focused on the right things and the right values. That lesson helped them to make their lives during and after the period of unemployment more meaningful and more filled with awareness and appreciation.

Looking at money through different eyes

In this chapter we will look at the reality about your financial situation, how you might start saving money now (by reducing expenses), and how you can prioritize which expenses are important and which are actually unnecessary. We will look at your attitude towards money, how it is tied to your sense of security, your status and self-esteem, and we will consider how you might change the way money functions in your life. Although money is a reality—and money does buy things that are important—we will examine how some of the more important things in your life might not cost very much, or might even be free. And we will look at how this more difficult time in your life might help you to establish more human values—values that are based less on materialism, less on things, and more on the meanings that you give to your relationships, your purpose in life, and the things that matter.

There are a lot of ways of helping your family—and of *being there* for them. Let's take a look at how your financial issues affect you and how you can handle them. And let's keep in mind that supporting your family is not the same thing as your paycheck. You are more than a paycheck.

1: Get the information

I continue to be amazed at how often people are upset about their finances, although they actually don't have the information available regarding how much they have, what they spend, and what they need. Money is one of the most emotional issues that we all contend with — all the more reason to get the facts. There are several kinds of facts that you need to grasp:

Savings: You need to look at how much you have in savings — both you and your partner. You may have a savings account, stocks and shares, or property, you may own one or two cars, you could have jewelry, and you might have a private pension. Whatever information about your assets that you would provide in applying for a mortgage is important information for you to look at now. Get the information together and share it openly with your partner. There should be no secrets. You are on the same team.

Expenses: Collect the information from your prior expenses for the last two months — including all credit card expenses that you can lay your hands on, details of your rent or mortgage, local taxes and other recurring bills such as electricity, gas, and telephone.

Accounting: Start keeping track of how you spend your money. For the next three weeks, you and your partner should keep a daily record of all expenses — checks, cash, debit and credit card use. Itemize each expense. Many people find that they are repeatedly spending small amounts that can add up to a lot more than you would think. A simple example might be buying coffee.

Let's say that you buy a cup of coffee at Starbucks every day for one year — price, $3.50 per cup. That comes to $1277 per year. If you brewed your own at .25 cents per cup you would spend $91 per year. This is a savings of $1186 per year. The same with buying lunch; if you saved $5 per lunch for five days, you would save about $100 per month. And you might eat more healthy food if you made your own lunch. These bills add up.

There are a number of sources of information about your expenses, including your paycheck records, your prior income tax returns, your bank statements, credit card bills, and any other information from your bank or investment records. Look at major purchases — such as a car — that would be something you might not buy for another five or six years. Since you are unlikely to have records of your cash payments, this will be something that you will have to start recording to get a better sense of where your money is going.

In any case, keep a budget of where you are spending your money. Think about which expenses are necessary and which are not. When possible, delay purchasing something — consider whether you really need it, whether there is a cheaper alternative, or whether you can get it later when your finances are more secure.

Use the chart below to keep track of your outgoings — or as a template to copy into your notebook.

Category	Weekly	Monthly
Food		
Restaurants		
Rent/mortgage		
Home (maintenance, repairs, plumbing, electrician, improvements, cleaning, supplies for home, etc)		
Insurance (house contents, car, personal, health, etc.)		
Taxes (income tax, local tax)		
Utilities (electricity, gas, oil, telephone, mobile phone, other)		
Entertainment (films, sporting events, other)		
Clothes		

Transportation (train, bus, taxis, gas, etc.)		
Car (Maintenance, parking, tolls)		
Personal (Haircuts, makeup, self-care)		
Hobbies		
Communication		
Recreation		
Supplies		
Child care		
Pets		
Gifts		
Charitable donations		
Payments on loans		
Credit card payments		
Education (tuition, private schooling, books, training, tutors)		

New sources of income: Collect information about sources of income. I know you lost your job, so that might be what you are focused on right now. But get the best information that you can about other sources of income. This might include any unemployment benefits (and how long you can get them), your partner's income, interest on savings, and other sources, if there are any. For most people, unemployment is a temporary setback—so you might be back earning a living in a month or two. But you cannot count on it, so try to look at the short term and the long term. Use the table below to compile your information.

Income	
Unemployment benefits	
Interest on investments	
Income from other family members	
Other sources of income	
Assets	
Private pension	
Savings	
Stocks and bonds	
Property (main)	
Car(s)	
Other properties	
Jewelry	
Other assets	

2: Consider where you can budget

One way of thinking about how you spend money is to categorize your expenses into needs and wants. Needs are expenses such as rent or mortgage, wants are those flexible and unnecessary expenses, such as the Starbucks coffee, the taxi, the latest electronic gadget, or other "preferences" that you really don't need.

As I indicated above, there are a number of items you can save on. These include repeated expenses, unnecessary purchases, and things that you buy only because of convenience or because you are driven by impulse. Make your shopping and buying more mindful, more frugal, more strategic. Why give other people your money, when you can save it for yourself?

Consider your phone bills—and your bills on your mobile phone or internet. Think about your subscription to cable television channels. Think twice before buying something. Just because you go into a store, it doesn't mean that you have an obligation to buy something. Just because you think something is a bargain, it doesn't mean you need it. How many pieces of clothing, or items that you have purchased in the past, are sitting around in your house that you never wear or use? We are drowning in unnecessary expenses.

Change your mindset about budgeting

Some people strongly resist keeping a budget and trying to save. They say, "I don't want to deprive myself," or "I don't want to feel poor." It's as if spending money foolishly is a sign of success. I recall a number of years ago I had a client who was very wealthy. He owned companies across the US. I commented: "That's a nice jacket you have on."

"Yes," he said, "they had a great sale at the store."

"You look for sales?"

"Of course I do. I never pay full price. I always look for a bargain."

This really impressed me. I realized that he had the same strategy in his business—always looking for ways to save money, always looking for a bargain. He was rich because he bought bargains. Buy low, sell high.

It's a good practice no matter what. You are very likely throwing away a lot of money. You don't need to.

A budget means less guilt when you buy

Interestingly, in developing a budget—finding out what you are spending and what you can afford—can allow you to make purchases with less guilt. A lot of people who are unemployed become extremely anxious about spending any money. You can get upset—or your partner can be upset—if you make a purchase that doesn't seem absolutely necessary. You might get into an argument about buying a tuna sandwich or a scarf. But the purpose of a budget is not to eliminate all expenses — or even all unnecessary expenses. It's to let you know what the information is. So budgeting can actually give you "permission" for purchasing things you don't need, because you can plan for some of these expenses in your budget. Your budget should help you find your balance, not deprive you of everything you want.

Using the table below, based on the information from **Keep a Budget**, think how you might plan to spend less. Put a tick next to each category where you might consider spending less. In the right-hand columns, indicate if this is a flexible expense (one that you can reduce without suffering a decline in your quality of life), and how much less you can aim for. Then indicate what your goal would be for this week (or month) and then keep track of what you actually spend. You might find that this targeted budget plan can produce real savings. (Don't forget, you can copy this information into your notebook if you'd rather not write down here.)

Planning on Reducing Expenses

Category	Could spend less	Current Weekly	Planned Weekly	Actual Weekly	Current Monthly	Planned monthly	Actual monthly
Food							
Restaurants							
Rent / Mortgage							
Home (maintenance, repairs, plumbing, electrician, improvements, cleaning, supplies for home, etc)							
Insurance (house contents, car, personal, health, etc.)							
Taxes (income tax, local tax)							
Utilities (electricity, gas, oil, telephone, mobile phone, other)							

Category	Could spend less	Current Weekly	Planned Weekly	Actual Weekly	Current Monthly	Planned monthly	Actual monthly
Entertainment (films, sporting events, other)							
Clothes							
Transport (train, bus, taxis, gas, etc.)							
Personal (haircuts, makeup, self-care)							
Hobbies							
Communication							
Recreation							
Supplies							

Category	Could spend less	Current Weekly	Planned Weekly	Actual Weekly	Current Monthly	Planned monthly	Actual monthly
Child care							
Pets							
Gifts							
Charitable donations							
Payment on loans							
Credit card payments							
Education (tuition, private schooling,							
Other							

3: Don't jump to conclusions

Losing your job and losing your income can be difficult to deal with. But a lot of what makes it even more difficult is what you are telling yourself about what has happened. I asked Brian what thoughts were going through his head about this:

"If I don't get a job, I won't be able to pay the bills. I will draw on my savings," he said.

"OK, so you see this going on for quite some time?"

"Yes, it could. Look, there are some people out of work for a couple of years."

"OK, so keep going with these thoughts, "If I don't get a job and I draw down my savings, then what will happen?"

"I'll run out of money. I'll lose my house. My wife will leave me."

"What's the worst outcome you can see?"

"I suppose I am homeless."

This string of negative automatic thoughts can feel devastating. But to carry this sequence of thoughts to its dire conclusions requires that you have to assume a lot of really negative things will happen. After all, Brian could get a job sometime in the future. He and Kathy could economize. They might be able to rely on unemployment benefits for a while. They could keep their house. They could even move to a cheaper place to live. His wife could stay with him.

Seeing things more positively

I like to think about all the reasons why none of these things would happen. Now, again, there is no guarantee, but there are lots of things that you can do to cope with your situation and the things that could happen.

First, almost everyone eventually gets a job—especially if they are willing to put effort into it, give it time, be flexible about the job, the pay and the location, and consider acquiring new skills. You have lost your job, not your life. You are still a living human being with intelligence, the capacity to work, the ability to solve problems. It's not over. It's just beginning.

Second, you and your family may find it quite illuminating to consider how you can start saving money. Most of us buy a lot of things that are next to useless. We don't need most of what we have. Your unemployment may be temporary — but the lessons to learn about economizing are lessons for life. This is a good time to start economizing — at least now you are motivated. I've found that a lot of people who have a financial setback are a lot smarter about spending in the future. This is your opportunity, however difficult it may be.

Third, don't assume that you will lose your house. Banks are not eager to repossess if new arrangements can be made. After all, banks are not in the property business, they are lenders. So before you assume that you will lose your house, realize that there may be ways of negotiating the financing. You might be able to extend the length of your mortgage or get financing at a lower interest rate.

Fourth, it's also possible that you could end up "downsizing" to a house or apartment that is more affordable. There is nothing absolutely essential about any particular house — after all, you lived a life before you had the house. Reducing expenses through moving into something smaller might be a way to reduce your stress. This might never be an issue for you, but it is a way that some people have coped.

Fifth, your partner might prove to be a source of support for you and the family. Some partners are not — some turn against the person who is out of work. But most husbands and wives pull together and try to solve the problem as a partnership. Rather than assume that you will lose your family, you might very well find out that your family is your major source of support.

Try to catch yourself with these "what ifs?" running through your head and then tell yourself, "Perhaps none of these things will really happen." Try to challenge these negative thoughts with more balanced, rational and helpful thoughts — indicating there may be adaptive ways of coping every step along the way. Always consider another way to look at it.

When things work out differently

There is no guarantee that everything will work out, but there is also no guarantee that the worst possible outcome will happen either. But what if some of these things did happen? After all, bad things do happen in this difficult life. Tom is a case in point. You may remember from Chapter One that he was ashamed and inclined to isolate himself before he came to see me. His wife, Becky, loved to spend money, and she loved to compete with the neighbors for the most expensive car, house, designer clothes, holidays, and so on. She was into competitive spending. Tom was able to keep up with their lifestyle until the company he worked for went bad and he lost his job, then he no longer had any money coming in. Becky began to nag him, humiliate him, and compare him to the other husbands who were doing so much better. Finally, after a year he moved out, into a small apartment and gave up his expensive car. He saw his daughter, Rachel, several times a week.

As Tom began to examine what had happened, he realized that Becky was actually the wrong partner for him. He said to me, "You know, Bob, I used to like reading books. I used to study religion and philosophy. I used to listen to music. My life with Becky was chasing after money that she would spend on things we didn't need. She stood for all the wrong values. I became a person I didn't like—constantly focused on money. Now, I live in a small apartment, but I really am happier. I have a better relationship with Rachel and I feel better about the person that I am."

Tom went on to describe how one day he stood on a small bridge near to his apartment and thought about his new life. It was better. And the bridge, in my view, symbolized that he had connected with something deep inside himself: his true values, his real self. He had been living a life of status and money, and it really wasn't him. The bridge took him back to being the person he really wanted to be.

Ironically, Tom may have lost his job, his money, and his wife, but he rediscovered who he really is. And he now knew that life without Becky could be a better life.

Take each step individually

Jumping to conclusions can get you to jump off a bridge. I suggest that you take each event, each fact, as a separate experience. Right now you have lost your job. You are collecting the information on how you spend money. You are beginning to keep a budget. There is no need to jump from what is going on now to what may never happen in the future. You have a lot of things to cope with right now and you don't need to solve problems in the possible future—problems that may never occur. Deal with each day—one at a time.

EXERCISE: WHAT MIGHT OR MIGHT NOT HAPPEN IN THE FUTURE?

Work through the following list to clarify your thoughts about the conclusions you are reaching:

- Are you jumping to conclusions?
- What do you fear will happen?
- How likely is it that your worst fears will come true?
- What are some reasons why each of these fears will not come true?
- How could you handle some of these possibilities if they did occur?

4: What is free?

I often think that I have a great advantage over most people when it comes to money and all its emotional issues. I grew up poor—I mean, *really poor*. My parents were divorced when I was not yet two, my mother had to receive welfare payments for a few years because our father provided absolutely no support, we lived in a housing project, and my brother and I never went to a restaurant until we went to college. There were no safety nets. My brother, Jim, and I worked for our savings—I had a paper route and rode my bicycle through the snow in the winter to deliver papers at 6:30 in the morning. We ushered at Yale sporting events to make money, and shoveled snow and cut grass to have a chance to buy a milk shake. We were always busy. We were poor, but we didn't feel deprived.

The one free thing I had was my library card. I walked almost two miles to the library to be able to sit there and read books that would take me to a different world, to different times, fuelling my fantasy of exciting possibilities. My library card was my freedom. My brother and I seemed to spend almost every day at the park across from where we lived—playing basketball, shoveling off snow from the court in the winter. There were always other kids to play with. We were never alone. Play was free—and fun.

So enough about my hard-luck story; here's the point: there are a lot of things you can do that are free. I would argue that they are the most important things. Here are some examples:

You can spend time with your kids. That's free—and fun. And your kids will benefit more from your attention than from some unnecessary gadget that other kids think they need. Talking to your kids, playing ball with them, playing with them, laughing with them, listening to them, all are free—and important.

You can read, listen to music, fix things around the house, make your environment a better place, help out with the chores, learn new skills, see your friends, go for walks, exercise, play sports, ride a bike, sing in the shower and relax—all free, and all important.

You can help the people in your life feel loved. It's free—but is really priceless. It doesn't cost you anything to tell your wife, husband, or your children, that you love them. It doesn't take a large salary to tell them you appreciate what they do, who they are and what they mean to you. You don't have to be bubbling over with compliments, but a hug, a kiss, a caress, a compliment can go a long way.

I remember the son of a wealthy man who told me that he felt emotionally deprived all through his childhood—his father and mother were too busy. "So tell me, Rob, what is the best memory you have of your father growing up?" I asked him.

"I remember when I was a little kid, I came into their bedroom in the morning and my dad let me get on top of him, and he was holding me and playing with me."

Strange how a little play and affection is worth a lot more than a bank account. A kid can't play and laugh with a bank account. Sometimes all a kid needs is a lap to sit in and a father or mother who will listen.

Exercise is free, by the way. You might say, "I can't afford to go to an expensive health club." Funny, when I was a kid, I didn't even know there were health clubs. But you can exercise at home, go for walks, practice stretching, get yourself in better shape. Is there a park near you? Then go to it.

Meditation and yoga are also free. OK, you might be thinking, "I'm not a new-age person, I don't need this Eastern mumbo-jumbo." Well, that's exactly what Karen said to me about yoga and meditation. "It's just not me," she said with considerable confidence and with a little disdain about the fact that I would even put her name and meditation in the same sentence. But much to her surprise and mine, she was willing to try it out. For months afterwards she would quote from lessons of wisdom that she had learned from her yoga class. And you can practice yoga and meditation on your own. Karen is like a lot of people who find that yoga is excellent exercise—it helps stretch and tone your muscles, and it makes you more flexible. Part of yoga is often meditation, reflection, acceptance and calming yourself in the present moment. We will talk more about meditation in a little while. But keep in mind: yoga, meditation, relaxation — anywhere, anytime, free.

You might not be a religious person, so this might be something that you skip over. But a lot of people find religion to be a comforting, meaningful, and enriching experience. One of my clients, an Orthodox Jewish man, told me that the most comfortable and meaningful time for him was morning prayers at the synagogue. He felt at peace, he felt connected, he experienced a meaning larger than himself.

According to the Pew Research Group[12], 40% of Americans are active in religious organizations. The research by the Pew Research Group in the US indicates the following: "Compared with those who are not involved with such organizations, religiously active Americans are more trusting of others, are more optimistic about their impact on their community, think more highly of their community, and are more involved in more organizations of all kinds."

Religious practice and attending a church, synagogue, or mosque can help in many ways. Many people who participate in religious services and institutions are able to connect with others in their community. Meeting weekly with others from a similar faith can help you feel connected, understood, and not alone. According to a Rasmussen Survey[13], 47% of Americans pray every day — or nearly every day.

If religion and prayer are meaningful to you, then you might join the millions of others who observe and practice their faith every day.

There may be people in your religious community that can help you find a job or provide leads for training. Religion often gives people a sense of hope and purpose, a value to their lives that is independent of money and social status. Psychologists may often derogate religion, but I have found that many of my clients, friends, and family members gain considerable support and meaning from their religious observance. And, it's also free.

EXERCISE: NEW WAYS TO SPEND TIME

Look at the following list to find new approaches to spending your time between jobs:

- Now that you have more time, you can do more things with your family.
- How can you be more supportive and more involved with the people you love?
- What can you do each day that is free?
- Could you spend more time exercising?
- Is religion part of your life? How could you get more involved?
- Could you consider meditation, relaxation, learning?

5: It's not what you have — it's what you appreciate

My office is just two blocks away from an expensive shopping area on Madison Avenue in New York City. One of the trendiest stores is Barneys, where floors are assigned to designer labels and where expensive jewelry greets you as you enter the store. Everywhere, people are concerned about their appearance, their labels, and the latest fashion. The only reason I ever go there is to meet a colleague who likes to have lunch there every few months. I find New York to be a temple of materialism, shallowness, and unnecessary expenses. And it may be my imagination, but the people there don't look very happy.

Materialism, fashion, being "with it," having the latest thing, are all part of our culture of deprivation amid affluence, but I think it's not so much what you have, it's what you are able to appreciate. You can have an expensive house and car, a wardrobe full of the latest fashion, and you can have prestige and power, but if you don't appreciate what you have and who you are, then you are impoverished.

Look around you and ask yourself, "What do I really appreciate in my life?" If you are feeling down and worried about money, you might focus on what you won't be able to have, buy or get. But what about appreciation? Here's a simple exercise for you to do.

EXERCISE: VISUALIZE LOSING EVERYTHING

1. Close your eyes. Imagine everything has been taken away. You have no senses (no vision, no hearing, no sense of touch). You have no memory. You have no family, no friends, no money, no possessions. You have nothing; you are nothing. You have disappeared.

2. Now, I am going to suggest a simple exercise. You can have one thing back at a time, only one at a time. I won't tell you how many things you can get back. It all depends on how much you can convince me that you really appreciate each thing. You have to be the Great Appreciator: the one who really understands what it means. The only way to appreciate is to imagine not having it.

3. What would you like to have back first? Convince me that it really matters to you.

I've conducted this exercise many times with many different people. I've tried it on myself, on friends, family members, on taxi drivers, strangers, and many of my clients. It always seems to reveal what is already there—what we have taken for granted, but what is really essential in our lives. Here are some of the responses:

"I want my eyesight back."

"What would you like to be able to see for five minutes—if you knew you only had five more minutes of seeing available?"

"I'd want to see my wife and my daughter."

"What do you want to see in them? What do you appreciate?"

"I love my wife: her smile, her eyes, her hair, the way she looks. We've been together for fifteen years, she is still beautiful to me."

"OK. How about your daughter? What do you appreciate about seeing her?" "Her face, her laughter, the way she's grown up. She's still my little girl. I love her."

"OK. You can have your eyesight back."

Another woman said she appreciated her son. "I know we have had some difficulties, but I've also learned from them. I've grown. He's had some hard times, but he's a good kid. I really appreciate his ability to keep trying, his strength. But also I appreciate the fact that he knows he's not perfect, he keeps trying. Knowing he is in my life is about the most important thing I can imagine."

So close your eyes and, while you are blinded to the world, look around you in your imagination. Do you appreciate the fact that you can hear, walk, talk, think, listen to music, laugh, play, give and receive love, touch the people who have touched and moved you? What would life be like if any one of these senses, people, experiences were to disappear forever?

"I never realized how much I have in my life," Rob said to me. "I just didn't think about it. I wasn't aware."

I like to start each day with some quiet time, some reflection, some appreciation. I am lucky to be alive, lucky to hear, listen, feel and be touched. It's all here, the most important things and experiences and people. If only you could open your eyes and ears and find it right in front of you.

EXERCISE: DISCOVERING WHAT'S REALLY IMPORTANT

Spend a few moments going through the following points:
- Imagine it's all been taken away. What would you want back? Why?
- Start each day thinking about what you appreciate. Focus on that.
- When you think about what you appreciate, is it really related to money?
- If it's not related to money, what does this tell you?
- What's really important?

6: What does money mean to you?

All of us have our own way of relating to money. It's one of the most emotional issues in our lives. For some, it's more important than love, sex, integrity, family, or health. People kill over money. People kill themselves over losing money. Ironically, a lot of psychologists are reluctant to talk to their clients about money, considering it "too personal." This is like your nurse saying, "I don't want to take your blood pressure because I don't want to invade your privacy." It's nonsense.

Ask yourself, which of the following fits you:

- Money is security.
- Money helps me build my self-esteem.
- I often compare myself with others — and what they have.
- I am envious of people who have more money.
- I feel embarrassed about how little money I have.
- I feel embarrassed that I have more than others.
- If I had more money, I could relax.
- I am concerned that I won't be able to support myself or my family financially.
- I couldn't live on less.
- I need to spend money to feel happy.
- Money is a sign of success.

If you are like a lot of people, you might find a little truth in some — or all — of these statements. We attach a lot of psychological baggage to money in our lives. When you think of money as "security," you might also say, "I want to have enough money so that I don't have to worry about it." Now, what's interesting is that I have heard wealthy and poor people say exactly the same thing. Money equals security. What is more likely the case is that your expectations and demands determine what you think you need. Let's imagine that everyone in the world had to live on 25% less. So we would learn to live on less. (Here is a hint: for the last 99.99999% of human history people lived on less than what they have now.) OK, perhaps you won't have the more expensive car, the designer clothes, flatscreen TV, iPad, holidays, cool furniture, restaurant meals, and whatever else you really don't need. Security is not what you have—it's what you think you need. Do you really need all the "stuff" you have? I doubt it.

Or perhaps you think of money as self-esteem. "I feel good about myself when I make a lot of money." That doesn't say very much about you that is good. How about trying this, "I feel good about myself when I am kind, loving, honest, and self-disciplined"? Now, that would be a legitimate reason to have self-esteem. Being a good person doesn't cost anything.

Or you might be caught up in comparing yourself with people who have more. So you lose your job, start economizing, and worry, "What will the neighbors think?" I have neighbors who are out of work and I still think of them as "my neighbors," some I think of as "my friends." I think they are people going through a rough patch. But what if I were the kind of obnoxious, judgmental person who thought less of them? Does that say more about you—when you are out of work—or more about the creepiness of some shallow people? Why should you care about what some shallow, unfeeling, uncaring person might think?

How do you know what people think about you?

You have no idea what people think. Are they telling you? Is it possible that some of your neighbors are out of work, worried about losing their jobs, or have family members going through a hard time? Tough times hit almost all households. It's not the material possessions that you have become attached to that really matter. It's whether you can build a meaningful life—a meaningful family—without having more than someone else. Here is another hint: in doing therapy for almost 30 years, I have never had anyone come to me complaining that their problems today—as adults—were due to not having enough material things when they were kids. But I have seen plenty of adults who grew up wealthy who were impoverished in the most important way: lacking love. Security in a family is more about love, understanding and kindness. All, free.

The pleasure of spending is short-lived

Let's look at your thought that you need to spend money to be happy. This is the "retail therapy" that a lot of us rely on when we are feeling empty, bored, unloved, or unhappy. You go to the store — preferably a shopping center with lots of options — and entertain yourself looking for "bargains." You look in the shopping bag at all the items you bought — which you have never needed — and feel momentarily happy. It's like having a drink — it works for a short while until it wears off — and then you are stuck with the bill: either your hangover or your credit card bill.

If spending money is what makes you happy, you need to find another way of making yourself happy. Materialism is an empty journey. Materialism fills an empty void in you with more emptiness.

This is the opportunity to re-evaluate your relationship with money. It's not the same thing as security, or legitimate self-esteem, and it seldom buys lasting happiness. I think of money — along with time — as "utilities" — that is, "What can I get with money or time?" Let's take time first. I like to limit the number of clients I see so that I can spend time with my wife, or reading, or relaxing. Time is a utility — it's useful to get me things and experiences that I really value. If I spent all my time making money, I'd have less time to enjoy my life. I call it "balance." In fact, now that you are unemployed, you have a lot of time that can be put to good use — following the many suggestions that I am outlining for you in this book. Make use of this time now, because when you get back to your job in the future, you won't have the richness of time that you have now.

Consider your needs vs. your preferences

Money is a *utility* — it's an exchange. Think about what you can get with money — and think about whether you need it. For example, you need food, clothing, and shelter. You get the money to purchase these things. But if you are making money a goal in itself — like people who simply want more — or if you use money as a way of "keeping score" — then you will be unhappy.

No matter how much money you have. Money is part of an exchange. But what is it you are buying? How much do you really need? Is it "need" or "preference"? You might prefer the $100 designer jeans, but you might be better off with the knocked-down price of $30. Is money the way to impress people—people who really shouldn't matter to you? Are you willing to make yourself miserable so that judgmental people who have shallow values will "like" you more? You decide what's important.

EXERCISE: YOUR FEELINGS ABOUT MONEY

Untangle your feelings about money by answering the following questions:

- What does money mean to you?
- Does money mean security? Self-esteem? Success? Status? The only way to buy happiness? A way to win? To keep score?
- What's wrong with these ideas about money?
- Are less expensive things that much less rewarding? If not, why not?
- What are some things that you like to do that are free? Why do you enjoy them?
- If you have more time now, how can you "spend your time" to get more meaning, pleasure, growth and purpose?

7: Even if money is a problem, what good will worrying do?

Even if you do everything that I recommend, money issues can still remain a problem. It's a reality for many people who lose their jobs. You can budget, economize, focus on what you can do for free, show love, experience appreciation, pray, go to church, meditate, do yoga, or exercise. All of these can be free or relatively inexpensive, but money can still remain an issue.

Yes, that is true. But after you have done everything you can that is adaptive in reducing expenses, is there any point to worrying about it? Think of worry as the repetitive focus on a negative thought: "What if I run out of money?", "What if I can't pay my mortgage?", "What if I take another five months to get a job?" I want you to examine if repeating these negative thoughts—over and over—is going to do any good. It's natural that the thought occurs to you—and probably natural that it is disturbing—but what good will it do to focus on it, repeat it, and get stuck with it?

You are probably thinking, "Are you naive? How can I not worry?" I know it sounds naive to you, but you can choose to compartmentalize your money worries and focus on all the other things that I have been describing. You can do constructive things—now—rather than worrying about the future. The future will come, whether you worry or not. You don't know the future. You might get a new job sooner than later. The future might take care of itself. Even if it doesn't work out as well as you might wish it to, there is no real advantage to worrying about future money issues.

I want you to consider two ways of looking at worrying about money: First, it's the repetitive nature of your worry; second, it's the ability to compartmentalize your worry. OK, you have had worries about money before—many times: the same thoughts, repeated incessantly. There is nothing new in the new occurrence of the worry. There is no new information. It's the same. Repeating it won't lead to any new solutions or insights. You are just nagging yourself. Consider putting the worry into a compartment and setting it aside to a time during the day when you can worry about your money problems.

Make an appointment with your worries

I call this "worry time." Arbitrarily choose a time—say, 4:30 in the afternoon. This is your time to spend twenty minutes on your money worries. Any other money worries that come up at any other time can be put down on a piece of paper. Just as you did for rumination, set up an appointment with that worry at 4:30 pm. You will find that you are able to do this (not always, but very often). The worries are delayed and compartmentalized to 4:30. Your worry time rolls around, you look at your list of worries and you find several things to be true: first, it's the same few thoughts, nagging you; second, you might be less concerned at 4:30 in the afternoon than you were at 11:00 in the morning or 11:00 at night; third, you sleep better, because you have assigned the worry to worry time, not to sleeping time. You feel less controlled and less trapped by your money worries. As a result, you can enjoy most of your day without having to answer to them.

Now, what can you do at 4:30 pm? Ask yourself the following questions, to put the worry to a test. First, is there any advantage to repeatedly worrying about this? The emphasis is on "repeatedly." Did you get the point the first ten times you nagged yourself about your worries about money? Do you need to nag yourself another ten times? Second, is there any productive action that you can take to make progress? Anything that you can do in the next twenty-four hours? I call this, "Your to-do list for today." Perhaps there is. You can budget, do things for free, look for a job. OK? Then do those things. They are more productive than worrying. Third, are there other rewarding and meaningful things you can do that have nothing to do with money? Well, that's what this chapter—this entire book—is about. Do rewarding things, meaningful things, action and experience in the present moment—rather than worrying about money.

Think of it this way. We will all die some day. You can spend every moment of your life worrying about dying. Or you can spend every moment of your life living a full and meaningful life. Which makes more sense to you?

EXERCISE: LOOKING AT YOUR WORRIES

During your worry-time appointment, use all the points listed here.
- Are you spending a lot of time worrying about the future and your money?
- What are the costs and benefits to you of spending time worrying about this?

- Will worry actually solve your problem?
- Is there anything that you can do today that will actually solve your problem?
- If not, then why continue worrying?
- What would be the advantage of accepting that you really don't know what the future might be?
- Could you spend more time doing productive things for yourself in the present moment?
- Set aside a worry time every day. Put off your worries until that time.

8: How can this help you establish better values and more self-discipline?

I think it is realistic to say that you are very likely to get another job and get your finances back on track. Almost everyone eventually gets back to work. I know this might seem overly optimistic to some readers, but that's what the facts tell us. But I want you to consider looking beyond the immediate situation to the bigger picture in your life. This involves two — related — issues: having more self-discipline when it comes to money, and setting the right values for your life.

Self-discipline

In every chapter in this book there is a message about self-discipline. It includes making your job getting a job, taking care of yourself, having activity schedules every day, pulling your weight at home with chores and support, being a better parent and partner, reaching out to the larger community, helping others, and making sure that you have a regular self-care program of exercise and diet. And money is now on your list of self-discipline.

We all spend more than we need to — often not saving anything in any given year. It's absurd. When you get your next job, keep in mind that keeping a budget, economizing, being more mindful of what you spend, thinking about what you need vs. what you prefer, escaping the treadmill of competitive spending and status-seeking are lessons for life. Don't just use them during the time between jobs. Use this for the rest of your life. Keep money in perspective as a means to buy things that you actually need, rather than what is on sale, what is convenient, or what makes you feel better for the moment. The best way to stretch your money is not to spend it.

This doesn't mean that you are deprived. It means that you get smart about money.

Setting the right values for life

Think about what you really value. I have pitted materialism against human needs and values. You, your kids, and your partner need love, understanding, appreciation, time together, and the ability to have fun. These are generally free and readily available. You can get your mind around the issue of money by doing the mental exercise, Visualize Losing Everything, that I described on page 134 — imagine it has all been taken away. If you start each day with appreciating what you already have — especially the relationships, your senses, the freedom, and the ability to grow and learn — then you are a richer person. If you chase after money as a way of defining your "worth," then you will find yourself chasing the wind. You will find yourself alone, lost and empty. The decision is yours.

EXERCISE: YOUR RELATIONSHIP WITH MONEY FOR THE FUTURE

Look ahead to when you will be earning again and think about your changed attitude to money:
- What if you changed your attitude towards money after you go back to work?
- In what ways could you be more self-disciplined?
- How could you change your priorities so that you get more meaning out of life?
- How can you put money in its place—so that you don't get too focused on it?

- How could you plan your spending and savings so that you are more on top of things in the future?
- How can you replace materialism with human purpose—and better relationships?

SUMMARY

We have looked at a lot of ways that money issues can affect your experience during this time between jobs. Of course, it's important to collect the information—find out what your assets and income are, what benefits you qualify for, where you are spending your money and how you can economize. This doesn't mean that money won't be a problem, though, it just means that you will have a better handle on the facts and ideas about where spending can be changed from wants to needs. In addition, we have examined how you might change your view of money and materialism, thinking about how what you really appreciate and value may have less to do with money and more to do with purpose and relationships. There are a lot of things that cost a lot of money, but the person who can build on appreciation, gratitude, awareness, and fun is the wealthier person. Money is just one value—it's more of an exchange for other things that may or may not have value.

Get the information Find out how much money you have, your savings, other sources of income, what you possess, and how much you are spending.

Consider where you can budget Keep track of what you spend and what you are spending it on. Try to identify other ways of making your budget go further.

Don't jump to conclusions Just because you are currently unemployed doesn't mean that you will never have an income. Identify your tendency to jump to conclusions and try to put things in perspective.

What is free? List all the things that you can do that are free and spend a lot more time focusing on those things and doing them. Are you able to enjoy and appreciate what comes naturally to us that is free? What does that tell you?

It's not what you have—it's what you appreciate. The greatest "wealth" is the ability to appreciate and show gratitude. What do you have in your life right now: relationships, interests, things, experiences, hobbies and opportunities? Do you really appreciate these things?

What does money mean to you? Does money mean self-esteem, status, security, success? How can you achieve these things without focusing only on money? Are there ways to be proud of yourself that don't involve it?

Even if money is a problem, what good will worry do? Often money can be a real problem, but it is a given for right now, and worrying about it won't help.

How can this help you establish better values and more self-discipline? If you learn to put money in its place and learn to appreciate more, show gratitude towards others, base your self-esteem on being a decent person rather than having possessions, you may be able to use this time to reassert true values of human dignity and human worth.

8

HELPING EACH OTHER: FOR PARTNERS AND FAMILIES

A lot of couples who are going through a period where one of them is unemployed have more friction and frustration than they have ever had before. They are worried about money, worried about maintaining their lifestyle, worried that they won't ever get a job again. In this chapter I look at how your partner and your family, if you have these, can work with you as a team during your time between jobs. This chapter is for both of you to read. You need to understand how each of you experiences this time and how you can both be supportive to the other person. If you are the person who is unemployed, you also need to attend to the needs and the frustrations of your partner. If it is your partner who is unemployed, you can also express your feelings and needs, but in a manner that is respectful and helpful. This can be a time that can bring you together in a common cause, or it can be a time that drives you apart. It will depend on how you use this time.

Try to bring it together. You won't regret working hard to build your lives.

Breaking the news — sharing the news

When Mark found out that he was losing his job, the first thing he thought was, "How am I going to tell Anna?" She had high expectations of him and she always seemed to push him harder — to make more money, climb higher in the corporate ladder, impress everyone with their lifestyle. They had been living beyond their means for several years, taking a mortgage on a house they really couldn't afford, and constantly competing with friends and neighbors for the latest in fashion, gadgets, cars, and holidays. They had been the "fake rich"—a family with a lifestyle that was maintained on maxed-out credit cards. What would Anna say?

When he got home he poured himself a drink—then another one. He found himself fumbling with his thoughts and his words, afraid to tell Anna. But he knew he would have to tell her. "I've got some bad news. They told me I'm being made laid off today."

She looked at him, scornfully, exasperated, angry, and contemptuous. "How could you do this to us? You really screwed up this time, Mark. All of our friends are going to think we are losers. I don't know if I can stay around for this. I mean, how are you going to take care of us? You can't do anything right. You've let us down—once again. Just like you always do. I should have married Jonathan. He's doing so much better than you. How could I end up with such a loser?"

Fortunately, this is just a fantasy. But it might be your fantasy. I hope it's not your reality. Imagine confronting a wife or husband who responds in this way? How would you feel? After you work out if you are sadder or more enraged, you might think, "This is the absolute worst way to respond to someone losing their job." You're right. No one should have to go through this kind of contemptuous humiliation. Losing your job is not a crime, it's not something that you wanted. You need love and support, not another obstacle to overcome. You have lost your job, you don't want to lose the love and respect of your family.

If your partner is unemployed, you can be helpful, or you can be hurtful. Perhaps more than any other time in the history of your relationship, this is the time when they will need you most. Keep in mind that it is hard enough on your partner who lost their job—it's not what they wanted to happen. They feel bad enough. Criticizing, ridiculing, withdrawing, or complaining will not help them get another job. It will only make things worse for the entire family.

Does unemployment wreck marriages?

It's interesting that the research on the effects of unemployment on marital satisfaction is not as clear-cut as you might think. In a review of the research on couples with one unemployed spouse there was no direct relationship between unemployment and marital dissatisfaction.[14] That's right! Some studies show that relationships get worse, but some research suggests that relationships can get better. It really depends on how you and your family cope together or turn against each other.

One thing is clear; if you and your partner have more difficulties in your marriage, then you are going to have more difficulties coping with unemployment. Although for some people, things get worse, for others, they can actually get better. You do have a choice.

Facing it together

Let's take a look at how a couple of families coped with unemployment. One client, Phil, lost his job at the company after eighteen years of being a productive employee. There was a downturn in the economy and a lot of people were being laid off. But his wife, Ellen, realized that he had done everything he could to do a good job and that he was a good man, a good father, and a good husband. It was hard enough for him. When he told her he was being laid off, she put her arms around him. There was a long silence as they heard each other breathing together. Ellen said, "Don't worry, Phil. We'll get through this together. We can cut back on expenses, and I know you'll get another job. We're in this together."

Phil wasn't the kind of guy who cried, but he felt tears falling down the side of his face, and he held Ellen tighter, breathed a little more easily, and whispered to her, "I knew I married the right person when I married you."

They realized that Phil would now have more time to spend with their son, Daniel, who needed a ride to school and would also love it if dad could be there at his football practice. "I was so busy at work for all of these years that I missed a lot of Daniel growing up. I now have some time to catch up with him," Phil told me, a little proud of himself for taking an interest in his son. "You know, now that I have more time to spend with Daniel and with Ellen, I realize that I missed them when I was working. Or, at least, I think now I should have missed them. I'm lucky to have them in my life." Now that Phil had more time at home he could help with the chores — the shopping, cleaning the house, getting the laundry done.

Phil told me, "Ellen and I wrote out the different things that we needed to do as a family. I hadn't realized Ellen was carrying the extra burden of a lot of these things that I just took for granted. I guess doing them has helped me appreciate what she's been doing all these years."

Seeing your situation from a new perspective

Another couple, Maureen and Lawrence, relied on both of their salaries, and when Maureen lost her job, they both got worried about their finances. Lawrence realized Maureen was feeling anxious and guilty. "I feel I have let you down," she said to Lawrence. "I want to pull my weight." Maureen had been doing two jobs for quite some time — doing most of the childcare and homemaking, and working full-time at the office. It was much harder for her to juggle so many things, and Lawrence had tried to be helpful, but a lot of the home responsibilities were falling on her. Lawrence said, "You know, perhaps you need a break from the job for a while. Perhaps you've been doing too much. We can cut back on some expenses and you can take some time finding some balance for yourself. In fact, when I think of it, it's hard to imagine how you have been able to do so much."

Yes, there are couples who do pull together, who are empathetic, supportive, compassionate, and collaborative, but it's not easy. You are likely to have your own anxious, and even angry, thoughts if your partner loses a job — and you might have a lot of concerns about how your partner will respond if it is you who finds yourself out of work.

Strengthening your relationship

You and your partner can use this time between jobs to practice the skills to build a better relationship—not just for now, but forever. I've seen some couples pull together during this time, using a lot of the skills that I am going to describe in this chapter. They focused on coordinating rather than competing; listening rather than criticizing; solving problems together rather than complaining about having them; and accepting difficulties while still working on them. It's really up to you. Which direction would you like to go in? If you are ready to make things better, then read on. If you are willing to change the way you communicate, then there is hope. Let's look at how you and your partner can pull together rather than pushing apart during this time.

1: This is about *all of you*

If you have a partner and a family, the experience of unemployment is one for you all to face together. It's as if one of you is "out there" looking for a job and the other is "in here" waiting for things to change. You and your partner are not living in a parallel universe where you never touch each other. Unemployment has direct effects on a number of factors that affect the family. These include changes in financing and budgeting, time spent together, dividing up work to do for the family unit, being a sympathetic and supportive partner, helping each other maintain and build hope, and brainstorming solutions to make things better.

It's likely that the period of unemployment will require new adaptations in how you spend money and what you are likely to do—or plan to do. For example, you and your family members may want to keep a budget—and live within it (I discuss this in Chapter Seven). That doesn't mean you are totally deprived of everything you want, but it may mean that you will all have to consider ways of being more frugal. In fact, these might be good habits to follow after this period is over. You will need to talk about budgeting in a collaborative and respectful way—not in a defensive or accusatory way.

Similarly, you might find yourself spending more time together. If your partner is unemployed, they will be spending some time looking for a job, but it may not be as much time as you might want them to be spending. That's because there is really just so much that one can do in a day to actively look for a job. So you may realize that your partner is home much more than before, and this might trigger some of your critical thoughts, such as "Why don't they just get a job?" It's not as easy to simply wish it to be so. But these critical thoughts may come to you, and it won't help anyone to start putting down your partner. You're human and you will naturally feel anxious and angry. You might feel anxious and worried that your partner will never get a job. And you might feel angry, because you are blaming them for the situation. These are normal feelings. But you can also stand back and realize that doing an emotional "dump" on your partner will only make everything worse.

How can each person help?

Let's think about the changes that each of you can make that might be helpful for the family in coping with this period in between. If the wife is the one who is out of work, what can the husband and children do to help? Can each family member think about ways of budgeting? Are there ways of being supportive to Mom? Can you think of positive and encouraging things to say to her? The same is true if Dad is the one who has lost his job. What can each family member do to be helpful to dad and to the family?

You should have a family conference meeting every week to discuss how to cope together during this time. This is a chance to brainstorm together, solve problems together. For example, Phil and Ellen sat down, first with each other, and later with their kids, to discuss how best to cope during. Phil told Ellen, "Look, I need to keep busy; I can't just lie around and wait to get a job. So I plan to spend some time every day doing something to look for a job. I can talk to the employment people, get in touch with people I know, look around for possibilities. But that's not going to take eight or ten hours each day. So try to help me think of things that I could do around the house or for the family that would help, so I will feel like I am of some use."

Ellen and Phil came up with a list of tasks that he could follow up on. These included taking the kids to school and picking them up, doing the shopping during the week, helping clean the house, paying the bills, and following up on other chores that needed to be done. Phil could also help the kids focus on their homework, read along with them on some of the assignments, and discuss the work they had to do. He wasn't as "absent" as a father as he was when he was working full time. He had time to be with them.

They put a list on the fridge showing Ellen's and Phil's chores, and Phil's list was a lot longer than Ellen's. This was actually really good because it helped Phil to stay busy, it gave him a focus every day, both he and Ellen could see that he was making a contribution and the household and family ran more smoothly. I encouraged both of them to look at the list every day and to add (or subtract) tasks. Having the list kept everyone focused on the idea that the family was in this together and that Phil was busy doing his part.

Contrast this with Steven and Amanda. Steven would get up late in the morning, hours after Amanda had left for work. He would walk around in his bathrobe all day, watching television or sitting at his computer surfing websites for nonsense. He didn't exercise, didn't help much with the chores, and resented Amanda when she complained. Steven's response to his day was passivity and rumination, mixed with self-pity. Some of this is natural for people when they are out of work, but these habits began to annoy Amanda, and this led to more arguments and more resentment for both of them. Steven felt that Amanda didn't understand how hard it was for him, and thought she was just nagging and complaining. And Amanda felt that he had given up on pulling his weight in the family. Amanda felt Steven had given up on his job, his family, and himself.

The choice is always yours. You can change things today—use this list to remind you of how you can approach this time:

- Try to pull together rather than pulling apart.
- This is about the entire family, not just one person.
- Divide up responsibilities and assign tasks.
- Everyone contributes.
- Post your tasks and follow up with each other.
- Have a family conference meeting.

2: Everyone has responsibility

We like to think of ourselves as individuals, facing the rugged challenges of the marketplace, doing it on our own. Our image of ourselves might be as a warrior, who is able to withstand all the travails of nature and, now, the marketplace. But nothing could be further from the truth. Society has been built over the centuries by families who worked together—almost non-stop—who belonged to communities, attended churches, helped out their neighbors, and cared for each other. We are better together than coping apart as individuals without any support.

I want you to think of your family—and friends—as a group of people with shared responsibilities during this time of unemployment. When a friend of mine was unemployed, I chatted to him a couple of times a week for over six months, supporting him, encouraging him to keep looking for the option that would work for him. It was an honor, in fact, to be there for him. If you are a friend or a family member of someone who is unemployed, think of this as the time when you can really matter, when you can really help. Perhaps your family member needs a phone call, someone to have lunch or coffee with, someone to go for a walk with, someone to laugh with. We are our brother's keeper.

Try to understand each other

If you are not the person who is unemployed, what can you do that would help the unemployed person in your family? Ask them. Perhaps they just want to know that you care enough to ask. Perhaps they want to know you are there to talk. Or perhaps they could ask you for suggestions, for leads, for help. Helping someone who needs help can make you proud of yourself, can make you feel that you are the kind of person others can count on.

If you are the one who is unemployed you also have responsibilities. You can't just assume that everyone is going to be patient if you aren't doing something to actively look for a job. They aren't going to be patient if you don't take care of yourself. Steven would just lie around, watching television, overeating, and being irritable and self-pitying. He wasn't doing his part in looking for a job, or of taking care of himself, helping with the chores around the house, and being part of the team. He was AWOL—absent without leave. He acted as if he was entitled to feel sorry for himself and passively lie around. Of course, he was really depressed and his passivity and pessimism were part of it.

Steven also had a responsibility to do something to help himself with his depression. If you have a problem, you have a responsibility to look for a solution. Use the list below to focus on how each person can be helpful:

- Everyone has responsibility for something.
- Teams are better than loners.
- Ask each other what would be helpful.
- What are you willing to do and when will you do it?

3: Talk about it

Many people who are unemployed feel ashamed and feel like a burden. They often say, "People don't want to be around me." But it may be that the unemployed person is isolating him- or herself. If your partner is unemployed and remains silent and aloof and isolates him- or herself on a regular basis, reach out, make an offer to talk, show some interest in what they are going through. Your partner might feel they are enough of a burden, that they have failed, and that they have let the family down. They might feel ashamed, all alone, as if no one wants to hear their story, or cares enough about them. Isolated and withdrawn in their own sadness, guilt, and shame, they begin to feel more depressed, ruminating and dwelling on the negative, feeling cut off from all the support that they once thought they had.

If you are the person who is unemployed and prone to avoiding difficult situations, you might find yourself pulling away from your partner. You may feel ashamed, as if you are a burden. Or you might feel your partner could never understand what it's like. You might even feel you don't have a right to talk about the difficulties you are facing. As a result, you pull away, remaining silent, brooding alone with your negative thoughts, feeling worse and worse, and alone in your own home.

If it is your partner who is unemployed, you might think that talking about the situation will sound like pressure or criticism. It will only bring up unpleasant thoughts and feelings. You might withdraw from your partner, partly because you are anxious and angry yourself, and partly because you think you don't know what to say or do. As the two of you withdraw more, both of you get depressed. In fact, the research on couples shows that if one partner is depressed there is an excellent likelihood that the other one will get depressed, too.

Disconnecting is not the answer

Problems don't get solved by withdrawing. You don't connect if you are living in a fortress.

Withdrawing from difficult feelings and discussions is perfectly normal—but it's also something you will want to overcome as soon as possible. You and your partner can support each other during this time. One way of breaking the ice is to talk about talking. Bill's wife, Ariel, said, "Bill, I know this is a hard time for you losing your job, and I want to be supportive. What can I say or do that will help you right now? If you just want to talk about your feelings, that's fine. If you want to brainstorm ideas, that's good, too. I need to know what will help you."

Bill said, "I suppose I just need to feel you are there if I am feeling down. Sometimes I feel all alone with my feelings, sitting at home all day."

By talking about what to talk about, you and your partner can come to terms about what you need during this time. Some people when they have lost their job just need to know their partner is there for them, some need to know they are willing to listen, some need to sort out their thoughts and feelings by sharing them, and some want to solve problems together and brainstorm. Others, at least for now, may simply want to be left alone. But the key thing is to start by talking about talking.

It's not only the unemployed person who needs to talk about feelings. The partner of the unemployed person also has his or her feelings, too. Many partners of unemployed people feel anxious, depressed, angry, confused, hurt, helpless, and hopeless. If your partner is unemployed, and you are going through a tough time, you may need your partner to be supportive to you as well.

You can be better together — by leaning on each other.

EXERCISE: HOW PARTNERS CAN HELP EACH OTHER

Build a bridge between each other for mutual help by thinking about these issues:
- Withdrawing, pouting and refusing to talk won't help.
- You have a right to the support of your family members.
- Reach out to the person who is most withdrawn.
- Talk about talking—what to talk about, what to do, when to do it.
- Ask your partner what they need to hear.

4: Talk so you will be heard

We've been discussing the importance of talking about things, but there are effective and ineffective ways of communicating. Some people, caught up in their negative thoughts and feelings about being unemployed, will focus excessively on repeated negative complaints. This is like the person who always puts a downer on everything: where you just go on and on describing how bad you feel, repeating yourself endlessly without taking a break. This repeated negative complaining is related to the rumination that we described in Chapter Six. When you ruminate, you get stuck on a negative thought or feeling and just keep repeating it to yourself, without solving a problem or making a change. Typical ruminative negative communication sounds like this:

- I can't believe that this has happened to me.
- Why does this have to happen to me?
- It's so unfair.
- I can't stand it.
- I can't get this stuff out of my head.
- I feel really lousy.

Ruminative complaining is not the same thing as simply having a negative thought or feeling. A negative thought can last five seconds. Here's an example: "This is crap." OK, we got the message. How many times do you have to repeat it to yourself or your partner? Every single one of the statements above makes sense to you. You are entitled to have these thoughts. But the nature of ruminative complaining is its relentless repetition—you just keep focusing on the same story over and over. And, unfortunately, you are bringing other people down with you.

It makes sense to talk about the negatives, but if you get stuck on the negative, you will lose your audience and feel worse in the long run. You have a right to your feelings, but there are more constructive ways of sharing them. Some people think they can do an "emotional dump," just say everything that is on their mind, go on and on forever talking about how bad things are. Three things will happen if you do the emotional dump:

You will feel worse, since you are only focused on the negative. The more you talk about negatives, the more negative you will feel. You will access more negative thoughts, memories, and feelings — and you will feel worse.

You will alienate the people who could support you. Your listener might start off feeling like they want to support you, but then they will feel overwhelmed, helpless, and even invisible. That's bad for both of you.

The problems remain unsolved. By focusing on doing an emotional dump you sidetrack yourself from solving real problems in the real world. We will look at this later in this chapter, but keep in mind that expressing sometimes may be good, but it won't solve your real problems.

How to change the ways you talk

Here are some guidelines to keep in mind so that you don't get stuck in your thoughts:

1. **Try to edit what you say.** Don't go on for long periods of time without interruption.
2. **Reduce the drama and the negativity.** You don't have to yell to be heard.
3. **Let the other person talk, too.** Ask them how they are doing. It's not only about you.
4. **If you talk about a problem**, talk about a solution. Balance expression with plans for action.

Let's take each guideline:

1. **Try to edit what you say.** One way of thinking about a conversation is that it's like playing tennis: both you and your partner hit the ball back and forth. If you are hogging

the conversation with repeated negative statements, your partner is going to feel left out. He or she will stop listening. Punctuate your statements with questions and reflections: "Does this make sense to you?", "What do you think about what I am saying?" Editing what you say also means eliminating the repetition. Your partner already got the message the first time.

2. **Reduce the drama and the negativity.** Your discussions about this between-jobs period does not have to be overly dramatic and negative. Raising your voice, yelling, pouting, being sarcastic may seem like "natural responses," but they only add to your own misery and the unhappiness of people around you. You can talk about difficulties without making it overly difficult to hear you.

3. **Encourage the other person to talk.** We already can see that editing and asking for feedback is a way of inviting an exchange. But it also may be helpful for you to show an interest in the lives of the other people in your life. How is your partner doing? What did they do today? What's on the news? What are some plans that the two of you can make? Getting the spotlight off you — at times — can help to improve the communication. After all, the family includes both of you, doesn't it? "I know I've been talking a lot about myself, and I was wondering how your day was. What did you do today?"

4. **Talk about solutions, not just problems.** For example, if you are complaining about feeling lonely, you can always add a few words about what you are doing to connect with other people. "I've been feeling isolated since I've been out of work. But today I went onto my Facebook page and sent out a few messages to some of my old friends. It was nice to get some responses. Carolyn wrote and said it's been a while since she's seen us, so perhaps we can get together with her and Doug." The thing that is great about discussing solutions is that it gets you out of your negative rumination state — it

gets you out into solving the problems, getting back into the world outside you. That's where the action is. And that helps your listener feel more optimistic about supporting you in making things better.

EXERCISE: COMMUNICATE WITH YOUR PARTNER AND FAMILY

Here are some reminders about ways to communicate when times are difficult.

- Find the right time to talk.
- Ask for feedback when you are speaking.
- Don't get stuck on being a downer.
- If you talk about a problem, talk about a solution.
- Try to edit what you say.
- Reduce the drama and the negativity.
- Let the other person talk, too.

5: Blaming won't help

Many family feuds during this time often start when one partner blames the other. One man told me that his wife turned against him during his period of unemployment, ridiculing him—in front of his daughter—and telling him that he had let them down. Needless to say, this made everything worse. Eventually he did get a job, but he also got divorced. "I realized she was never on my side, it was all about her."

Partners of unemployed people often have a lot of angry thoughts. See if any of these are familiar to you:

- You did this to yourself.
- It's all your fault.
- You let us down.
- We can't count on you.
- You just lie around doing nothing.
- If you don't get a job right away we will end up homeless.

If you look at these thoughts—and if you say them—I guarantee that everything will get worse. (No one has ever told me it really helped when their partner blamed them, humiliated them, or labeled them.) Let's examine each one.

Replacing Negative Thoughts with Helpful Ones

Your negative thoughts about your partner	More helpful thoughts to have
You did this to yourself	It's doubtful that your partner intentionally lost their job. People lose their jobs all the time. There may be other factors involved: changes in the company, the economy
It's all your fault	This is another blaming thought that won't help anyone. Unemployment feels like an individual experience, but it's really part of the economy
You let us down. We can't count on you	Your partner is not doing this to you, it's something that happened to them. It's not like your partner planned this out to harm you and the family. You could be unemployed, too, not because you are negligent, lazy or incompetent but because unemployment can happen to anyone. And, you are over-generalizing by saying that you can't count on anything from your partner. If that were true then you wouldn't be let down right now. Losing a job is a temporary setback not a permanent loss of ability to help out. In fact, your partner can help out right now by doing things with and for the family that can be beneficial
You just lie around doing nothing	This is another over-generalization. Your partner is reading this book and doing some of the things suggested here. In fact, your partner will be keeping an activity schedule listing all the activities for each day of the week. When you look at that you might see that there are a number of things he or she is doing

If you don't get a job right away we will end up homeless	This is very likely fortune-telling and catastrophic thinking. You are predicting a future that is bleak and horrible, based on your emotions, not the facts. Is it really true that if your partner doesn't get a job this week that you will become homeless? It's possible, but doubtful. What good will it do to make these dire predictions?

You can also examine some of your beliefs about communicating with your partner who has lost their job. Here are some examples of beliefs some people have that might contribute to more problems.

- I need to keep at my partner to motivate him/her to get a job.
- I have a right to complain. After all, it's hard on me.
- My partner let me down. I need to tell him/her they can't do that to me.
- I need my partner to hear and agree with all of the things that I am feeling and thinking.
- I just can't help myself. I'm too emotional not to just say what I am thinking.
- There's no use in talking with him/her. It's a waste of time.

If any of these thoughts are your thoughts, then you are probably nagging, criticizing, complaining, ruminating, feeling sorry for yourself, feeling angry at your partner, or just brooding and feeling alone, refusing to answer questions. None of this is good.

Let's take a look at each one of these beliefs about communication and see if there is another way to look at it.

Your negative thoughts about communicating	More helpful thoughts to have
I need to keep at my partner to motivate him/her to get a job	This is the nagging theory of motivation. You believe that you need to keep repeating yourself, keep the pressure up, and that will motivate your partner to get a job. It won't. It will

simply create more problems for both of you. More arguments, more ignoring questions, more anxiety and anger. You can be more effective if you approach this in a collaborative way, talking about what each of you can do to make things better. You can take an approach of "mutual problem solving," where each of you comes up with ideas of things to do

I have a right to complain. After all, it's hard on me	You have a right to a lot of things and certainly you have a right to complain, but will it really help anything? Will you feel better if you drag out your complaints? Will your partner get a better job because you are complaining?
I need my partner to hear and agree with all the things I am feeling and thinking	Why does your partner need to hear every thought and feeling you are having? Do you need to hear every thought or feeling they are having?
I just can't help myself. I'm too emotional not to just say what I am thinking	You can help yourself. Do you say everything that you think and feel in public all the times? Of course not. You have a filter. You think about the consequences. What will the consequence be if you say everything that you feel? You do have control
There's no use in talking with him/her. It's a waste of time	This idea that you can only refuse to communicate is not helpful, either. There are effective, respectful and collaborative ways of discussing things. Simply pulling away and giving up will lead nowhere

Leaving the blame behind

Blaming and nagging your partner who is unemployed will not achieve results, but you may not realize the effect that your words may have on them.

EXERCISE: LOOKING CLOSELY AT BLAMING AND NAGGING

Look through the list below to focus on the kinds of things you might be saying and whether you think they would be helpful if they were said to you:

- Are you blaming and nagging your partner?
- What are the advantages and disadvantages of blaming and nagging?
- How would you feel if someone talked to you this way?
- When you blame your partner are you discounting the positives, labeling them, focusing on the negative, over-generalizing and judging them severely?
- Take responsibility for what you say. Are you trying to convince yourself that you are entitled to blaming and criticizing? Do you think you don't have any control over what you do? Are you blaming your partner and then justifying this by blaming them for your own behavior?
- How would you challenge your idea that you need to blame and criticize your partner to get them motivated?
- How would support, encouragement and mutual problem solving work better?

6: Be a better listener: the power of active listening

If your partner is unemployed and you want them to communicate with you, it's essential that you become better at listening. One way of thinking about how to listen is to ask yourself how you want your partner to feel after they have opened up to you. Do you want your partner to feel that you care about their thoughts and feelings, that you respect them, that you have patience, that you are on their side, and that you support them? Or do you want your partner to think that you are contemptuous, judgmental, rejecting, competitive, impatient, bored, or frustrated with them?

What makes a good listener? Some people think that good listening is the same thing as saying nothing, just silently and passively sitting there and "listening," like a tape recorder that doesn't say anything. Let's say your wife has lost her job and she feels she needs to talk about it. Let's assume she is like most people—she wants to feel that you understand her, respect her, and care about her feelings. Well, you might not be doing a great job of this, if you do or say the following when she is talking:

- Sit silently and say nothing while she is talking.
- Interrupt her and say, "I got the message, you don't need to repeat yourself."
- Say, "Snap out of it and move on."
- Tell her, "You're complaining too much."
- Say, "You're unrealistic."
- Tell her exactly what she has to do to solve her problem—if she hasn't asked you to solve the problem.
- Be sarcastic, condescending, or dismissive.

You might say, "I listened. I heard what she had to say, I just don't want to hear it again." It's understandable that as a listener it's taking some work to hear it again, but how much work is really involved in that? I can imagine several thousand things that might be more difficult for you to do than spend a few minutes listening to your wife complain or describe how she feels. But you might think to yourself, "Look, if I don't interrupt, if I don't tell her she's going on too long and whining, she will go on forever. I've got to put an end to it."

Or you might think, "She's just complaining. I've got to get her to solve problems, not focus on feeling." Of course, the irony of this jump to problem solving is that unless your partner believes you care enough to hear the feelings, you won't get to solve any problems. In fact, you will have created a new problem: "You don't care about how I feel."

These are the thoughts of a poor listener. Communicating contempt, boredom, or sarcasm for the message and the messenger will only make matters worse. Jumping to problem solving will mean that problems become magnified, not solved.

What can you do?

Fortunately, there are some simple rules to follow to be a good listener, and you can start today. If your partner is talking about something that is bothering them, you might try the following:

Rephrase what they say: "I hear you saying that you spent a lot of time today looking for a job and there just wasn't anything out there." By rephrasing you communicate exactly the message that you heard. It also gives the speaker a chance to correct your misinterpretation of what they said. Sometimes we rephrase what we thought the speaker intended (for example, "You don't think you should have to look for a job"), rather than what was said ("No, I understand I have to look for a job. It's just a real pain to have to do this.").

Empathize: Identify the feeling that your partner is sharing with you: "It sounds like you were feeling frustrated (angry, anxious, sad, hopeless, helpless, like giving up, etc.)." This communicates that you care enough about your partner's feelings to notice them. By recognizing—clearly—that your partner feels frustrated, you are connecting with their experience so they know that you know and that you care enough to know. It's often not about facts as much as it is about feelings.

Validate: Try to find the "truth" for your partner in those feelings: "I can understand it would feel really frustrating to be looking and to find nothing today, since you are trying hard to find the next job." By finding the reasonable truth in having the feelings that your partner has, you communicate that they make sense, they are not alone, they have the feelings that a lot of other people would have, and that you respect their feelings enough to validate them and normalize them.

Ask for more: "Are there other thoughts or feelings that you were having about this today?" When you ask for more, you invite your partner to share whatever they need to share, you are making time and space for them to connect with you—and for you to connect with them. You are showing patience, respect, and inclusion.

Think about each step in this Active Listening model—rephrasing, empathizing, validating, asking for more. What are you communicating by listening in this manner? I think you are telling your partner that you are really interested in their feelings and experiences. You understand why they feel the way they feel and you respect their right to their feelings. You are communicating that you have time for listening, and you care enough to hear more.

Your non-verbal signals

Another part of good listening for the partner of the person who has lost their job is the non-verbal communication that you engage in. For example, when you are listening, do you make faces, look down or away, occupy yourself with your computer or other distractions rather than looking directly at the speaker? Does your voice sound impatient, or does it sound accepting and open? Are you crossing your arms across your chest, or are you sitting loosely and openly directed towards your partner? What are the signals you are sending?

By using these active listening skills, you automatically have a go-to plan for listening. Rather than showing contempt or sarcasm, you can go into this "mode," rephrase, validate, ask for more, and find that it is a lot easier for you, as a listener, to accept your partner's thoughts and feelings rather than withdrawing or jumping at them.

EXERCISE: LISTENING

Use the list below to find out what kind of listener you are:
• Are you a good listener or a poor listener?
• Do you think that listening and validating will open a can of worms?

- Do you think that listening patiently is simply indulging whining?
- Are you sending out non-verbal signals of indifference or contempt?
- What is the consequence for you and your partner of being a poor listener?
- Try Active Listening Skills:
  1. Rephrase
  2. Empathize
  3. Validate
  4. Ask for More

7: Solve problems together

Did you ever play basketball or baseball as a child? There are five people on each basketball team and nine for baseball. But imagine that the other team only had one member against your five members. Unless that one-member team was a professional player who is seven feet tall, your five-member team would win. Teams win against loners. The same thing is true for families and friends of the unemployed.

You and your partner—and your entire family and circle of friends—can all team up to solve problems together. We have already discussed how this is about *all of you*—not just the single person who is unemployed—but I want to expand more on teamwork and solving problems together.

Let's face an obvious set of facts:

1. Unemployment can lead to problems for the entire family.
2. Conflicts within the family are best solved if everyone works together to solve them.
3. Sharing the responsibility to solve the problems removes the burden of blame on one person.
4. By working on problems together, you build more positive feelings. By blaming one person and telling them it's their problem you divide the family, increase resentment and defeat your goals.

Here's an example of the opposite of mutual problem solving: "Karen, you're the one out of work, so it's your problem. You got yourself into this situation, so it's up to you to solve the problem. Don't dump your problems on the rest of us. You aren't pulling your weight. I have enough to deal with without having to deal with your problems." It's pretty clear here what the message is! This is rejecting and isolating the unemployed person. They will now think, "I was fired from my job, and now my family is rejecting me." Could there be anyone who would be better off receiving this approach of blaming and isolating?

As I said, focusing on mutual problem solving—where you and your partner, your family and friends all pull together—empowers everyone. Teams beat individuals.

Help your partner who has lost their job realize that you know how hard it is, but gently suggest that you are open to brainstorming ways of solving the problem. For example, you might say, "It's a hard time and you probably feel discouraged. You're human, and that's natural. But if you like, we can brainstorm together and think about strategies and things to do. Let me know if that would be helpful." Validating the difficulty of being unemployed can help open you both up to working towards solving real problems. But if you don't offer some validation of how hard it is, your partner might think, "You don't really understand how hard my life is. All you want to do is make things better for yourself." Problem solving is often a balancing act where you acknowledge the difficulty of the problem while suggesting the possibility of a solution.

Working through step-by-step

Let's go through each of the steps in mutual problem solving and see what it would look like in your family. Let's say Karen has lost her job and Mike, her husband, wants to work together with her to make things better. Mike not only wants to communicate respect and support for Karen, but he also wants to work towards solving some problems in the family and in their relationship. Here are the steps.

Invite your partner to solve problems together: You can suggest to your partner that you would like to work together to make things better. This is an invitation, not a demand. It's communicated with the openness that the invitation might get rejected right now, but could be open for future consideration. Mike: "Karen, I can see that this period of being out of work is a difficult one for you and I wonder if we can work together to find out how we can make things better. Would you be willing to talk to me about solving some problems together so that things are better for all of us?"

Indicate your role in the problem: When you invite your partner to solve problems, you don't want to communicate the idea that the problem is your partner. You don't want to say, "You are creating problems for all of us." A better way of reducing the sense of blame is to suggest that you—yourself—have been something of an impediment in solving problems. Perhaps you have been critical or silent, or you haven't brought up problem solving before. But by opening with the idea that you are also part of the problem—and part of the solution—you will reduce the likelihood of labeling your partner as the problem. Mike: "I know I could have done more to be supportive of you. Perhaps I could have asked how I could be more helpful. I am willing to work together with you, if you wish, to make things better."

Focus on one problem at a time: You can't solve all the problems at once, and trying to do this will only demoralize all of you. You and your partner should prioritize the problems that you want to work on by creating a problem list and agreeing on the top-ranked problem. You can begin by inviting your partner to make separate lists of some problems that you both can work on. For example, you might have problems dealing with arguments, family chores, childcare, finances, job hunting, exercise, or other problems. Mike: "Karen, I know there are probably a number of things that we could work on to make things better, and I wonder if it might be useful for us to make up a list of a few things we would try to work on. Perhaps you can make a list of some things, and I could also make a list, and then we could decide which problem we want to tackle first."

By suggesting that each of you has a separate list, you are communicating that each of you has legitimate needs and priorities, and it's not just you telling your partner what the problem is. If both of you work as a team in identifying mutual goals, you are more likely to work together towards accomplishing those goals. In this particular case, the problem they selected is how Karen can spend her time during the day doing things that are helpful to the family, while balancing her job search.

Brainstorm solutions: Often, when we think we have a really good idea, we believe it's the *only* idea. But in mutual problem solving you want to try to be creative. The more possible solutions that you generate as a couple, the more likely you are to find a good-quality solution that you both can settle on. In this stage of problem solving, you can each offer a number of solutions — without evaluating them at this point — just to create a large number of possibilities. Mike: "Let's see if we can come up with some possible solutions, Karen, so you can both search for a job and help out with some of the family things. Perhaps we can just come up with five ideas each — and then see if we could agree on one or two of them to try out."

Rank the solutions: After you have generated the solutions, you might rank them in order from the most to the least desirable. Then you can see if there are some solutions that seem mostly agreeable to the two of you, and you can discuss the pros and cons of each of these top-ranked solutions. Karen: "OK, I think it might be a good idea for me to spend some of the day going over our finances and bills, and doing some of the shopping. I also think it's a great idea if we could both brainstorm possible ways of my looking for a job, since you [Mike] have a lot of connections, as I do, and I am more likely to find someone I could network with."

Set up a plan to take action: The two of you have now moved very close to solving some problems. It's time to set up a clear plan of action. This involves specifying the behavior that each of you will engage in, when you will do it, and how you will know that it is done. Like any behavior you want to change, you will be much more likely to do it if you keep track of it. I suggest having a list of tasks for each of you—and to post this list in a conspicuous place (the fridge is a good place, since you open that door several times a day). Mike and Karen: "OK, so we agree that Karen will work on the bills and the other chores in the house, and get this done by Friday. Mike will make a list of possible contacts for Karen to pursue. Both of us will do this by Friday and report back."

Review the outcome: It's important that you view your mutual problem solving as an ongoing process that you track and revise and make better together. At the end of the next week, look at what the two of you have done, separately and together. Check what the outcome was: did you make progress, did you feel better or worse, were there some roadblocks, did you not follow through? It is even helpful to recognize when you have not done the tasks, because then the two of you can look at what got in the way so that you can change it and overcome the roadblocks. Mike and Karen discussed the outcome. Mike: "I made a list of some people we might contact, but I didn't follow through with any emails or calls. I suppose I was busy and didn't give it the priority it deserves. I let you down." Karen: "I did some of the bills and got some of the chores done, but I didn't put in enough time looking for a job. I realized that I find it really depressing and frustrating to look. I could do more."

Revise your plan: All plans are up for modification. It would be an unusual plan that worked the very first time. Either one or both of you might not carry out the behaviors that you committed to. You are both human. In a sense, experimenting with a plan by engaging in some behavior is a way of finding out what is the next problem to solve. In the case of Mike and Karen, they realized Mike's problem was that he got caught up in work and didn't give the job search for Karen the priority he said he would. So he has to examine whether he is willing to set aside the time to contact people to help Karen. He has to examine his negative thoughts (if he has them), such as "It won't help. It's her problem, not mine." He can then challenge these thoughts: "You don't know if something will help unless you have tried it. If Karen is having a problem, we are all having a problem. I can be part of the solution." And Karen can examine her own negative thoughts—which, ironically, are very much the same as Mike's. Revising a plan helps you make it better and helps you identify the roadblocks to change.

The advantage of mutual problem solving is that you have a team effort to pull together to solve your problems. No one is to blame; everyone has some responsibility. You don't have to feel alone and you don't have to feel powerless. Sometimes people say, "Why should I admit I am part of the problem?" The simple answer is, "If you are part of the problem, then you are part of the solution." That's real power.

EXERCISE: TEAMWORK

Work through the following list to start solving your problems together:
- Are you more likely to solve problems as a team?
- How would you be more empowered if you shared solving the problem?
- If you think it's only your partner's problem, how does this make you helpless?
- Use mutual problem solving skills to move things forward together.
- Invite your partner to solve problems with you.

- Indicate your role in the problem.
- Focus on one problem at a time.
- Brainstorm solutions.
- Rank the solutions.
- Set up a plan to take action.
- Review the outcome.

8: Reward every step forward

As we have seen, when you are between jobs this can cause problems with your partner and family. If you are the one who is unemployed, you might feel frustrated, guilty, ashamed, hopeless, lonely, and helpless in doing anything of any value. You might feel that you are losing your identity. And if you are the partner of someone who is unemployed, you might feel that your partner has let you down, you might resent their passivity, or you might feel they aren't pulling their weight. All of these thoughts and feelings are common in families of the unemployed and I hope that you are getting some ideas of how to counter these and deal with them.

I've suggested that you look at this as a shared experience, where both of you take responsibility, validating each other, solving problems together, pooling your resources and reducing blaming and criticism. This is hard work. I always realize when I suggest that my clients do something that might be helpful it can often lead to their telling me, "You make it sound so easy, but it's not." It is often the case: making things better might be harder than you could imagine.

That's why you need to reward each other more. Given all the stress of this time in your lives, you might think that all you are doing is dealing with problems, complaints and negative moods. What a drag.

I am going to suggest that you and your partner do three things together:

First: Catch Your Partner Being Good.
Second: Plan Some Fun.
Third: Make Your Partner Special.

Let's take each one in order.

Catch your partner being good

Let's say that there are some behaviors that you would just love to see your partner doing. For example, if your wife is unemployed, you might want to encourage her to spend some time looking for a job, networking with people, learning new skills, exercising, seeing her friends, helping with the kids. Each of these are positive behaviors. Here is the challenge for you. Every time you see your partner doing anything that is positive over the next week, write it down, put it on a piece of paper on the fridge door, and tell them how happy you are to see them doing these things. For example, you might say, "I was really happy you spent some time exercising today. It must make you feel good to be active. It makes me feel good to know that you are taking care of yourself."

Now you might think, "This sounds patronizing to give your partner credit for exercising or helping with dinner." It might sound trivial to write it down for him or her to see. Sounds like a fair criticism, but I have used this simple technique of "catch your partner being good" and "give them feedback" countless times. In almost every case the partner whose behavior is praised is grateful that what they do matters. One woman said, "I didn't realize you noticed." It's a simple technique—positive tracking. Try it and see if it helps.

You probably don't need any training in catching your partner messing things up. That's not a problem for you, if you are like a lot of families; however, you might have a negative filter and only see the "negatives," then you blow them up in your mind and dwell on them and then complain about them. You don't need more of that. But you could use some extra focus on catching the good and rewarding it.

Plan some fun

Just because you are unemployed it doesn't mean that you and your partner can't have fun. You don't have to sit at home, ruminating, passively isolating yourself and waiting for the next argument to start. One of my clients who was out of work realized that he and his wife weren't doing much together, so I suggested that he think of something inexpensive to do that might be fun. He realized there were cycle trails near their house and that they used to enjoy riding their bikes. That weekend they got their bikes out, packed a picnic lunch, and went for a bike ride. It was better than Prozac.

There are a lot of fun things that couples—and families—can do together. I always like to ask people what they used to do when they were dating—when they were trying to win each other over. In fact, most people, when they are first dating, don't have a lot of money, so these activities tend to be fairly cheap to do. One couple remembered they used to like cooking together, trying out new recipes. So they got out some new recipes and made a meal together. It was like old times.

Make your partner special

Most of us want to be special to the people who are special to us. If you are unemployed, you might not feel very special right now. You might be down in the dumps—even feeling like a burden. If your partner is unemployed, what can you do to make them feel special, important, and valued by you? Well, you can always tell them, "I love you," or "I need you," or "I missed you." That seems to work most of the time. But there might be small, even sentimental, things that you can do. Perhaps remembering a special time together, remembering something that is special to your partner, even reminiscing about shared moments. One man who was unemployed remembered that his wife liked parrots. He was walking around the city and came across a store that sold cheap trinkets. He found parrot earrings that cost almost nothing. He wrapped them up, wrote a little note, and gave the gift to his wife. He said, "I was thinking of you and I remembered how much you love parrots." She reached out and hugged him.

You get a lot further by noticing the positives, labeling them, and being a cheerleader. Rather than nagging and criticizing, notice the positive steps your friend or partner is making and say, "That was terrific you made those calls today," or "That was wonderful that you sent out your CV." Also reward activities that are simply healthy behaviors, such as exercise, seeing friends, taking classes. You build confidence on positives.

EXERCISE: FIND WAYS TO BE POSTITIVE TOGETHER

Actively work on ways to be positive with your partner by acting on the following:
- Are you focusing primarily on the negative?
- What would be the advantage of focusing more on the positives?
- Catch Your Partner Being Good.
- Plan Some Fun.
- Make Your Partner Special.

Finally, there is nothing better at times than a supportive and objective friend. You don't want your partner to become the only source of support. Think about supportive, kind, understanding, and objective people, then see if you can share your experience with them. Don't overload them with complaints, but edit what you say while balancing it with an honest expression of your thoughts and feelings. I always think that if you are going to talk about a problem with a friend, be ready to talk about a solution that you are willing to consider. My friends have talked to me about a lot of problems, and I feel honored to be helpful to them. That's what friends are for.

SUMMARY

Many people who lose their jobs worry that they will eventually lose their family, too. When they receive notice to leave, some people think, "How will I tell my wife/husband?" They think, "I've let them down," "They have counted on me." If your partner has lost their job, you also might have some anxious thoughts: "What will we do now? How are we going to pay the bills?" Or you might have resentful thoughts, "Now, it's all up to me."

If you are part of a couple or family you will do better if you think of this time as a period when you pull together to be more supportive, while each of you takes some responsibility for making things better, each of you contributes to the family.

Use the ways I have described to approach this together, by reducing blaming and nagging, overcoming withdrawal and pouting, actively talking so that you are heard, and using skill in listening with an open mind. If you use these techniques you don't have a guarantee that you won't have arguments, disappointments and even despair at times—you are both human and your family is going through a hard time. But you have a choice about whether you face this in a constructive manner or whether you fall back on old habits that will only make matters worse.

Learn from this experience It may be hard to imagine, but some people have told me that this was a time that they realized how much their family meant to them. And how much they needed them. Remember the basics I have covered in this chapter and practice them as you work together:

- This is about all of you.
- Everyone has responsibility.
- Talk about it.
- Talk so that you are heard.
- Don't blame your partner—it won't help.
- Be a better listener: practice the power of Active Listening.
- Solve problems together.
- Reward each other.

9

STOP WORRYING: LIVE FOR NOW

Brian worries every day about whether he will get a job. "I get up in the morning, and I think, 'I have nothing to do.' I feel I am waiting for the 'work day' to end—so I can act like I am a normal person who has a job. I hide in my apartment. I worry about how long it will take me to get a job. When will this agony end? When will I be able to move on? It's like I am waiting every hour of the day, every day. And I just don't know when it will happen. I feel I am waiting to live my life again." Karen feels the same way. But she also says, "I just can't stand not knowing when I will get a job. I really feel I need to know right now. This uncertainty is killing me." Both Brian and Karen are waiting for life to start again, worried about the future, unable to enjoy their present life. They feel as if they are killing time until they can get on with living. They are in purgatory, waiting to be released.

If you are like a lot of unemployed people, you are a worrier. What do we mean by "worry"? You can think about your worry as repetitive negative thoughts about the future. It's not simply one thought, "Perhaps I won't get a job," it's the same thought—or group of thoughts—repeated over and over. Your thoughts might sound like this: "When will I get a job? I wonder how long it's going to take. What will I do until then? I can't believe I'm in this situation. Will it take another month? Three months? A year? What if I never get a job? How am I going to live?"

These thoughts seem intrusive to you—they are unwanted, barging in on your mind at any time of the day or night. You try to respond to them, and answer them, but eventually you try to suppress them. You are struggling with these thoughts, thinking that you have to get rid of them. You think that because you don't have the answer, you need to worry until you do. Because you are dealing with worries about the future you have less ability to concentrate, less energy and focus on solving problems today and less of an experience of your life in the present moment. When you sit down to read something, you find these thoughts impinging on you. "How can I read when I am so worried about the future?" You might even have these thoughts while reading this book: "I can't concentrate on what he's saying. I keep thinking about what might happen. How will this get me a job?"

Worrying: your fears about the future

In Chapter Five I described how rumination works. This is when you go over past events in your head, trying to make sense of what has happened. But you may also be deeply concerned about the future and worry about it in the same way. This chapter explains what you may be going through. Your worries about the future are perfectly natural, but you can also ask yourself if you are spending too much time with your worries and whether you are giving them too much importance. For example, you are spending too much time with your worries if you find yourself worried at all hours of the day and night, have difficulty sleeping because you are worried, can't enjoy your present life because of worries, or if you get anxious or depressed when you are worrying. You may go to bed with your worries in your head and have difficulty falling asleep. You may wake in the middle of the night and think, "I need to know when I am going to get a job." Brian had debilitating insomnia; he couldn't sleep, beset with these worries almost every night. He couldn't just surrender to sleep because he had to know what the future will be.

Your worries may be repetitive negative thoughts that keep coming back—the same thoughts over and over. You find yourself hijacked by these thoughts—as if you experience your worries as an intrusive visitor that you are required to spend time with. You think, "Will I ever get a job?" and then you can't seem to just set this thought aside and do other things. You are pulled into the thought, residing in it, trying to answer it, and trying to make sure that you have covered every possibility of how things could turn out. You feel your worries are ordering you around—as if they appear and then you have to do something. You feel responsible to your worries: "I think I might not get a job, and then I think I have to make sure that I work out how I will absolutely get a job." It's as if your worries are like a fishing pole: the worry is the bait, you grab onto it, and the worry pulls you in all directions.

Your attempts at removing the worry

Sometimes you try to suppress these worries, saying to yourself, "I am not going to think about it." But that doesn't work for very long. Perhaps a few minutes pass by and then the worry pops up again. You think this means that your mind is out of control, you can never set this aside, never get away. You think, "I need to get these worries out of my head, stop worrying, I need to stop it immediately." But this doesn't work, which just convinces you that you are out of control and need to get more control. So you worry that you don't have control of your thinking. You try yelling at yourself, perhaps silently in your head, "Stop this worry," and that just makes you feel more frustrated.

What can you do?

In a similar way that we dealt with rumination, in this chapter we will look at how your worry makes sense to you, what you are trying to accomplish with your worry, and whether it is working. When you worry, you are living in the future—and it's the most negative future that you can imagine. So understanding your motivation to worry—and whether it is really accomplishing anything—is essential. We will also look at the costs to you of worry—what it keeps you from doing or experiencing. Worry is an escape from the present moment. You can either worry or live your life now. We will also examine the benefits of accepting uncertainty and relinquishing some control—over the things you cannot know now or control now. Your worry about your job prospects may also have a sense of urgency—that you need to know *right now*.

Do you really have a choice when it comes to your worries about the future? Are there any really effective ways to set aside this nightmare of the future? The answer is "Yes!" There are things you can do that will allow you to live more in the moment and let the future take care of itself.

In contrast to the way you worked on problems with rumination about past events, we will examine alternative ways to think about time—especially the possibility of both stretching time and living in the present moment. There are alternatives to worrying about the future—and you can begin your new approach to your worry today—right now—by recognizing that you actually have a choice. You can spend time with your worries—locked in combat with your mind—or you can spend time living your life. We will see how this is possible. It's a way of taking your life back, a way for you to live for the Now rather than suffering about what could happen in the future.

Let's turn to what you think your worry will do for you.

1: How does your worry make sense to you?

Like a lot of worriers, you may treat your thoughts as if they are facts. Brian said, "I keep thinking I won't get a job, so the more I think it, the more likely it seems that I won't get a job." Predictions are not facts. You can predict a lot of things—floods, winning the lottery, planes crashing, a beautiful or handsome movie star falling in love with you, levitating above the couch in your house, becoming a homeless person, turning into a vampire—but these predictions, no matter how often you make them, don't always become facts. Don't believe everything you think, don't count on everything that you predict. Since almost

everyone eventually gets a job—if they are willing to look, willing to give it some time and willing to be flexible—your worries
about never getting a job are predictions that may never come
true.

On the other hand, facts and thoughts are different. You can
have the same negative prediction a thousand times but the job
market doesn't revolve around your mind. It has a reality of its
own. Getting a job or not getting a job is different from worries
about jobs. Thoughts are not facts.

Needing to know now

The problem is that you want the answer immediately. You
demand it: "I just have to know!!!" Both Brian and Karen are like
a lot of people who are out of work—they worry about the
future; they think that if they don't know right now about how
things will turn out, they can't enjoy their lives. They have a
sense of urgency about knowing, and they seem to predict the
worst. It's hard being unemployed if you think you need to know
right now, since your mind gets stuck on trying to work out what
is going to happen. The more you think about it, the worse you
feel. And the more you demand certainty right now, the more
helpless and frustrated you feel.

You may think that worrying makes sense. After all, you
don't have a job and you don't know when you will get one. So
you probably think, "Of course I worry. What else am I supposed
to do?" You may think, "I have to worry, I have no choice." If you
are a worrier about your future job and financial prospects you
probably have a number of thoughts about your worry. Ask
yourself if any of these seem to fit the way you think:

- I can't help myself from worrying.
- My worry prepares me for the future.
- I need to worry so I won't be surprised.
- My worry will motivate me to help myself and solve
  problems.

- Worry is a sign of responsibility.
- I pay attention to my thoughts.
- I find my mind so busy I can't concentrate or pay attention to other things.
- It's hard to remember all the things I need to remember.

Let's take each of these thoughts and see if they are true:

"I can't help myself from worrying" implies that if a negative thought appears at the doorstep of your mind, then you have to engage with it, answer it, control it, or suppress it. Brian said, "I don't understand what you mean by saying that I have a choice. When the worry comes to me, I don't have any choice. It's just there. I can't escape from it." This makes sense to a lot of worriers, but it's actually not true.

I said to Brian: "Let's say you are worried about getting a job and your wife walks in and tells you there is a call from your brother. Do you say to her, 'Tell him to call back. I am busy worrying'?" Brian immediately realized that almost anything could interrupt his worry, including any distraction that he could imagine. "So if a phone call can interrupt your worry, then it means that you have a choice as to where you put your thinking."

"My worry prepares me for the future": Does it really? Researchers have found that 85% of the things that we worry about never happen. And 79% of the time worriers say that they handle things better than they thought they would. You prepare yourself for a future that never happens and you underestimate your ability to cope with real problems when they do happen.

Shift your attention

I suggested that one of the ways of thinking about worry is that it all depends on where you want to place your attention. "Look around the office here and tell me how many objects are blue."

Brian looked around, described the color of some book covers and some paintings. "Now, you have immediately shifted your attention to other things in the room—and your worry came to a standstill. We call this "attention deployment," which is simply another way of saying that you are able to shift your attention, and you probably remember that we did a similar exercise in Chapter Five to deal with rumination.

Make a time for worrying

Attention deployment is important because one of the techniques that you can use to put worry in its place is to delay the worry to another time during the day in the same way that you allocated a time for rumination in Chapter Five. For example, let's say that you notice that you are worried at all hours of the day and night. The worry pops up and your mind is hijacked. But you don't have to be hijacked at that moment. You can decide to worry at another time. You can set up a time—every day—to focus on your worry—I call this "worry time." You can make an appointment with these worries. So if you find yourself worried at 10:00 in the morning or 12:00 at night, you can set it aside, write it down, and have an appointment at 4:30 in the afternoon.

This means that you can then direct your attention to something positive or neutral in the current moment. You can redirect your attention to listening to music, doing some chores, looking at the sky, taking a walk, playing with your dog or cat, or getting something done. Worry time is a very simple, very powerful technique. You might think, "I can't set worry aside." Try it for a week and see if you can. You might surprise yourself.

Brian used the worry-time approach. Initially, he said, "Are you kidding me? How can I set aside my worry?" I urged him to give it a try, experiment with worry time, see what he could do with it. He tried it. He would write down the worry when it occurred and set it aside until later. This helped him significantly with his insomnia. He could say, "I will get round to the worry tomorrow."

Why you may feel it is right to worry

You may think that worry is a way to avoid surprise, get motivated, be prepared, or that it is a sign of your responsibility—"*I need to worry so I won't be surprised*" and "*Worry is a sign of responsibility*." It's good to be prepared and good to be responsible, but is your worry the best way to accomplish these goals? Let's take the issue of being prepared. Prepared for what? You might say, "Being out of work for a long time." OK, that's a good thing to be prepared for. But rather than worry about it—repetitive negative thoughts haunting you over and over—you might take some action to be prepared. This might include budgeting, acquiring new job skills, networking, exploring job options that are not as lucrative or that require your moving elsewhere. These are actions that are productive, need planning, and are practical. But worry is just a lot of useless repetitive negative thinking.

Let's take another set of thoughts or experiences that you have about your worry—"*I pay attention to my thoughts*", "*I find my mind so busy I can't concentrate or pay attention to other things*", "*It's hard to remember all the things I need to remember*." Your worries about future job prospects means that you are spending a lot of time scanning your thoughts, examining what is going on inside you (feelings, thoughts, images, memories), and trying to keep track of all this noise at all hours of the day. It's like your mind is a radio station, lots of channels shifting back and forth, and lots of static.

One of the reasons worriers get stuck in their head is that they actually worry they will forget what they should be worried about. This is like trying to immediately recite all the telephone numbers of all the people that you know. Your mind goes on overload and you can't remember what you should really attend to. Just because you have a thought doesn't mean you have to think about it. You can notice it, observe it, and wave it by. "I noticed that worry, and I said, 'See you later.' "

You can notice, but walk on towards your goals

Think about what I just said. You can have a thought, notice it, and walk on by — walk past the thought, leave it behind, focus on the goals that are in front of you. How can this be? How can you walk past a thought? Here's how:

Think about these thoughts as irrelevant to your goals right now — your goals in the present moment. Let's imagine you are at the airport and your plane doesn't leave for two hours. You are sitting there reading a magazine. There are lots of announcements being made, people chattering, babies crying. But you say to your mind, "Hey, mind, don't mind that. It's not relevant. Your plane doesn't leave for two hours. You don't have to pay attention. It's just background noise."

If you are like me, it might take a few minutes to get into being able to ignore the noise. But you do it. You do it every time you travel. The same thing with these worries; they show up in your mind — "Will I ever get a job?" — and you can now say to yourself, "I've heard that before. There's nothing useful for me in spending time with this thought. I have more important things to do right now — like living my life."

You can think about the worried thought as static on a radio that you are no longer listening to. It's just there. Who cares? No one is listening. It isn't saying anything you need to hear. You hear it, but you don't really pay attention.

What does your worry achieve?

Now that you have examined whether your worry will motivate you, keep you from being surprised, solve your problems, or help you be responsible, you can now answer one question about your worry "*I pay attention to my thoughts*" — that might help you set it aside more times than not: "Is your worry productive?" By "productive" I mean, does it lead to a to-do list today? Just like rumination that keeps you stuck in the past, worry keeps you stuck in your head. It doesn't accomplish anything. Will it lead to a solution to your problem — getting a job — today? If not, it's unproductive. And, not only is it unproductive, it's destructive. The more you worry, the more depressed you become. The worse your concentration, the less you focus on solving real problems in real time in the here and now and the less you live your life. So I have indicated that you do have a choice—you can set it aside, put it into a compartment, write it down, make an appointment with it—wait until later for worry time. And then get on with your life in the present moment.

EXERCISE: CHALLENGE THE REASONS FOR YOUR WORRY

Work through the list below to clarify in your own mind whether you feel that worrying is helpful to you.

- Do you think that your worry will keep you from being surprised, solve your problems or get you motivated?
- Is it working?
- Or is worry trapping you with useless repetitive thoughts? Does it interfere with concentration?
- Does it keep you trapped inside yourself? Are you unable to notice what is going on around you?
- Do you think of your worry as a thought that you cannot escape?
- Redirect your attention somewhere else. What happens to the worry?
- Postpone your worry to worry time.
- Will your worry lead to any productive action? If not, set it aside.
- Do productive and rewarding things rather than worrying about the future.

Accept uncertainty and give up control

When you are out of work, you don't know for sure when—or if—you will get that next job. You don't know for sure what the job will be, how much it will pay, whether you will like it, or whether you will be able to keep it. If you worry about this, you are probably having a hard time tolerating the uncertainty of being out of work and not knowing when things will work out for you.

Take a look at some of these thoughts and ask yourself if any of them seem familiar to you:

- If I don't know for sure how things will work out, I can bet they won't work out well.
- Uncertainty is bad.
- I need to know for sure how it will work out.
- Once I have certainty, then I can relax.
- If I worry I might be able to reduce this uncertainty.
- If I get reassurance, I can feel more confident.

Brian was like a lot of worriers who are unemployed: "If I don't know for sure that I will get a job, then it's really bad. Not knowing means that anything could happen. It's hard to live your life if you don't know how the future will turn out."

Uncertainty is a part of daily life

Uncertainty about the future is not the same thing as a bad outcome. You can be uncertain about the weather next week, but that doesn't mean we are going to have a blizzard or a hurricane. You can be uncertain about whether someone driving on the highway is drunk and will lose control and kill you, but that doesn't mean you are really unsafe. Uncertainty is neutral. It simply means you don't know something for sure.

In fact, you accept uncertainty every day. You accept it when you drive your car, eat food in a restaurant, start a conversation, or choose to watch a film. The possible outcomes might be infinite, but you are willing to place your bets and accept some uncertainty. In fact, imagine the opposite: imagine if you knew everything for sure. It would be like Bill Murray in *Groundhog Day*, living each day with the same conversations with the same people—ultimately, boring. Repetitive sameness is a guarantee of boredom. Uncertainty just means that there is a range of possibilities.

Uncertainty is not a bad thing

Take your thought, "I need to know for sure that things will work out." Why do you need to know for sure? If you don't know for sure, what will happen? Can you imagine that you will have to be hospitalized with some dreaded "uncertainty disease"? The doctor in your imagination says, "I don't know what we can do for him. He doesn't have certainty. It looks like a hopeless case. There's nothing we can do for him. Does he have a living will?" Nonsense! You don't know for sure what will happen every day—you even don't know for sure about the lives of your loved ones, or your own life. You might prefer knowing for sure about your future job—or whatever you are worried about, but your preference is not a necessity. It's an illusion.

Why can't you relax if you don't know for sure? Don't you sleep every night? How is that possible, if you don't know for sure? Should we wake you up, if you fall asleep, and tell you to find out for sure that you will get that job? And if you don't know, we won't let you go back to sleep? Should we have the *uncertainty police*?

Of course, you can relax, eat, digest your food, play, have fun, learn, make love, listen to music, and do everything else. Imagine the following absurdity: "Sorry, darling, we can't have sex tonight. Not until I know for sure that I will get a job." This is another powerful, but nonsensical, belief that we trouble ourselves with. You can say, "Even though I don't know for sure, I think I'll just spend some time relaxing." Letting go and relaxing is letting go of uncertainty. When you drop your arms and let go of uncertainty the world does not fall apart. The job will come when it comes. You have to live for now.

Worry as a guarantee of certainty

Let's take your other two thoughts about eliminating uncertainty: "If I worry, I might be able to reduce this uncertainty. If I get reassurance, I can feel more confident." How will worry guarantee certainty? You might think that you will be able to work it all out, maintain your confidence that everything will — *guaranteed* — work out. But you know, from experience as a worrier, that your quest for certainty only leads to more uncertainty. That's because you can't accept what's possible, since anything is possible. "I could be kidnapped by men and women from outer space" — that's possible. But eliminating uncertainty is not possible. After all, your worry is another word for *imagination.*

Since you don't need certainty — and worry only leads to more uncertainty — you can drop your quest for certainty and accept. "I don't know right now what the future will be, but I can try to improve my life right now." That's the whole message of this entire book. It's about your time between jobs. Who knows what will turn up in the future? But during this time you can do a thousand things to make your life better. Your life right now begins when you give up — for this moment — on knowing and controlling the future.

Putting off enjoying your life until you know for sure what the future will be is like the man who decided to put off sex until retirement. Not a good plan.

Will reassurance help you?

You may think that seeking reassurance will get you that certainty that you believe you desperately need. You ask your partner or your friends, "Do you really think I'll get a job?" They reassure you, "I believe in you. You are fantastic. It will work out. Count on it." So now, with the reassurance, you feel better for — fifteen minutes. Then you say to yourself, "How do they know? They are just trying to make me feel better. They can't predict the future." Then you go back to worrying.

Reassurance is just another failed strategy to get the certainty that you don't really need. You do need to live your life — today — in the midst of uncertainty, not knowing for sure what the future holds.

Imagine saying to an 18-year-old boy or girl, "You can't live your life until you know how it is going to turn out." Nonsense, once again! Living your life means that you accept whatever comes—and you live it fully, for now, in the present moment. Fully. You don't need a curtain line to get on with the show.

EXERCISE: ACCEPTING UNCERTAINTY

When you look deeply into your fears of uncertainty you discover that there are other ways to deal with it. Work through the list below:

- Uncertainty is neutral. Just because you don't know for sure is no proof that it will be bad.
- Which experiences do you accept with some uncertainty? If you are willing to accept uncertainty every day for other things, why not accept uncertainty about getting a job?
- Why are you unwilling to accept uncertainty?
- What would your life be like if you never accepted any uncertainty? Can you imagine living a life where you required certainty about everything?
- Can you accept uncertainty and still live your life—for now? Accepting what you don't know can help you live a life in the present moment.
- Why has reassurance-seeking proved so useless? Would you really believe someone if they said, "It will all be OK"? Why not give up on reassurance?
- Give up some control about what you cannot control—control what you can control. What are some things in your life today that you do control?
- Putting off living for the present moment because you don't have certainty is like wasting all of your opportunities until the final curtain. Live the life that you have now.

3: Is everything so urgent?

Karen kept thinking that she needed to know, right now, how the job search would work out. She would wake in the middle of the night, half asleep, tired, unfocused, and say, "I don't know if I will ever get a job. I really need to know." This sense that you need the answer right now keeps you up at night and follows you around all day, stealing your life from you. When we are anxious, we often have the sense that something is urgent. It's like a fire alarm going off in your head. "I need the answer —IMMEDIATELY!" At times you feel that you are running around, trying to put out fires in your head. "What if I don't get a job?" and "What if I run out of money?" —and then, you are off and running trying to answer each thought, get certainty, prove it is wrong, solve every problem. It's like these thoughts are banging on the door, they will rush in and destroy you—unless you do something.

Doing nothing might be the best strategy.

But you can't just "do nothing" about the future when you have these worries. You think you need the solutions right now. You think you need the answer immediately. That's because you are telling yourself that you can't just let it happen, let it be.

Here are some typical thoughts about time urgency that you might have.

- If I don't have the answer right now, then everything is going to fall apart.
- I can't wait to see how things will work out.
- I can't stand not knowing about the future.
- It's hard for me to stay in the present moment.

You are not alone. We all tend to think that there is some urgency to finding out something that is important to us. It could be finding a job, money issues, whether your partner will leave you, or whether you will ever be happy again. Anxiety is your perception that there is a threat and your sense that there is a catastrophe about to happen. Anxiety is nature's way of telling you, "Get the hell out immediately!" It's nature's way of scaring you so much that you won't tolerate another second.

The reality is that right now you don't have a job—and you are looking for a job. It's not the same thing as gasping for air while the oxygen is depleted from your diving tank. Living your life daily is not the same thing as an emergency. The job can wait.

But you shouldn't have to wait to live your life. You are "in between" jobs, not living a life in limbo. Every day is your life. Live it every day.

Thoughts are only — thoughts

As strong and real and awful as this all feels, your thoughts about the future are in the same category as a tiger running towards you, or a fire in the basement. They are only thoughts. Thoughts are not going to eat you alive while the tiger uses his claws as dental floss. Thoughts are not flames jumping through the floor, consuming you and your family. Thoughts don't kill.

Actually, thoughts are minute, almost imperceptible, electrochemical events in your brain. No one dies from a thought. "I am sorry to tell you, Mrs. Jones, but your husband had a difficult thought and he didn't find the answer, and he just dropped dead. Yes, we have seen a lot of this 'urgent thought disease' in recent months; people dropping like flies because they weren't able to get to the answer in enough time."

What are true emergencies? Try *not* to circulate your blood, for example. Now, if you fail to do that for more than a few minutes you will most certainly die. But having the answer to your random worrisome thoughts about a job or finances is not in the same category. We are not going to cut your throat open and perform a tracheotomy so your air passage can get some oxygen to your urgent thoughts. Thoughts are not emergencies.

Thoughts pass

Negative thoughts are like burps; they come and go.

Let's take your thought, "I can't wait," as another story you are telling yourself which has already proven to be false. Of course you can wait. You are already waiting. The idea "I can't stand it" or "I can't wait" is really more like a thought about a preference: "I would actually prefer not to wait." You might yell and scream at yourself and tell yourself you can't wait to get the next job, and that you need to know right now, but stomping your mental feet, protesting that you don't want to wait and cannot wait will only frustrate you more.

Try rephrasing this as a preference: "It might be nice for me to know how things will turn out, but I will just have to tolerate the uncertainty and the frustration." In fact, if you give up on the goal of immediately having the answer, you will be a lot less frustrated. If you focus on making the current moment better, you will empower yourself. You are more likely to find pleasure and meaning in the present moment than in a future that may or may not happen. Let's turn to the present moment—now.

EXERCISE: THINKING DIFFERENTLY ABOUT YOUR SENSE OF URGENCY

It's worth working through your worries to find out how you can change the way you are thinking at the moment.

- What are some examples of your sense of urgency?
- Do you have the feeling that you need to know right now?
- What is the cost and what is the benefit to you of having this sense of urgency?
- Can you still look for a job and live your life without scaring yourself to death?
- What is the evidence for and against the belief that you absolutely need to know immediately if you are going to get a job?
- If you turned off the urgency, would you be able to enjoy daily life?
- Try to focus on the current moment and slow down your thinking.

4: Focus on the now

When do you taste something? In the present moment —now—and then it is gone. Put a raisin in your mouth. Let it roll over the top of your tongue. Feel it, feel the texture, the taste, the size of the raisin. It is a raisin in the present moment in your mouth. As you focus on a raisin, the rest of the world disappears—for one moment in time.

When do you breathe? Now—and then you exhale. You notice your breath coming in and going out. Each is a separate now and each now is gone in a moment. As you focus on your breath, moment to moment, you are not worried about the possible futures that your imaginative worried mind could create. You are simply in the moment of your breath. Now. Then, the now is gone.

When do you see and hear your child laugh? Now, and then the laughter subsides. Each experience, each breath, each laughter, and each tear that is shed is experienced in a Now that is a present moment and then passes to another present moment — *ad infinitum* — one after the other. Let's take the current moment — this Now, this moment at this time. Notice how you are sitting, notice your feet, your legs, how they are arranged, notice your shoulders, notice your hands. Each moment that you notice yourself, you are living in the present moment. Until I asked you to notice yourself, you probably were only focused on what you were reading — or thoughts about the future or the past. Each moment you miss that is in the Now is a moment lost forever.

Lost in the future

Worry is always about the future — never about the Now. You predict that bad things might happen, your mind races ahead of you towards a life that may or may not ever end up the way you think it might. As you live in the future that you imagine you have shifted away from the present moment. You are staring out into the space of your future life, with no anchor in the present. You are temporarily lost. You have left the present moment.

Come back to the present moment, and your worries will evaporate — at least for now.

What if you were able to concentrate on the present moment and just notice what is in front of you? Well, my kitten, Katie, is sitting on my desk next to my monitor as I write this. She is looking out toward a squirrel. She is completely in the present moment. Focused, alert, tail wagging, ready to pounce. Needless to say, she is not a worrier. She — like all cats I have ever known—lives in the present moment. Moment to moment, focusing on what is in front of her, experiencing a stream of images, sensations, tastes, touches, and sounds. Perhaps you could become a Zen cat—you should be so lucky.

Just as we discussed in the chapter on rumination, you can use mindfulness to cope with your tendency to jump ahead in your mind to a future that may never occur. Focusing on the here and now and watching it come and go is a great exercise in freeing yourself from your worries.

Let's take your breath. You are breathing every moment of the day. But how often do you stop to notice your breath? Notice it now.

EXERCISE: FOCUS ON THE HERE AND NOW USING YOUR BREATH

1. Take a few minutes to sit quietly.
2. Notice how your breath goes in, then out, then in again. Bring your awareness back towards your breath.
3. Notice the in and out, where your breath is. Do not control it, do not judge it. Notice it. As you notice your breath you will notice that your mind goes elsewhere—to other thoughts, hearing sounds, remembering things. Acknowledge these thoughts and sounds and gently bring your awareness back to your breath.
4. If you close your eyes, notice your breath as it goes out, saying to yourself, "Letting go," and let the breath leave you. Bring your breath back to you, noticing the flow, like water, like air, like a moment that comes and then is gone.

This mindful awareness of the breath is an exercise that you might do each day. Try it for fifteen minutes, if you can. Just notice what you are noticing. Watch your mind drifting away from your breath, drifting away from the present moment. Watch your mind telling you, "I have things to do" or "What good will this do?" Yes, your mind is busy running away from the present moment, judging it and trying to control it. Awareness of the present moment is the first step in living more completely in the Now.

To be aware is to be awake.

Give up on the future — live Now

During this time between jobs, you would be wise to live your life Now rather than think you are waiting for your life to begin when you get a job. After all, you have to live every day, every moment. If you are living in dread, driven by worry, focused on regrets, anticipating the worst, predicting catastrophes — then your life, for Now, will have disappeared. You can take your life back by giving up on the future. At least, for now.

You might say, "How can I focus on the present moment if I am worried about getting a job?" Yes, you are right. If you only focus on your worries about the future, then you cannot live in the present moment. But let me ask you this: "If you are born and then die 85 years later, how can you enjoy any moments in your life if you know you will die eventually?" Living life is not preparing for the end. It's living your life. Living is — by nature — in the present moment. Laughing is in the present moment. Crying is in the present moment. Anything with "ing" is in the present moment. You would not say, "How can I enjoy this hotdog if I know I am going to die in fifty years." Enjoy it now.

"I am enjoy*ing* the hotdog." "I am liv*ing* my life."

Take notice

Noticing is another experience of the present moment. Right now, along with Katie the kitten, I am noticing the squirrel outside. And now, in the present moment, I am noticing Katie's ears. They are directed towards the squirrel. (I suppose she is trying to pick up on the conversation the squirrel is having with her.) I am noticing the grass and the trees. I am noticing the bare branches, here in January, in Connecticut. I am noticing the sky, the sun. I am filled with the present moment. I am — almost — a cat.

EXERCISE: NOTICING NOW

When we relax and just notice what is around us, or simply notice our breathing, it can be a peaceful way to remind us that Now is the most important time:

1. Look around you where you are sitting. You may be at home or on a bus or train. Wherever you are is your present moment.
2. Notice the objects around you. What colors are they? What shapes do they have? What are these objects immediately around you? Until I asked you to notice you may not have seen them with your mind's eye. You walked past them, sat among them, lived in their presence, but they were not present to you.
3. Open your eyes while you open your mind and take it all in. Do not judge what you see. Just absorb it.
4. Are there any sounds that you hear? Is there traffic outside, voices, the wind, sounds of music or television? What do you hear? Perhaps there are no sounds and you notice the silence. As you are noticing, you are living. You are awake.
5. Return now to noticing your breath. Where is your breath at each moment? Notice it coming in, flowing in, like water, like gentle water flowing into you. And notice it flowing out, letting go. As if you are watching the waves very gently flowing in and out on the beach. Each wave is a moment that comes and goes. Life is an infinite series of these moments. Be aware and awaken to the moment in front of you.

Now is where your life is.

EXERCISE: CHANGING YOUR FOCUS

Push your worries and sense of urgency to the background by focusing on the Now. Use this recap to remind you of the benefits of living for the moment:

*   Place a small piece of food in your mouth. Notice it. Focus on the Now.
*   Focus on your breath. Notice it going in and out. Experience only the Now.
*   Notice how each breath comes and goes. Each Now is gone in a moment. Each moment is a new Now.

- If you focus on Now, you are not worried. At least for this moment.
- Practice mindful breathing each day. Focus on where your breath is.
- Give up control and judgment of the Now. Just observe.
- When you notice your worries about the future, bring your attention back to what is happening in the Now.
- What is around you? What can you see, hear, touch, smell, feel?
- Live each day, each moment—if possible—fully aware of the Now.

5: Make the most of now

You are practicing being more aware of the present moment. Each day you are practicing your mindful awareness of the breath. Each day you are shifting your attention to the present moment in front of you. Taking it all in, living and experiencing what is in the Now. Your experience of time is less focused on the distant future, the worries about what may or may not happen, and you are committing to awareness and living where you are, in the Now, for now.

As you are aware of what is happening around you in the present moment, however, you may also notice and say, "But the present moment is boring and empty at times. I have nothing to do. There are times I feel miserable, depressed, empty, and lonely. How can I live in the Now when it really is so lousy?"

These are fair observations on your part and deserve your attention. One way of living in the Now is to plan for many moments that may be difficult. For example, I like to think of having a menu of things I can do that will improve the present moment. This could include talking with my wife, playing with Katie the kitten, listening to music, working out, watching a movie, listening to the news, going for a walk, meditating, breathing in the present moment, cooking food, reading, taking a bubble bath, playing basketball, looking up information, talking to a friend. You need your own menu of things to do in these present moments. Rather than sitting passively and ruminating about the past or worrying about the future, you can spend this present moment doing something that is fun and interesting that involves growth, relaxation and play, or whatever it is that makes a present moment a moment to experience.

Simple things that you can enjoy

Make a list of simple things to do, and keep adding to the list. Assign these things to yourself every day. If possible, ask other people what simple things they have enjoyed doing. Brian noticed that one of his neighbors enjoyed going for long walks in the morning. It wasn't something he had ever tried. He needed to lose a few pounds and his doctor told him he should exercise, so he began going for walks in the morning. He took his mp3 player and listened to music. He began to walk three miles each day. He was outside, noticing the trees, the sky, the change in seasons. He felt the air against his face in the winter. It woke him up. He listened to music he enjoyed when he was in high school. Brian thought this walking, noticing, listening, and feeling was the best time of the day.

That time was Now.

EXERCISE: FINDING PLEASURABLE ACTIVITIES

Work through the list below to help you find ways to keep your mind busy while you do something pleasurable:

- Develop a menu of rewarding and pleasurable activities.
- Keep adding to this menu every week—every day, if you can.
- When there are moments that you find difficult, turn to your menu and do one of the things listed on there.
- Stay focused on the activity. Notice if your mind drifts towards worries, and bring your attention back to your activity.
- Each activity is a present moment in a Now that will be gone. Cherish the moment while it lasts.

6: Stretch time

When you are out of work you find yourself focused on getting the answer as soon as you can—"When will I get the job I need?"

Solving the problem immediately is a natural part of anxiety. But it only adds to your anxiety if you are focused on the immediacy of your demand — getting it Now. You may not have the answer for a while.

Most people who are out of work get a job in a few weeks or a few months — some linger on longer. You might not know when it will happen — but you still have to live your life, every day, in this time between jobs. For example, you may remember Harry from Chapter Five who had been a chronic ruminator since he was a child. Harry was in his fifties and was out of work for five months. He was worried about when he would get a job. He told me, "I have been trying for months, but it's not easy. I have to get something near where we live, since we are not going to move, and there aren't a lot of jobs around here." I thought for a minute, realizing that Harry had excellent job skills, was a very good worker, but that he really needed to think of giving himself more time. He did have a severance package that fortunately provided him a bit of a cushion, so I asked him, "What if you gave yourself another six months? Why the urgency to get something now?" Harry looked at me and said with a smile, "I never thought of it that way. You're right. There is no urgency for me to get a job right now. I can continue looking for a while."

This was an excellent example of the value of stretching time. With more time, he could consider more possibilities. The job market was always fluid, jobs were periodically coming available. He could stretch time for more months, network more, perhaps even acquire new job skills. Stretching time gave Harry more freedom and more options.

Now Harry was in an enviable position because he had a severance package. Stretching time for a possible six months more was not going to cause immediate financial hardship. But he may be unusual in having this kind of cushion. Many people will not be in that position, so increasing the search time for finding a job may require major economizing at home. It may require going into savings, borrowing, downsizing. All of these are unfortunate realities, but it is always possible to consider alternatives to the sense of urgency. Almost everyone can live on less — at least for a while.

What are the implications for you if you stretch time?

Ask yourself if it is possible to give yourself a wider window of time to look for a job. If you changed your expectations and gave yourself a few more months, what would this mean? Would it relieve some of the psychological pressure? Would you be able to consider more options? What would be the costs to you and your family? Would there be some cutbacks in spending? Are there resources you could draw on? I am offering this as a suggestion, and it may be harder for some than for others. Harry was able to get a new job in a few months after our conversation. It was a good job, not ideal, but it did allow him to move on to working, earning, and using his skills. But he told me that giving himself permission to stretch time was immensely helpful to him.

Another way to stretch time is to think of your current unemployment as one point in time. Your life may go on for decades beyond the present moment. Let's say that you are thirty years old and you can expect to live another fifty-five years. If you are unemployed for several months (or even longer) at this point in your life, does it really have as much impact on your entire future life?

This is what I would call your "time-horizon." Let's say that you have been out of work for two months. Let's assume for right now that you might be out of work for another four months. (You might get a job next week, but let's just play out this mental experiment.) Now, if you are out of work for six months and you live another fifty-five years, what real difference will it make over the long run? You might have another thirty years of earning. You might take your next job and then "trade up" to a better job in another year of two. You might acquire new skills and get even better work later. Your current unemployment is not a permanent disability from which you will never recover.

If you think about your future earnings over the next thirty years, how much money would that be? If you subtract out the loss of income during the current period of unemployment (while taking into consideration any unemployment compensation), what percent of your total life-time earnings is represented? When I have asked people to do this kind of calculation it really helps them put into perspective that the current setback is a temporary and—for many—ultimately a minor setback.

Putting your period between jobs into perspective over a lifetime

Increasing your time horizon for future earnings and future work not only will allow you to see more options in the future, but it will also help you to recognize that this current problem is a small percentage of your total life. Imagine this: what if everyone in the world was "required" to go through five months of unemployment? This would be a built-in expectation. How would everyone in the world consider how they cope with this and put it into perspective? It might sound a bit unrealistic to imagine this kind of situation, but a lot of people will have a period of unemployment at some time.

What if we all built this into our expectation—at some point we will all be—or could be—unemployed? Then the question would be, what would your expected life-time earnings be? Well, by definition, your lifetime earnings would be what you would expect to earn if you were never unemployed, minus the loss of income during the period of unemployment. This would represent a very small percent of your total lifetime earnings. For example, if you expect to work for a total of forty years, then the loss of six months would be 1.25% of your total lifetime earnings. (This would be with the unrealistic assumption that during the six months you would have absolutely no unemployment benefits.) If we adjusted for unemployment benefits, it might represent about 1% of your total lifetime income. That is, you would be losing 1% of your total lifetime earnings.

I think almost all of us could survive on 1% less over our lifetimes.

By stretching time, getting a longer time horizon for future earnings, you can consider the high likelihood that you will be able to recover your earnings, move forward, put this in perspective, and get on with a productive life. Losing a job is hard—but it is not a death sentence.

Stretching time helps us realize that the financial difficulties and the need to economize may be temporary. It may have almost no long-term implications for our quality of life. You will have time to recover, time to earn again. You might be delayed in buying things you like, but so what? You may have to wait to take that vacation you dreamed of, but it can wait for you. You may have to wait for the new car, but you can live for now.

Stretching time allows you to put the current setback into perspective of a larger life, with more chances for earnings, more opportunities to recover, more of an ability to get on with productive work.

This is just a moment between jobs.

EXERCISE: COULD YOU STRETCH TIME?

Look at the following points to help you decide whether you really need to have a new job right now.

- Are you telling yourself that you need a job immediately?
- What is the evidence for and against the idea that you need a job right now?
- What would be the costs and benefits of extending your time for searching for a job?
- What additional things can you do to improve your searching if you give yourself more time?
- If you got a new job in the next couple of months, how many more years of being employed could you expect?
- What would be your total lifetime income from the beginning of your employment in your early adulthood to your retirement?
- What percentage of your lifetime income is represented by your lost income during your current period of unemployment?
- If your current unemployment represents a small percentage,

what is the evidence that you will be able to recover financially in the future?

SUMMARY

Yes, it might be nice for you to have all the answers right now. It might be great to have that job right in your hand and to know that this time between jobs is over and you have now moved on to the next stage in your life. But things don't happen until they happen and you won't know them until you have that knowledge.

You don't have a crystal ball—but that doesn't mean that there are real fire alarms going on, the house is burning down, or that life is imploding on you. Life is an everyday experience. Every day is a series of moments.

Practice mindful meditation Daily practice of mindful meditation can help you become more aware of the present moment, slow down your sense of urgency, allow you to give up control, and experience the present moment. Mindful awareness of the present allows you to let go of worries about the future.

Your worries are your imagination The present moment is reality. All rewards, pleasure and experience is in the present moment. Why live your life in a future that may never occur, when you can improve the present moment and turn off the alarms in your head?

The job will come when it comes You can keep in mind that you can slow down your thinking, turn off the alarms, focus on the present moment and live your life in the current moment in time. You cannot control the future—it hasn't happened. You might be able to control the present. And you might be able to enjoy the present moment, which is the life between jobs.

Worry is always about the future Living is about the Now. Keep the following in mind:

- Ask yourself, "How does my worry make sense to me?"
- Accept uncertainty and give up control.

- Is everything so urgent?
- Focus on the Now.
- Make the most of Now.
- Stretch time.

10

GETTING OUTSIDE YOURSELF

You don't live in a world without people and connections. You were meant to talk to people, get support and support them. When you are unemployed—and you don't have the regular contact with your co-workers—it's easy to become isolated. It's easy to feel all alone, but it doesn't have to be that way. Brian thought he was an outcast from life. Unemployed and sitting at home brooding about how bad things were, he no longer had the daily contact with his friends at work. He remembered how he would arrive at the office at work, take his coffee out of the bag, and joke around with his colleagues, Laura and Frank, before he had to get down to getting his work done. In fact, he enjoyed the office because he always had someone around to talk to. Now he felt lonely, with nothing to do, and he wondered why his friends from work seemed to have no contact with him since he left. "I thought they were my friends," he said, looking down at his hands as if he was trying to make sense of something. "It's as if I disappeared from their lives."

Brian did have friends outside work, but he said, "They're too busy. They're working during the day and they have their families at night. No one has time for me." And, since he and Jane had broken up after dating for a year, he didn't have her either. Not that Jane would have been any consolation—she was continually complaining that he didn't make as much money as her ex-husband. But at least it was something to do—hanging out with her. That had ended four months before he lost his job. "I lost my girlfriend, and then I lost my job," he said. It's been a great year for me, hasn't it?"

I asked Brian what his typical day was. He looked at me with an empty hopelessness in his eyes, his voice becoming softer, more tentative and sadder. "I usually feel there is no reason to get up in the morning. There's nowhere to go, no one to see. I wake up at around eight, lie there thinking about how my life really sucks, try to get back to sleep. It's hard. Sometimes I just lie there for an hour, thinking, feeling sadder. When I get up I make some coffee, have some toast, watch the news. It just seems to repeat itself. I sometimes don't get dressed until the afternoon. Why bother?"

"Do you see anyone during the day?"

"Are you kidding? Who is there to see? I'm alone."

Understandably, Brian felt lonely, sad, helpless, unsupported, and despondent about the future. The reality was that he was out of a job, didn't have a girlfriend, and he had lost contact with the structure of going to work and seeing his friends and colleagues. That was the reality. But he was coping with this reality in a way that was making everything worse. He was isolating himself, taking a passive role, giving up before he could get started, and brooding about how bad things were. He was taking a bad situation and making it worse. It was time for a change. You won't get anything done by *waiting* for things to happen.

1: Turn passivity and isolation into action and engagement

There is nothing bad that can't be made worse. OK, you are out of work; perhaps you are living alone, but there are better ways of coping than simply lying around waiting for life to get better. Throughout this book I have been repeating the message— perhaps nagging you—that you can take responsibility and take action and do something different. It *can* be different. Isolation, passivity, rumination, and worrying are choices that you make. They are terrible ways to cope—and they may come to you automatically, but there are better alternatives.

I suggested to Brian that it was time to get a plan and carry it out. His current strategy of passivity—lying in bed, moping around his apartment, and isolating himself—was just adding to his depression and helplessness.

"Are you willing to make some changes and take some steps to making it better?" I asked.

"What steps?"

"Is what you are doing really helping?"

"No, I feel miserable."

"OK. Let's come up with a plan to take action to deal with your passivity and loneliness. It's going to require you doing things differently, even doing things that you might feel uncomfortable doing. Are you willing to be uncomfortable?"

Brian said, "I'm uncomfortable now."

I told Brian that we needed daily goals, daily assignments, that would get him out of his isolation, out of his apartment and out of his ruminating head. We were going to identify possible sources of support and contact, possible activities, possible networks and groups. And he would have to take the first steps to initiate contact and follow through. But first we would have to deal with his shame and embarrassment about being unemployed. You will remember that we looked at the self-esteem issues that arose through feelings of shame and embarrassment in Chapter Four. Here we look at how isolating ourselves can make these feelings worse.

EXERCISE: LOOKING AT THE EFFECTS OF PASSIVITY AND ISOLATION

Work through the list below to focus on the consequences on your feelings of passivity and isolation.

- Is passivity and isolation making you feel worse?
- Why do you feel worse when you are passive and isolated?
- Are you willing to develop a plan to take action?
- Are you willing to set daily goals? Weekly goals? What do you

want to experience and accomplish that can take you out of your head?
- Are you willing to do things that are uncomfortable that can help you make progress?

2: Overcome your shame

In Chapter Four we discussed the shameful feelings you might have about being out of work. You think of yourself as a different kind of person, as someone who has a mark on you, as if you are inferior, a burden, a disgrace, a forgotten man or woman that no one would want to be around. Being unemployed is a condition of unemployment, it is not a disease. You are still the person you were when you had a job. You are still a complete human being, still someone with intelligence, values, the capacity to give and receive, and the ability to relate effectively with other people. Once you get past your shame, you can open up your social world and get out of the shell in which you feel trapped. But how do you do that?

Let's look at Brian's thoughts—what was he telling himself that was making him feel ashamed? "I feel so embarrassed being out of work. I often think other people are looking at me and thinking there is something wrong with me. I think they are thinking I must have screwed up, perhaps they think I did something at work that caused me to get the sack. I wonder if they think about my ending up homeless, a burden. I think that when I am talking to someone, they are probably thinking, 'I don't want to be around this guy. He's so depressing.'"

Brian thought people looked at him and could see right through him. He was doing a lot of mind-reading about how other people were thinking—with almost no evidence that anyone had these thoughts. In fact, it may be that people were not thinking about his unemployment—or might not even know about it. I know when I meet someone and they tell me they are unemployed, I do think about it. I wonder what it is like for them. But invariably the conversation turns to something else. They might be talking about their family, politics, neighbors, films, their interests, or the latest gossip. People talk about a lot of different things. But Brian felt he was wearing a big "U" around his neck and people were thinking, "He is unemployed."

Test your shame-thoughts

We've already seen how your thoughts can make you miserable—and these thoughts are guaranteed to make you unhappy. But thoughts can be true or false, and you won't know until you examine them. These shame-thoughts can be tested, put under your mental microscope.

First, as I have mentioned before, you might wonder if anyone you are talking to has ever been unemployed. Perhaps they actually know what you are going through. Or perhaps they have a close family member who has been out of work. Perhaps being unemployed is normal, almost a universal experience for families, friends, and self.

Second, given the fact that there are always millions of people who are unemployed, it's possible that people think that someone can lose a job because of problems with a company or with the economy in general. Perhaps it's an external reason, not something intrinsic about you. I've known a lot of people who have lost their jobs in construction, services, finance, law firms, public relations, media, college teaching—even psychologists! The job market is fluid and sometimes a job flows out and takes you with the flow.

Third, why would someone think that you are going to end up homeless? Almost everyone gets another job. Unemployment may be longer than you want it to be, but it is almost never permanent. That would be a pretty unusual outcome for someone who has lost a job to end up homeless. Do you think others are thinking that all unemployed people end up on the street? I doubt it.

Fourth, it might be that someone might think it's depressing or awkward talking to someone who is unemployed. But does it have to be depressing? My sense is that it really depends on what you are talking about. If you continually dwell on the negative, it can be a downer — not only for the other person, but also for you. But you don't have to ruminate and complain when you talk to people. In fact, you might actually talk about the things we are going to discuss in this chapter. And I'll bet if you do, it will make both of you feel better.

It's always better to talk about the action you are taking to make things better than the sense of feeling trapped and defeated. What you talk about is really up to you. It can bring both of you up or put both of you down.

3: Identify friends and family — and reach out

If you are going to build your support network, you need to start with the people that you already know. You might start with your family — your parents, siblings, cousins, aunts, uncles, and in-laws. There's a good chance that some of them have gone through periods of unemployment, so they may know what it is like. Since you have more time on your hands, you might have more time to talk with them, see them, and do things together. Brian was able to turn to his brother and spend some time visiting him. It was actually a good experience for both of them. His brother, Dan, was able to feel useful and supportive, and Brian was able to feel a lot less alone. They had dinner together, talked on the phone, emailed each other. This turned out to be a big support to Brian.

Some people are reluctant to turn to family members because they feel embarrassed about their unemployment and they don't want to lean on someone. Carol was one of these people who thought she should be able to handle everything on her own. Although she had two brothers and a sister, she said, "I don't feel comfortable talking to them. They all have jobs and families. Why would they want to hear from me?" I asked Carol if her sister, Lara, were out of work if she would feel comfortable talking with her.

"Of course, I'd want to be there for her. She's my sister."

"Is there some reason that Lara would feel differently about being a sister to you if you are unemployed?"

Carol began to realize that she had a double standard. She thought she was a burden, but she would have thought it would be OK if her sister turned to her. "In fact, when I think of it, I would actually feel bad if my sister didn't turn to me if she needed support." Carol realized that one of the things you want to do if you are a sister or a friend is to support them. You want them to turn to you when they are in need of you.

Carol reluctantly reached out to Lara, called her on the phone and told her that she was out of work and that she was looking for a job. As they talked, Lara told her about some of her friends who had been laid off in recent months and how she was worried about losing her job. "There have been so many layoffs in my business, and I worry that I'll be next. In fact, it could be me calling you for support. So I'm glad you reached out to me." Knowing Lara was on her side was a relief for Carol. They began to brainstorm possible leads, people that Carol might contact for possible jobs, and thought about how to expand her network, how to keep herself busy, and how to lift her mood. "Let's have lunch next week and catch up on things," Lara said.

Reconnecting

You will want to connect with people in addition to your family. I asked Brian to go through his list of contacts and rate people into three categories—those who would be good people to see for job leads or for social support, those of moderate relevince, and those of the least relevance. Close friends, former business or work colleagues, professional contacts, and other people with whom Brian had closer relationships were the first category. He was able to identify a number of old and current friends—some who could be a source of social support, some who might be professional leads. We decided to start focusing on these people first.

Brian said, "I haven't been in contact with some of these people for over a year."

"So what? If one of these people contacted you after a year, what would you do?" I asked.

"I'd think it was unusual, but I imagine I would be curious about what was going on with them."

"When was the last time someone contacted you who hadn't been in contact for some time?"

"About six months ago, my friend Phillip emailed me after Christmas and said it had been too long since we had talked. We emailed back and forth and set up a lunch and, you know, it was really good seeing him."

"You know, Brian, it's so easy to fall out of contact with people. We get busy with work and family and other things. People move and it feels awkward to initiate that contact, but perhaps it's worth a try."

Brian decided he would contact three old friends and see if he could get together with them. "But what do I talk about when I see them?" he asked.

"You might talk about what you talked about when you last saw them."

Brian recalled that they often talked about his friend's family—what the kids were doing, their latest holiday, sports teams, politics, mutual friends. Sometimes they would talk about work.

"Now that I think of it, a few years ago one of my friends, Ed, was out of work, and we talked about how he was coping with that. I remember he told me that he felt he got blindsided at work, suddenly they just laid him off, and he was fairly pissed off about that. I could understand that. Especially now."

I wondered how Brian responded to Ed's loss of his job.

"I tried to be supportive. I could see he was going through a rough time. He was trying to pick up some freelance work until he could get back on his feet and find a full-time job. He told me he was watching his expenses."

"Sounds like your experience, to some extent, doesn't it?" I asked.

Brian began to realize that unemployment happens to his friends and family and that, at different times in life, you could be the one giving support or the one getting support.

Most people will be supportive

Brian's quest to connect with his friends and contacts had mixed results—but, overall, he said, it was helpful. Over the next few weeks he met with seven old friends and colleagues. When he got around to discussing his current position of being out of work and looking for the next job, several of his friends were very supportive. Two mentioned how they had been out of work in the past, and one of them described the layoffs that had been happening where he was. Some of them suggested possible leads, companies that might need Brian's experience, each of them encouraging him to keep his hope up and to keep busy looking.

One guy, though, was visibly nervous, seeming to fidget when Brian mentioned he was out of work. "He began looking down at his fork, as if he wanted to end the conversation, as if he wanted to get out of there." Brian was disappointed in this friend's response and couldn't work out what was going on. I said:

"Well, it's hard to know what is going on in someone else's mind, Brian. But some people have a hard time dealing with real emotional issues. They feel awkward and uncomfortable. Who knows? Perhaps he was thinking he didn't know what to say to make you feel better, as if that was his job. Or perhaps your situation reminded him of something he fears; losing his job. Sometimes people just have a hard time with the serious things in life." As Brian thought about this guy he realized that this was exactly what he had thought about him in the past—he was a rather superficial person who just liked talking about sports, telling jokes, and getting his work done. He was a private person, in fact, someone Brian thought was hard to get to know. And this interaction confirmed his view of him. Yes, sometimes people will let us down.

Widening your network

Knowing that most of Brian's friends and colleagues were supportive and encouraging, and could even give him ideas for leads, was helpful to him. This spurred him on to contact more people on his list. I asked: "Brian, has it occurred to you that some people might actually like to be in a position to be supportive—even if it might be awkward? It can make you feel useful, important, and good about yourself to support someone who is out of work. It's not always that way, but it could be that way with some of these people."

We discussed how someone might feel in business talking with someone who was out of work. If he were on the other side, he might think, "Why should I have to deal with this? It's not my problem. This guy is out of work, and he can't help me." But we then looked at the other side: "This guy is a good person, he's talented. This could happen to anyone. If I do him a favor, I create a lot of good will. I can feel good about myself if I help someone. I'm no worse off if I am supportive and, who knows, he might return the favor one day." We discussed how this view of a network empowered people who participated in networks. I said, "If you are a player in a network, you create a lot of obligations and goodwill. People begin thinking of you as the person who helps his friends. Perhaps some of the people you contact might feel that way. I hope that when you are back working and someone approaches you, that you will reach out to them."

Multiply your leads

Brian's categories included people who were not close, but could be a source of a network. I suggested that he ask each person he spoke to if there were two people they could recommend that he contact to learn more about what was out there. Some people were able to name a couple of others, some were not. But expanding your network by multiplying your leads is a good way of "penetrating the market" out there. Some jobs are through word-of-mouth, some through public listings, and others through agencies. I know I like getting personal recommendations from people when I'm looking for future staff members because I feel they have already done some of the screening, and people will know what I am looking for and what kind of person I am like to work with. But multiplying your leads by having one lead connect to another lead is an effective way of dramatically expanding your possibilities. People may say "No," or "I don't know," but you only need that one lead to pay off.

Filling in with part-time work

Joe lost his job at the factory and had a small severance package with benefits for a while, but he knew that this would run out after a couple of years. He and his wife, Sarah, had a small amount in savings, but with two kids in school and a mortgage, he worried about making ends meet. Joe had lived for over twenty-five years in the small town where they were now, so he knew a lot of people. But there was no factory opening up, no big hiring going on. His cousin, Martin, had a landscaping business—which doubled in the winter cutting branches from trees and clearing snow. "You know, Joe," said Martin, "I could use you in my work. It's only part-time, although sometimes you might work more hours because of the weather or the jobs, but it's work, and I can pay you enough to make it worth your while." Joe always liked working outside, so he took the job.

When I talked to him about the period after losing his job he said, "You know, I am always working now. It's not that I have anything full-time. But I work for Martin, helping with his work, and I also do other odd jobs and help out with the school part-time. It pays the bills."

I looked at him with a great deal of admiration and said, "You are incredibly resourceful. It's amazing how versatile and determined you are. I really think you should be proud of yourself for working so hard to make things work out."

The value of the contacts you have made

Every job that Joe got was through family, friends, and other contacts. He was able to piece together the support he needed to keep his house and support himself and his family.

Reaching out for connection and support doesn't always work. But it's far more productive than isolation, passivity, and rumination. You won't know until you try. Some people will be supportive, some may have leads, others may not know what to say, and still others may not return your calls. You find out about people when things are tough, and you can remember who was there—and who wasn't.

EXERCISE: CREATE A NETWORK

Start to build up a useful network for finding employment by working through the points below:

- Make a list of people you know—from close friends and family to people you are barely acquainted with.
- Think of this list as your "prospects" for a network and categorize them in terms of how useful they might be in developing social support or looking for a job.
- Identify your negative thoughts about why it might be difficult to contact these people. Challenge these negative thoughts.
- Is it possible that almost everyone on this list has been unemployed, worries about losing their job, or has a close family member or friend who has been unemployed?
- When you contact people, explore additional contacts that they might know. Expand your network.
- Could some people feel good about being supportive?
- If you got just a few sources of support, would it be worth it?

4: Become a volunteer

Karen told me that she spent most days hanging around her apartment with nothing to do, waiting to hear if one of her job applications had been picked up. "It's like I am killing time, and it's killing me. I hate feeling so useless, so invisible." Actually, Karen's negative thoughts came from a good place—she wanted to feel useful and to connect with others. Her job had provided a lot of that, but she was isolating herself in her apartment, feeling ineffective, cut off from the world. We had to change that.

"Have you ever done any volunteer work?" I asked her.

"Yeah. When I was at the university, I used to teach inner city kids and volunteered at a local care home. When I first moved to the city, I remembered missing my dog from home, so I volunteered at an animal shelter. Actually, I didn't work with the dogs so much as helping socialize the cats. I used to play with them. I wasn't really a cat person, but I got so hooked on cats that I adopted one. I still have her. Her name is Samantha."

"What do you think about doing some volunteer work now?"

"I don't know where to start," she said, beginning with the first thought that every depressed person seems to have: "I don't know how to do it." I suggested that we do some research together.

Helping others can lead to helping ourselves

In most towns and cities you simply can Google the word "volunteers" with the name of the town/city, and you will get a large number of possibilities. You can also look in your local newspaper. You can volunteer to help with children, elderly people, and people who are ill, housebound, or who have memory problems. You can volunteer to help with animals, charities, or organizations who need assistance with fundraising, such as the local hospital, and any number of other possibilities. Even rural areas have lots of possibilities for volunteering.

You may think that volunteer work is a waste of time. You might think, "How is this going to help me get a job? That's my problem right now." Yes, it may be one of your problems—not having a job—but volunteer work can help you address another problem: how you take care of yourself. If you had a choice between volunteering to help someone else and sitting around your house or apartment ruminating and worrying about the future, which direction would you want to go in? If you help someone else, you might be helping yourself.

Another step on the employment ladder

I actually think volunteer work can help you get your next job. If you are volunteering, you are expanding your network, getting yourself out there, creating goodwill, giving people the right impression about you. Every person that you contact and make a good impression on is a potential lead. One could lead to a job interview. You never know. Another reason that volunteer work can help you is that you can talk about your volunteer work on your next job interview. What will it say about you? I think it will say that you are active, involved, responsible, altruistic, and caring. That sounds like the kind of person I would want to hire. People may want to help you if they see that you are helping other people. How could it hurt?

Feeling useful, being appreciated

When looking for volunteer work, you could ask if there is any volunteer work at your local church, charity, or hospital. You would immediately be part of that community—and it will be a community of people who care about other people: good people, people who reach out, people who can reach out to you. You will feel useful and better about yourself, you will get out of your isolation, and you will make a difference. In some cases, volunteer work can help you connect with people who then help you find work that pays. One of my clients, who was out of work, volunteered to work on research. They eventually hired her full time. Another, an out-of-work architect, volunteered at his local church community, and he eventually got commissions to design homes.

Karen decided to help an eleven-year-old girl with her homework, "I found this great volunteer group that has us helping kids in the inner city with their school work. I'm working with a girl who lives with her grandmother and aunt, and she's really very sweet, but things at home have been pretty rough. She lost her mother, who was a drug addict, and never really knew her father. We're working on her math and science together, and I can tell you that it's a real challenge. But sometimes I feel like I'm her friend, not just her tutor."

"How does that make you feel, Karen?"

"That's just perfect for me."

Giving and helping through life

Of course, volunteer work doesn't have to end when you get your job. I think all of us should give back—preferably on an ongoing basis. Reaching out beyond yourself helps you feel you are doing the right thing. You matter to someone else. They don't care if you don't have a job—in fact, it makes their lives easier—you are more available. Someone looks forward to you turning up, someone counts on you. It reminds you, too, that others have problems, others may be worse off than you are right now. I always feel that when I help someone, I am helping myself. I'm reaching out beyond my petty needs and connecting with the real world. There's always someone out there that needs you. Everyone has something to offer.

EXERCISE: LOOKING DEEPER INTO VOLUNTEERING

You may never have thought of volunteering before. Use the list below to help you think about it in more detail.

- Have you ever done any volunteer work? What was it like?
- What do you think of people who do volunteer work? Do you have positive thoughts about them? What are these thoughts?

Perhaps you could direct these thoughts to yourself when you
volunteer?

- What are the possible advantages of volunteering?
- Would you feel useful, good about yourself, that you are making a
  contribution?
- Could you meet new people—caring and decent people—who
  are also involved in volunteering?
- Could any of these people be a source of social support or networking for a job?

5: Take a course

If you think you might be out of work for a while, it might make
sense to learn something new. There are community centers,
colleges, and universities, and even private companies that
provide courses—and training—that can enhance your life, build
skills you might need, and connect you with other people. Most
courses have to be paid for, but some will be subsidized if you
are unemployed, and your unemployment benefits office will
also know if you qualify to attend a free course to develop new
skills. Some organizations will also give you a grant to attend a
course providing you meet certain criteria. You can Google
"courses for the unemployed" and see what comes up.

Steven had been out of work for some time. An aspiring
actor, he wasn't getting any paying jobs. He was talented, but
there were thousands of other talented people. He decided to
investigate taking a course in using computer software in an
office so he might qualify for office work. Steven was a quick
learner and he was now getting skills he could use in the
marketplace. The great thing about it was that a local college was
offering the course for free. He felt he was making progress,
building his ability to support himself, and meeting new people.
Learning how to do office work wasn't the "coolest" thing from
his point of view, but it did help him overcome his fear that he
would be permanently unemployed.

Courses don't have to be career oriented, however. They can
be fun, meaningful, interesting, and growth oriented. Karen

remembered that she used to like to draw, so we discussed the possibility of taking a course on drawing in a local art class. It was informal; she could just show up, bring her charcoal and pad, pay the small admission charge, and draw the model. She said, "I feel I can just let myself get lost in the moment when I am drawing. It focuses my eye and my mind on the contours, the light and the darkness. I can express myself without thinking about a job or bills to pay." Karen was rediscovering something she thought had been lost forever; the ability to be creative and expressive. The class included people of all ages and of all walks of life, all kinds of people. She began to talk with people in the class and made some new friends. But she told me that it was a sense of personal freedom to be able to go to the class and just express herself. "I wish I had more time for this when I was working."

I said, "It depends on the priorities that are important to you, Karen. Weren't there people in that class who had full-time jobs?"

Get fit

Of course, the healthiest kind of class to join might be an exercise class. One of the risks of being unemployed is that you have less physical activity and can do more emotional eating, which can lead to weight gain, high blood pressure, and higher cholesterol levels. None of that is good for you and all of it can be prevented. In the next chapter we will go into more detail on self-care during this time between jobs, but right now I want to mention the value of an exercise class—or a yoga class—or both.

I go to a local health club several times a week, and I also workout on my own. That's my style. But I notice a lot of people coming into the club on a regular basis to exercise. They get a great workout, but they also get to interact with each other. Some facilities have "water exercise classes" which are less stressful on your legs, but provide you with a great opportunity to work out with other people. Again, it's all about getting out and doing something with other people. And you can get into better shape as you do it.

Yoga classes are terrific for a number of reasons. First, yoga is a great way to stretch, build strength and flexibility, and calm your mind at the same time. Second, yoga is a form of meditation for many people, helping to reduce stress and learn the ability to stay in the present moment—where you are not worried or ruminating. And, third, you might find some interesting, warm, intelligent, and caring people in the community of yoga practice. I see people almost daily who are walking through the city streets carrying their yoga mat. They are eager to get to their class, eager to stretch, eager to meet their friends, and make new ones. One of my clients told me that yoga had changed her life. She described how she not only got into better shape, but how it also helped with her eating, her stress, her sleep, and her outlook on life. At her class, there were inspirational messages that they contemplated on weekly. I often had the sense that I wish I had come up with those ideas, but I was glad to learn from her. She also told me that she was meeting some really kind people—people she could talk to, people who were accepting, and people who were living a healthier lifestyle.

Think about a change of direction

Some people decide that this time between jobs can be extended rather than shortened so they can actually add to their skills and credentials. One way of looking at this time is to do a realistic assessment: would you be better off if you had more credentials behind you? For example, some people decide to go back to college—either part-time or full-time—to add to their CV and skills. You might look at the different courses offered in your area to determine if it makes sense to get new training, and even plan on changing your career goals.

Carl was an example of someone who "faced the facts," as he told me. He had been a professional musician, very talented, but work was hard to get and he spent a good period of time being unemployed. He decided he was tired of not having money on a regular basis and tired of waiting for the next job to come along, so he went back to college and took courses on computers. He had an excellent mind, and liked tinkering around with his computer and learning new programs. He especially liked the idea that he was increasing his potential marketability. After six months of concentrating on this new interest, he was able to get a job with a company that valued his new skills. The great thing about working with information technology is that it is always changing, you are always learning, and you are almost always in demand. Carl was able to keep up his interests with music, playing occasional gigs after work, and using the new technology to compose creative music. Learning more doesn't always mean giving up everything else.

Other people think about going back to college full time for a couple of years. During economic downturns, there is an increase of applications to colleges and graduate programs. Some people think, "The job market is telling me something. I may as well take a step backward right now in earning an income — take a course for a degree — and eventually increase my earning potential later — and for the rest of my life." Advanced training and degrees dramatically increase your earning potential and marketability. It's a real commitment, a real loss of income, an increased cost, but it may be something to consider.

There are lots of different kinds of classes to take — exercise, yoga, drawing and painting, classes to acquire new skills and classes on any topic. You're never worse off from learning or connecting with new people. It helps get you out of yourself. It makes your life more interesting. And, who knows, you might find someone who can help you move to the next stage in your life or help to make the current situation a better experience in living.

EXERCISE: MOVING FORWARD WITH ACTIVITY AND LEARNING

Look at the following points and consider whether you might enjoy joining a class for fun, relaxation, fitness or learning.

- Are there things you wanted to learn about but didn't have the time? What were they?
- Research courses and training in your area. Identify several possible directions to pursue.
- What would be the advantages and disadvantages of courses and training?
- Are there government agencies, colleges, organizations or businesses that provide training opportunities?
- What new skills or credentials could you obtain that might help you pursue new opportunities for work?

6: Connect with networks and clubs

We were not meant to live life alone. When you are unemployed, you may feel you have lost that daily social contact, that sense of identity, and that daily structure in your life. You wake up in the morning and feel there is nowhere to go. But there is always somewhere to go—somewhere to be. You don't want to get trapped in your head, ruminating, regretting, and worrying. You need to get outside of yourself.

There are lots of potential networks to join, so that you can get involved. Probably you already belong to at least one of these online networks—perhaps you belong to Facebook or LinkedIn, or some other social network. The great value of these online networks is that they are free and they can continue to expand your contacts. You can start with the friends you already have on your social network (I will use Facebook here, although you may belong to other networks—or you might just be joining). Each of your friends on these networks is a potential source of connection and support. For example, Lydia had been out of work and was feeling down. I suggested she get more active on her Facebook account, and she began posting some information about her son and daughter. Three of her old friends responded. One said, "Haven't seen you in a while. Let's get together." Another one "liked" her posting. I urged her to make plans. She got together with one of her old neighbors from where she used to live before her divorce, and they had lunch. It was a relief for her. Another friend, who she saw two weeks later, encouraged her to get back into looking for a job and, in the meantime, connect up with some volunteer work. (I liked this since it was reinforcing what I was talking to her about.)

Getting to grips with messaging

Some people find it helpful to use the messaging and chat features of social networking sites. This allows you more "real time" interactions and can help you strengthen your connections. You can make comments about people's postings on music, movies, politics, personal issues, travel, or whatever your interests are. I am convinced that many people on these networks are eager to expand their own support, so it's mutually beneficial and rewarding.

You might be hesitant to connect on the social networks because you feel embarrassed about being out of work. You have two choices: either mention it, or don't mention it. I am convinced that almost every single person you contact on these networks has either been out of work, or has a close friend or family member out of work. Do you think people will "unfriend" you if you don't have a current job?

Discover a network of interests that suit you

People meet other people through their interests. We have already seen how volunteer work can bring you together with other people—and keep you involved in feeling useful and productive. But you might have other interests that you want to follow up on. A lot of sports equipment stores have listings of hiking and biking clubs; meditation and yoga centers have listings of people who want to get together and share interests; there are book clubs or reading groups; and there are groups that your church might have where you can share your values and interests.

If you are a professional or businessperson, there are organizations where you can connect with people in your field. You don't have to have a current job to belong. In any case, you can check with your professional or business interest groups to see if there are meetings or events. Many of these organizations have speaking events, networks, or even support groups. Look into it and follow up. What do you have to lose?

Most schools, colleges, and universities are interested in keeping their past students and alumni connected with each other and with the school or university. You can check out your classmates from school and college on social networks such as Facebook and LinkedIn, and you can also contact the schools themselves to find out if there are any alumni events. I've found it to be immensely valuable to connect with some of my old friends from college. You have much in common with people from your past, and it makes sense to reach out and meet them again. Sometimes your former school may want a volunteer to help out with contacting former classmates or in getting involved in the school's activities and development.

Some universities provide support for graduates seeking employment. You should contact your university to find out if they are involved in anything that can be helpful to you. Some of my former university peers are heavily involved in contacting others, arranging luncheons and other events, connecting on a listserv (an electronic mailing list) where people keep up with what is going on. I have made new friends from these kinds of discussions—people I never knew at university but who I wanted to get to know because of our exchange on the listserv. It's a great way to expand your network. And it's great to get out of your isolation and rumination.

EXERCISE: USING SOCIAL NETWORKING

If you've never used social networking sites, you may feel uncertain about them. Use the list below to get started.

- People are always looking for other people to share interests and activities. Could there be someone out there who might like to know you?
- Explore social networks and identify possible friends or new people with similar interests. Connect.
- Look into clubs, interest groups, professional organizations and any other opportunities where people might connect. Go to these events.
- Contact your former school, college or university and find out what activities and mailing groups are available. You might connect up with someone you haven't seen in years.
- Get involved in professional or business groups where you can network.
- New people are a source of support, shared interests and possible leads for jobs.

7: Become a tourist

This might sound like a far-fetched thing for you to do, but bear with me for a few minutes while I explain what I mean. The key thing is getting out and getting outside of yourself. This can involve networking, clubs, courses, volunteer work, connecting with classmates and old friends, and lots of other proactive strategies. But getting outside yourself may literally mean "getting outside." I like to think about making yourself into a tourist and taking advantage of your local possibilities.

For example, if you ask anyone who lives in a big city when was the last time they went to a museum or art gallery, or walked around a public garden, or even visited some of the noteworthy architectural or historical sites, they will often look at you and say, "I don't have time for that, I have a job." Well, that must mean that if you don't have a job for now, you have time for those things.

Periodically, I like to think of myself as a tourist wherever I am. Earlier in my career I lived in lots of different places — New Haven, Connecticut; Washington, DC; Cambridge, Massachusetts; Berkeley, California; Boulder, Colorado; Vancouver, Canada; and Philadelphia, Pennsylvania. I now live in New York City. In each city, I turned myself into a tourist. Wherever you are, there are places that you would take a visitor. It could be interesting museums, buildings, exhibitions, clubs, or sports events in the place where you live. Take yourself. Be your own tour guide. I am constantly rediscovering New York City, and I've lived here for decades. Or think about the natural beauty in your area and visit the countryside, coastline, and rivers; look at the hills and historic sites, walk through the old towns, find out what there is to see. You can get a lot of information on the websites of the towns and countryside near you. Everyone is trying to promote the attractions where they live. Get up and go — and carry your imagination and curiosity with you, now that you have the time.

Seeing what you have taken for granted

You don't have the excuse that you are too busy working. Just think about the advantage you have right now as a tourist where you live. You can walk along the streets or footpaths, admire the architecture, walk on the beaches, take a canoe on the river or the lake, learn about art in a gallery, listen to a concert, go to a dance, sample the food in the tiny restaurant tucked in a forgotten place you have never visited, and live fully in the place that surrounds you. Walk across any bridge crossing the river in a city and you will find people sauntering along, looking back over the city and watching the boats going by. When you do this, you see the city in a new light. You can live in a city all your life without really seeing it. Now is the time!

EXERCISE: WHERE COULD YOU GO AS A TOURIST?

Think about where you live and how you could enjoy more of the interesting places:

- Now that you have time, you can explore and enjoy the area where you live.
- If you were showing someone around your area, where would you take them?
- Identify the places, buildings, museums, concerts, events and natural settings in your area—and take yourself there.
- Think of yourself as a tourist where you live and take part in life where you are.

SUMMARY

Throughout this chapter we have examined ways that you can get outside yourself and get involved in the real world. Isolating yourself, sitting at home watching television, ruminating, feeling ashamed and waiting for things to change will guarantee your misery. The great thing to keep in mind is that you have the choice to make things better. There are literally millions of people out there—many looking for a connection, a friend, someone to help out with volunteer work, someone with whom to share interests. We live in a world crowded with lonely people. But now it's up to you to make it different.

Don't spend this time between jobs isolated, ruminating, passive and worried. If you do nothing but wait for the next job to appear, you will not only waste the opportunities to make your life better but you will also probably decrease the likelihood of getting the next job.

Being active—and being proactive (making things happen)—is always a better formula for living a full life. Your life can be fuller or more empty during this time. It's up to you.

Consider your attitude about making plans, taking action and tolerating some discomfort. It's part of empowering yourself. Passivity is not the key to success. It's the guarantee of helplessness.

Think about how your irrational, but powerful, thoughts about shame get in the way of taking charge of your life and getting you out of your cocoon. You can challenge these shameful thoughts by normalizing the experience of being unemployed and normalizing the fact that everyone knows someone who has been unemployed. Get past your view that unemployment is a kind of disease or mark of disgrace. There is nothing evil or immoral about losing your job. You have a right to take your life in your hands and live it with other people. By reaching out and identifying possible sources of support you overcome your feelings of helplessness and hopelessness. Each person is a possibility.

You can feel more useful and find more meaning in your life, by helping other people. I think all of us should do volunteer work at some point. It helps you realize that you matter to others and that you can make the world a better place. Volunteer work brings you in contact with other volunteers—people who care, and people who can care about you.

You can also get outside yourself by taking courses, acquiring skills, even building your credentials. Some may cost you, some may be free, and some may change your life. You can also reach beyond your current isolation by connecting with social networks and clubs—finding people with common backgrounds, interests and the willingness to participate in activities. There are millions of other people out there. How many do you need to make your life better?

Become a tourist in your own home area. You were too busy while you were at work; now you have the time. It's your opportunity to discover what has been around you for so long.

11

TAKING CARE OF YOURSELF

For many people who are unemployed, the time between jobs is not only lost time, not only a time of increased depression and anxiety, but also a time when the worst habits of self-care develop. One client, John, was a great example of this dissolution and decay. He had been employed for several years and knew that he was likely to lose his job, but he took a passive attitude about looking for alternatives while still employed. He had no plan. Rather than anticipating losing his job and needing a new one, he had been passive and done nothing. He had done no networking, no searching—he just sat there and waited for the axe to fall. It did fall.

When he was laid off because of a company downturn, the only person who was surprised was John. Initially, he complained and thought of himself as a victim (which was understandable, even normal), but then sank into a pattern of passivity, isolation, and decline of self-care. He would sleep late, then stay up late at night watching television, surfing the net and perusing pornography. Alone at home while his wife was at work and the kids were at school, he sometimes didn't get dressed until late afternoon. His eating habits became the source of momentary pleasure, mindless compulsion, and self-destruction. Stuffing himself with junk food, he would munch on potato chips and cookies, raid the fridge for more ice cream, and sit in front of the television in an almost hypnotic state.

Never exercising, smoking more than ever before, John also began to drink during the day, often hiding the empty bottles under the furniture. John thought he needed more relief from his stress, so he began smoking marijuana during the week when everyone was out of the house. His motivation to look for a job declined along with his health. Every day had the same grey, foreboding quality, accompanied by the worst habits of self-care.

Poor health is often triggered by unemployment

Sadly, John's story is not unique. Unemployment—even the fear of unemployment—is characterized by a wide range of self-destructive, unhealthy behaviors. People who learn layoffs are coming—but who have not been laid off yet—show an increase in cholesterol levels.[15]

Stress hormones increase, digestion is compromised, and sleep is impaired. During the time between jobs, many people show an increase in alcohol consumption, smoking, drug abuse, and overeating. There are also increases in obesity during this time—the result of a decreased effort in working, plus passivity and compulsive eating. As we discussed in Chapter One, the unemployed have lifetime risks of cardiovascular disease that are substantially higher than those never unemployed. The habits you follow during this time might result in an early death, but it doesn't have to be this way.

1: Make your health a priority

Being unemployed can affect your health. Harvard researcher Kate W. Strully has found that unemployed people over the course of one and a half years are twice as likely to develop problems with diabetes, high blood pressure and high cholesterol[16] as people who have never been unemployed.

In fact, in a review of research from fifteen countries over the past forty years, Dr. Eran Shor and other colleagues have found a significant long-term increase in mortality related to prior unemployment. Men are more likely to be affected by job loss than women—men having a 78% increase, and women having a 37% increase in mortality.[17] Unemployment has consistently been linked to increased smoking, poor nutrition, reduced quality of health and overuse of psychoactive drugs.[18]

Don't let a life of poor health start here

It's essential to focus on your health care during this time, since the effects of poor health care can last indefinitely — especially if you develop the wrong habits. In fact, one of the first things I recommend to people I counsel who are unemployed is that the greatest risk at this point is their health. Veronica was unemployed and came in to see me looking somewhat disheveled. Her hair hung loosely over her face, her clothing looked unkempt, even her walk as she came into my office was characterized by a slump and a slouch that suggested that she was depressed in almost every cell of her body. (I know that's an exaggeration, but that's how she described herself.) Her physical being was demoralized, closed down and collapsing.

I asked Veronica to describe her typical day — from the moment she woke up to the minute she went to sleep. "There's no one time that I actually get up. It depends on when I go to bed. Since I have nothing to do during the day, it doesn't seem like there is any time I need to be up. I could get up at nine in the morning, or two in the afternoon. I lie there, sometimes for an hour, sometimes falling asleep again, sometimes in a half-sleep state of mind. I don't always shower. I'm embarrassed to say, this, but I just don't care. There's no one around, it doesn't matter what I look like. I eat throughout the day, sometimes just putting some junk food in front of me while I sit and watch television. The hours drift by. There's no purpose, it seems. I hardly see people anymore." As Veronica looked down at the floor, averting her gaze, her voice trailing off into a whisper.

"I'm sorry. I didn't hear what you just said."

"I said, 'I'm such a waste of time.'"

I said to Veronica, "One of the key things during this time is taking care of your health. It sounds like you have been experiencing a lot of depression recently, and that you have closed down physically and perhaps mentally. I wonder how you think you might feel if you got more active, had a healthier diet, exercised regularly, and had a normal sleep schedule."

"I'm sure I would feel better," she said, "but that's a lot easier to say than to do. I just don't have any motivation, I have no energy. I feel tired all the time. And the ironic thing is I am tired, but I am doing nothing."

"Perhaps you are tired because of your lack of activity. It could also be that your diet is robbing you of energy. The sugar, carbohydrates, and fat take a lot of energy to metabolize and digest, and this could be a vicious cycle for you: poor nutrition, overeating, inactivity, fatigue and more overeating and passivity. I think we need to work on breaking those habits."

"I know. I used to take care of myself. It's hard to believe that just last year I was running four times every week. I weighed twenty pounds less. It seems like such a long time ago."

"You were feeling better when you were acting better. The hard thing is to act better when you are feeling down. Let's try to work on taking care of your health. That could be something that you can start working on today — and then work on it every day."

If you are spending a lot of your time in passive isolation, then you might be at risk of a cascade of poor health problems. Let's take an honest inventory.

EXERCISE: THE HONEST INVENTORY OF LIFESTYLE CHOICES

On the table below, circle the items that are true for you and answer the questions where appropriate (if you would rather not write in the book simply note down the relevant information in your notebook)

Sleeping (circle the items that are true for you)	Not enough sleep Too much sleep Nightmares Irregular habits Too many naps

Difficulty falling asleep
Waking early and can't get back to sleep
Waking suddenly, feeling anxious
Finding it hard to get out of bed in the morning

Eating (circle the items that are true for you)

Eating too much
Eating too little
Not eating regular meals
Too many snacks
No appetite
Eating sweets, too many carbohydrates
Eating when I am not hungry
Eating more when I am feeling anxious or sad
Eating without thinking about what I am eating
Feeling a compulsion to eat
Feeling I can't stop
Regretting what I have eaten
Eating larger portions
Not eating enough

Alcohol consumption: have you ever experienced any of the following? (Circle the items that are true for you)

Consuming more than five drinks in one day
Not able to recall events the night after you drink
Feeling an overwhelming need to drink
Driving while intoxicated
People close to you thinking you have a drinking problem
Drinking to reduce your anxiety

Smoking

Do you smoke? (cigarettes, cigars, pipe) How much?

Drug use

Which prescribed or recreational drugs do you use?
How often?
Do you ever take prescribed drugs in a manner not consistent with how they are intended?
Do you mix drugs with alcohol?

Exercise

How often do you exercise?
Which exercises do you do?
Does your doctor think you are unable to exercise?

Look back at your answers to these questions and ask yourself if your current health habits are causing you to have problems. Be honest with yourself. Don't normalize problematic behavior. We know that the period of unemployment is a high-risk time for health issues—and these problems can perpetuate bad habits that can become a lifetime risk. Given the fact that you have more time now to focus on helping yourself, I suggest that you make your health a very high priority.

I often say to my clients, "I want you to become obsessed with a healthy lifestyle." Perhaps it's too much to ask you to turn this into a "boot camp," but I think of this time between jobs as your time to take care of yourself.

EXERCISE: PAY ATTENTION TO YOUR HEALTH

Use the list below to remind you that now is an important time to care for your health:
- Unemployment is a high-risk time for health problems.
- You are likely to develop problematic habits of sleep, diet, exercise, and drug use.
- Take an honest inventory of your lifestyle choices and identify the areas where your health habits are less than optimal.
- Consider focusing on changing your habits now.
- If you are healthier, you are less likely to be depressed, and more likely to be effective.

2: Getting a good night's sleep

If you are anxious and worried, you may have difficulty with sleep. You may be lying in bed, tossing and turning, trying to get to sleep, or you may wake in the middle of the night or early morning and be unable to get back to sleep. Insomnia is a common problem for the unemployed, as it is for anyone who is anxious, and difficulty with sleep can make you more prone to anxiety, depression, irritability, overeating, and increased passivity and isolation. Look at the questionnaire below, which was developed by Dr Colin Espie of the Faculty of Medicine at the University of Glasgow.

EXERCISE: SLEEP PATTERNS

In the text below circle the appropriate number, depending upon how true you feel each of the following statements are for your typical sleep pattern (or write it in your notebook if you prefer).

	Never true	Seldom true	Sometimes True	Often true	Very often true
1. I can't get into a comfortable position in bed	1	2	3	4	5
2. My mind keeps turning things over	1	2	3	4	5
3. I can't get my sleep pattern into a proper routine	1	2	3	4	5
4. I get too worked up about not sleeping	1	2	3	4	5
5. I find it hard to physically 'let go' and relax my body	1	2	3	4	5
6. My thinking takes a long time to 'unwind'	1	2	3	4	5
7. I don't feel tired enough at bedtime	1	2	3	4	5
8. I try too hard to get to sleep	1	2	3	4	5
9. My body is full of tension	1	2	3	4	5
10. I am unable to empty my mind	1	2	3	4	5

11. I spend time reading/watching TV in bed when I should be sleeping	1	2	3	4	5
12. I worry that I won't cope tomorrow if I don't sleep well	1	2	3	4	5
13. I have got into bad sleeping habits	1	2	3	4	5
14. It's just because I am getting older	1	2	3	4	5

Source: Espie, C.A., Lindsay,W.R., Brooks, D.N., Hood, E.M., and Turvey,T., "A controlled comparative investigation of psychological treatments for chronic sleep-onset insomnia," Behavior Research and Therapy,1989;27:79–88

Now answer the following questions:
- Which one of the above statements is most relevant to you?
- Are there other factors associated with poor sleeping for you?
- If so, please describe them.

Slowing down a busy mind

The quality of your sleep can affect almost every aspect of your feeling of well-being. You may be having difficulty sleeping because you are worried about getting a job, worried about finances, or ruminating and dwelling on the negative experiences you have already had. Psychologists know that insomnia is primarily due to "excessive mental activity" — you are lying there in bed and your mind is at full speed, churning one thought after another. The good news is that there are useful techniques for getting control of your sleep.

Proper sleep depends on good "sleep hygiene"

You should keep in mind that your brain establishes daily patterns of activity of wakefulness and sleepiness. This is called "circadian rhythms," which reflect the daily cycle that makes you sleepy at a regular time. However, if you go to bed at different times, take frequent naps, or use stimulants, the circadian rhythms are thrown off. Moreover, not getting enough sunlight during the day will also interfere with circadian rhythms, since your brain activity is "woken up" when you get sunlight. An important component of proper "sleep hygiene" (or good sleep habits) is regularity of sleep onset and waking. One of the goals of this sleep-hygiene program is to increase the efficiency of your sleep. Efficiency means the amount of time that you spend in bed as related to the amount of sleep that you actually get.

Let's take a closer look.

Keep track of your sleep: Write down the time you go to bed, fall asleep, wake in the middle of the night, and finally wake up. What time do you get out of bed? By keeping track of your sleep, you will get a better estimate of how much sleep you are really getting and whether the program I am describing here will help you. Many people with insomnia underestimate how much time they actually sleep. You may find that your sleep patterns vary from day to day. That will be valuable information to see what might interfere with your sleep.

EXERCISE: KEEP A SLEEP LOG

Keep track of the time that you go to bed and fall asleep every day, using the chart below as a template. Place an "s" in each box when you are sleeping and a "w" in the box when you wake. (The table begins at 7.00 pm and ends at 11.00 am. If your sleep occurs at other times, keep track of those times). Also note the naps that you take during the day, since these will affect your sleep patterns. What is the total amount of sleep that you get on each day? Ideally, you should do this for the next eight weeks.

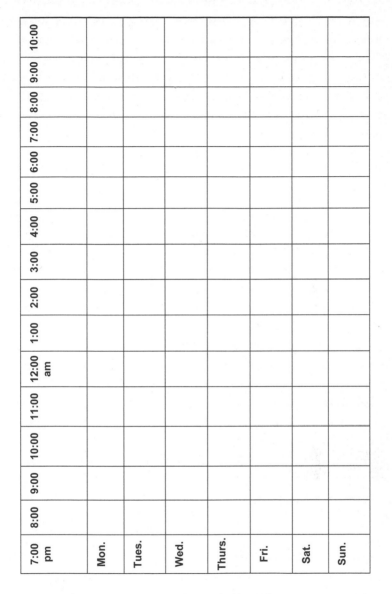

	7:00 pm	8:00	9:00	10:00	11:00	12:00 am	1:00	2:00	3:00	4:00	5:00	6:00	7:00	8:00	9:00	10:00
Mon.																
Tues.																
Wed.																
Thurs.																
Fri.																
Sat.																
Sun.																

Have regular times for going to bed and getting up: Many people have dysregulated sleep because they go to bed at irregular times. As we have seen, your circadian rhythms need to be regularized. I suggest that you try to go to bed at the same time—*if you are tired*—and wake at the same time each day. If you have to choose between regularizing going to bed and waking, choose waking. Let's say you want to start getting up at 7:00 a.m. If you are sleepy, go to bed at 11:00 pm. If you are not sleepy, go to bed later—but get up at 7:00 am. You might be tired the first day or two, but your brain will start sending messages to go to sleep at 11:00 pm. Avoid naps during the day, since they throw off the circadian rhythms.

Develop a wind-down time before bed: At least one hour before you go to bed, do something relaxing, or even boring. For example, you might take a warm bath before bed, listen to relaxing music (not agitating and irritating music), read something that is not too intellectually stimulating (I like to read history books because they tend to put me to sleep). Avoid using the computer, avoid intense emotional discussions, and avoid anything that is too emotionally provocative. You want to wind down.

Use the bed for sleep and sex—only: One of the problems for many people is that they associate the bed with a lot of mental activity. Don't use the bed for watching television, checking email, reading (other than a quick read before sleep), or talking on the phone. The bed needs to be a "signal" for sleep. It's OK to have sex in bed, since this will help to relax you. Your sleep environment should be relaxing. Is it too hot, too cold? Is there excessive noise? Try to remedy these problems if you can. Getting a relaxing night's sleep is essential. Your bed and environment should be comfortable.

Write down any worries or negative thoughts three hours before bedtime. Since much of insomnia is due to excessive mental activity, you need to get those thoughts out a long time before you go to bed. I suggest writing these down at least three hours before bedtime and then examining them using some of the techniques that we have discussed. You can use the form below to write down those thoughts and challenge them. Get this done hours before bedtime.

EXERCISE: CHALLENGE YOUR NEGATIVE THOUGHTS

Identify your negative thought and use the questions below to test or challenge it. Sometimes negative thoughts reflect certain distortions in thinking (mind-reading, fortune-telling, catastrophizing, labeling, all-or-nothing thinking, discounting your positives or over-generalizing). Which distortion are you using? You might also think about productive action that you can take. Problem solving is often a useful technique for dealing with negative thoughts. Not all thoughts have an answer and you might consider the advantage of accepting some uncertainty or some unfairness. Do you really need the answer right now?

Negative thought	
What thinking distortion am I using?	
How would I challenge this thought?	
Is there any productive action to take tomorrow?	
Can I accept some uncertainty or some difficulty—and still get on with life?	
What advice would I give a friend?	
Conclusion	

Eliminate food and drink before bedtime: Many people eat heavily before bedtime, or drink excessively. Any liquid may interfere with sleep since it may lead to urinary urgency during the middle of the night. Similarly, heavy or spicy foods interfere with sleep — as will alcohol. Try to eliminate these from your diet at least four hours before bedtime.

Get up if you are thinking too much: You don't want to lie in bed ruminating and worrying. If you are lying in bed for more than fifteen minutes with your mind racing with thoughts, get out of bed and go into another room. Sit quietly and do something boring. Don't do anything that requires a lot of mental activity. If your mental activity in bed was based on worry, use the form above for handling these thoughts. For example, identify your negative thought, the distortions you might be using, then challenge these thoughts, use problem solving, if that is relevant, and consider accepting either uncertainty or difficulty for now.

Practice healthy habits during the day: The quality of your sleep at night will depend on the healthy habits you practice during the day. This includes eating, drinking, smoking, and using drugs. Reduce caffeine intake, because this can stay in your system for many hours. Increase exercise during the day and get more sunlight. Sleep quality will reflect the quality of your daily life.

Give it time: You won't reverse insomnia overnight. It takes a while to practice new habits and to reprogram your brain's circadian rhythms. Sleep time is surrender time, so you might find that it will take a while to let go, abandon the active negative thoughts running through your mind, and slip into sleep. But it can be done.

If you follow this plan of sleep hygiene and reducing worry, you are likely to improve the efficiency of your sleep. It will take time. You are retraining your brain, stabilizing your circadian rhythms ,and developing new "associations" between your bed and sleep. The good news is that with proper sleep hygiene — and by challenging and dealing more effectively with your negative thoughts—you may find yourself more alert, less moody and more able to concentrate on important goals.

EXERCISE: ADDRESS YOUR SLEEP PROBLEMS

Use this list to recap on the importance of dealing with sleep problems if they arise.

- Sleep problems are common for unemployed people.
- Your sleep is affected by your worry, your sleep habits, and your increased mental activity.
- Keep track of your sleep: when you go to bed, when you fall asleep, if you wake during the night and when you finally wake. How many hours of sleep are you getting?
- Use the sleep hygiene program:

1. Have regular times for going to bed and getting up.
2. Develop a wind-down time before bed.
3. Use the bed for sleep and sex—only.
4. Write down any worries or negative thoughts three hours before bedtime.
5. Eliminate food and drink before bedtime.
6. Get up if you are thinking too much.
7. Practice healthy habits during the day.
8. Give it time.

3: Develop healthy eating habits

One of the great risks of this time between jobs is that you may be developing some harmful eating habits. We have already seen how a history of unemployment is associated with an increased risk of cardiovascular disease, high cholesterol and many other preventable health risks. This is a good time to focus on healthy eating and becoming mindful about what you put into yourself. It will require patience and attention, and will probably involve some frustration.

Sometimes you have to do what is hard now so that it can be easier, and better, in the future.

EXERCISE: YOUR FOOD INTAKE PATTERNS

Look at the questions below and answer each one honestly (remember you can write answers in your notebook if you prefer). It's important to recognize your eating patterns since they can affect your energy, attitude and overall health. When you are completing the questions, keep in mind that this can be a guide to what you might need to change.

Do you eat a balanced diet from the five food groups (grains/pasta/starchy vegetables, dairy, vegetables, fruit and meat (fish, meat and poultry)?

Yes _____ No _____
Which of the above food groups do you not eat enough of?

Do you eat at least five servings of fruits and vegetables each day (example: 3 fruits, 2 vegetables)?

Yes _____ No _____

Are half the grains you eat whole grains?

Yes _____ No _____

Do you eat a diet high in saturated fat (you eat mainly from fast-food restaurants, or you eat a lot of hamburgers, sausages, cold cuts, cheeses, biscuits, cakes, fried foods, butter)?

Yes _____ No _____

Do you drink soft drinks, fruit juices, sweetened foods, or cakes, pastries and other foods sweetened with sugar or other sweeteners'

Yes _____ No _____

Do you eat large portions (one serving of pasta is one handful; one serving of meat is the size of a deck of cards)?

Yes _____ No _____

Do you eat salty foods such as canned soups, processed foods and fast foods?

Yes _____ No _____

EXERCISE: YOUR HEALTH HISTORY

Put an X next to any of the following medical problems you have now or have had in the past (or write them in your notebook).

Problem	Past	Present
Diabetes: —type-1 —type-2		
High blood pressure		
Cardiovascular disease		
Stroke		
IBS (irritable bowel syndrome)		
IBD (inflammatory bowel disease or Crohn's)		
Lactose intolerance		
Bowel irregularities (chronic diarrhoea or constipation)		
Obesity		
Underweight		
Cancer – type:		
Osteoporosis		
Alcohol intake of more than two drinks per day		
Smoking		

Renal (kidney disease)		
Drug addiction (including marijuana)		
Swallowing problems		
For women only		
Are you:	**Yes**	**No**
Pregnant		
Lactating		
Perimenopausal (a few years prior to menopause)		
Menopausal (cessation of your period for over a year)		

Look at your responses to the medical questions and discuss your medical history and your needs with your doctor. It is important to get the proper medical attention during your period of unemployment—just as it is at any time. Since we know that unemployed people have both short-term and long-term risks for health problems you should be sure to see your doctor, practice the best health habits, take whatever medication is required and have regular checkups. You can use your period between jobs to get a better handle on your health—through diet, eliminating tobacco, increasing exercise, and practicing meditation and relaxation.

EXERCISE: THE EMOTIONAL TRIGGERS

The following problems can all result in erratic food intake (lack of balanced meals), inadequate food intake, loss of appetite or overeating. Tick—or write in your notebook—any that have had this effect on you.

Depression
Anxiety
Loneliness
Feeling emotionally empty

Anger
Feeling 'spaced out'

Now, look back at your answers to these questions. In terms of your current diet, is there a balance in your diet? Are your portion sizes too big? Are you eating high-fat, unhealthy foods? Is your eating related to your emotions? Each of these factors is important. While you are unemployed you will have a lot of opportunities to overeat, to eat while you are emotional, and to eat the worst kinds of junk foods. Because you have more time to act on your emotions, you may find that your eating has gone out of control.

Take control of your eating

There are three components to getting things back on track: balanced diet, heart-healthy diet, and portion control. With the proliferation of fast foods, mindless automatic eating, increased use of saturated fats, sugars and carbohydrates, and increased portion sizes, it is no wonder that a majority of adults are over-weight—and many, are significantly obese.

The basic dietary guidelines

Since we know unemployment is associated with an increased risk of cardiovascular disease, it is essential that you attend to your diet on a daily basis.

Balanced diet

Every day you should consume foods from the five food groups. These five groups include grains, which are the best source for energy; protein, which are the building blocks for cells; dairy, for strong bones; and fruits and vegetables, for disease prevention because of their antioxidants. There are many other reasons for consuming from each of these food groups, but these are the basics. In addition, everyone needs fat in order to cushion your organs and make hormones; however, it is the type of fat that is important. The best choice is monounsaturated fats. This type of fat is found in nuts, natural peanut butter, avocados, and olive oil. Just remember that fats have 9 calories per gram, so even if they are heart healthy, they are still caloric. In contrast, protein and carbohydrates have only 4 calories per gram.

Heart-healthy diet

The key to a heart-healthy diet is to consume a diet low in saturated fats. Foods high in saturated fats are ice cream, pastries, pies, biscuits, cakes, most cheese, many red meats, salami, ribs, sausages, the skin on chicken and turkey, fast foods that are fried (such as French fries, fried chicken, fried fish) and, of course, hamburgers/cheeseburgers. More healthful choices are roasted/grilled chicken (without the skin), or baked or grilled fish and turkey. When looking at a product label, check the saturated fat category. A low saturated fat product is 1 gram or less. We live in a real world, so it is hard to stick to 1 gram or less. It is acceptable to have up to 2.5 grams per serving if you are not a coronary risk.

Portion control

Portion sizes have grown substantially over the last thirty years. The size of the average serving plate thirty years ago was about 10 inches (25 cm) in diameter! Today, plate size is much larger. How many times do we go to restaurants and see on the menu a 10oz (280g) steak? What is the appropriate portion size? It's a lot smaller than almost any restaurant will serve. The appropriate portion of meat is 3oz (85g) — the size of a deck of cards. When you sit down and eat a piece of meat, ask yourself how much larger than a deck of cards is that piece of meat? If it is larger than a deck of cards, you are overeating the meat portion. One serving size of carbohydrate — such as pasta, rice, or potato — is the size of a fistful. In addition, your plate should be divided up with half your plate covered with vegetables, one-quarter of your plate meat/protein 3oz (85g), and a quarter of your plate carbohydrates.

In addition, try to limit your salt intake. You don't always need to add salt to your food, and you can choose to avoid foods that are high in sodium. If you eat out in restaurants or fast-food outlets, there is a good chance you are exceeding the recommended amount of salt in your diet. The best rule is not to add salt while cooking or at the table and, if possible, do not eat canned soups, processed foods, ready-meals, and fast foods. All these products are very high in salt and not healthy.

Unemployment and the reduced economic resources available can result in decreased nutrition. This compromised nutrition often results in malnutrition of various degrees, which can lead to lower productivity and effectiveness, reduced ability to concentrate and plan ahead, and prolonged unemployment.[21]

Eating and emotions

Your eating may be determined by your emotions. For example, you may binge eat if you are feeling anxious, angry, or emotionally empty. The binge gives you a rush of pleasure, temporarily distracts you from your emotions, and leaves you feeling a little spaced-out, as if nothing matters. You may also find yourself eating "mindlessly" — not paying attention to what you are doing. Sitting in front of the television or the computer, you shove junk food into your mouth. All of this leads to an unbalanced diet, weight gain, and eventual risk of high blood pressure, diabetes and cardiovascular disease.

Pay attention to your eating. One way of doing this is to keep a food diary. Keep track of what you eat, your emotions when you are eating, and what you are doing when you eat. Note the portion size, if possible. Simply monitoring your food and mood can help you to pay more attention and get more control. Also, plan ahead. We often tend to respond to how we feel and what is in front of us. You might be inclined to overeat, or eat the wrong foods if you simply respond to the food that is available — or the food listed on the menu. Therefore, plan ahead when you are not feeling emotional.

Make a commitment to stick with your balanced diet and your portion control. Eat more slowly, paying attention to each bite. Don't eat and do something else at the same time—this is called multiphasic eating, which results in overeating and eating the worst kind of food. Think beyond the way you feel. For example, you might be feeling anxious and empty, so you want that piece of cake. But the cake will only bring about five minutes of pleasure. You then will have consumed 500 calories you don't need—and you might regret that for the next day. Tolerating a little frustration while committing to a proper diet can help you gain control over your problematic eating.

Finally, there are some people who feel so depressed that they just don't eat very much. Malnutrition can result from a loss of appetite. Your malnutrition can then lead to lower energy, lower mood, lower activity—and more depression. I had a client once who just didn't eat very much at all—she said she didn't have an appetite. Despite my urging her to eat a regular diet, she refused. She eventually collapsed in a store and had to be taken to a hospital. This changed her mind and she began to eat a more balanced diet. Ask yourself if you are getting enough of the five food groups that I have outlined above. Are you eating enough to give you energy? Are you skipping meals, going for many hours without food? Planning ahead also means planning to eat.

EXERCISE: EAT HEALTHILY

Use the list below to remind yourself of the essentials of eating well:
- Unemployment is associated with poor eating habits, poor nutrition and weight gain.
- The long-term result of poor eating habits is an increased risk of high blood pressure, cholesterol, diabetes and cardiovascular disease.
- Follow the guidelines for proper eating: a balanced diet, a heart-healthy diet and portion control.
- Don't let your emotions dictate your eating.
- Plan ahead.
- Learn that tolerating a few minutes of frustration can keep you from gaining pounds of fat.

4: Get regular exercise

Research on depression shows that regular aerobic exercise is as effective as antidepressant medication for mild depression. Many people who are unemployed find themselves living a passive life of isolation, inactivity, and lethargy. The less you do, the less you want to do. But exercise may be one of the most important things you can do to take care of yourself. If you take regular exercise, you will lose weight, have more energy, improve your mood, help with your concentration and memory, and improve your cardiovascular system. Exercise activates your endorphins, which serve as an antidepressant chemical in your brain. It's like getting the benefit of Prozac without the downside.

You don't have to be an Olympic athlete to enjoy the benefits of exercise. Unless you are a regular and vigorous devotee of exercise, you can now start doing more than you did before.

What's your exercise level today?

Let's do an honest evaluation of your current exercise program:

- What is your typical exercise at the present time?
- Do you exercise daily?
- For how long?
- What exercise do you do?
- Do you have any health problems that might interfere with exercise?
- Have you had a physical examination recently?
- Does your doctor think that there are certain exercises that are not appropriate for you?

Before you try any new exercise program, you should consult with your doctor. If your doctor agrees that you can exercise, then you need to have a plan. But before you have a plan, we need to look at your motivation. I am sure that if you are not exercising on a regular basis, you have lots of reasons for not doing anything. I like to think of these as excuses, even if you call them "reasons."

First, what are the advantages and disadvantages of exercising? I'd like you to think carefully and clearly about this, since you are telling yourself a lot of things that might keep you from doing anything that is helpful. I have already described some advantages — weight loss, strength, energy, mood, cardiovascular health, endorphins. You might also feel better knowing that you are actually doing something. We know that doing something to help yourself usually helps you feel more effective. Doing nothing seldom helps.

Why you don't exercise sufficiently

You are sure to have lots of reasons not to exercise. Let's look at them:

- I'm so out of shape that nothing will help.
- I don't have the energy.
- It will be too painful and unpleasant.
- I feel embarrassed working out. People will laugh at me.
- I can't afford to join a gym.
- I don't want to exercise.

All of these are terrific reasons not to exercise. In fact, they have been "working" because you haven't been exercising. But all of them are false. All of them keep you from making progress.

Let's start with the first one:

"I am so out of shape": Well, isn't that exactly why you should be exercising more? Isn't that why it is useful? Exercise is "cumulative" — it builds up, accumulates its effects over time.

If you are very much out of shape, isn't it possible that if you exercised for a year, you might be in better shape? Is it possible that you could make progress — even if you are not perfect? Isn't it possible that you can keep things from getting worse?

You don't have to expect a miracle to make progress. If you are very overweight, even obese, some exercise on a regular basis can help you lose weight, feel more energized, have more strength, get more stamina and improve your mood. Yes, it's hard, but it's also hard to be out of shape.

"I don't have the energy": That sounds like a great excuse. That will certainly work well in keeping you from doing anything. But exercise generally will improve your energy level. Even if you are tired after you exercise, it's a "good tired" — you feel tired from doing something useful. In fact, it may even happen that you feel more energy after you exercise. Perhaps the energy comes after the behavior. Set up an experiment for the next two weeks. Rate your energy before and after exercise. What do you find?

You might say, "What if I have less energy after I exercise?" Why is that so important, so bad? Imagine that your energy level before exercise is 4 on a 10-point scale. After exercise, you find that your energy level is 2. OK, I imagine that is possible. Then what will happen? Will you have to be hospitalized because your energy level is lower? Or will you simply have to rest? Once you realize that energy comes and goes, that exercise can often increase your energy, and that even a decrease in energy — temporarily — may be a sign that you have achieved a lot of exercise, then you can set aside the "Energy Excuse" and get on with it.

"It will be too painful and unpleasant": That sounds like a very good reason to do nothing. But is it true? First, of course, I am assuming that you have checked with your doctor and that you have permission to exercise. Second, I am assuming you are starting slowly, if you haven't been exercising, and that you will build up gradually. There is no urgency to accelerate your exercise program. But assuming that you start slowly, why would a little more exercise result in pain? You certainly don't want to start exercising by pushing yourself too hard, lifting weights that might strain you, or raising your pulse rate too high for too long. But mild and/or moderate exercise need not do that. How about your thought that it is too unpleasant?

Set up an experiment. Start by doing a moderately paced walk for twenty minutes. Before you start, predict on a scale from 0 to 100 how unpleasant it will be (100 is equivalent to the most unpleasant experience you can imagine. For example, being burned over half your body would be 100). Then go out and do your brisk walk. How bad was it?

I doubt that it was as unpleasant as you thought it might be, but let's say it was moderately unpleasant. For how long was it unpleasant? Was there anything positive in doing a walk for twenty minutes? Why is it so bad to have to experience a little unpleasantness in doing your exercise? What will happen if you have to tolerate a little frustration? One way of thinking of unpleasantness is to use the concept of "constructive discomfort," which we discussed in Chapter Six. This means that some of your discomfort is used as a means to an end. It is useful. It helps you accomplish a goal. It's like thinking of discomfort as an investment.

"I feel embarrassed working out": Perhaps you think that you don't look as attractive as other people, or that you don't look as young and fit as the people who "usually" work out. Working out has become a fashion statement for some people. First, you can work out at home—in the privacy of your own living room. Some people find that turning on a television channel with an exercise routine—or a yoga class—is the easiest and most convenient thing to do. It's right there. Second, if you are concerned with what other people are thinking, which people are you talking about? Are you concerned that people might think less of you if they see you jogging along the street, or that you don't look so great in your exercise clothing? Well, what if they actually did think that? Are they thinking and talking about it all day long? Is word going to spread? Is your life really going to be affected?

I go to a health club several times a week, and I get onto the treadmill, turn on the television, or listen to my iPod—and I don't even notice other people. If I notice people, it's whether they might be using a weight-lifting machine I want to use. My goal is to exercise, not keep score of the people at the health club. But what if someone thought, "There's someone really out of shape! And they are exercising!" Why would that thought bother you, if you are out of shape you already know that? If they think there is something wrong with someone out of shape exercising, then — well — they are irrational. Why should you care about that? Keep in mind that the purpose of exercise is to take care of your health, not to gain the approval of strangers who, by the way, are not really thinking about you.

"I can't afford to join a gym": Why do you need a gym to exercise? Why can't you watch an exercise program on the television or internet or borrow a DVD and just do it at home? Why can't you go for a long walk — or even go jogging? Do you have a bicycle? Go for a ride (and wear a helmet). You can stretch, do sit-ups, run on the spot. You can get a football and go to the park. You can also check the websites of the parks departments of your town. There may be some facilities that are free. There are lots of free activities that are available, if you are willing to look into it.

"I don't want to exercise": That makes sense, especially if you think it will be unpleasant, painful, and a waste of time. But the real question should be, "Is exercise something that could be good for me?" and "Am I willing to do some things I don't want to do in order to improve myself?" In fact, almost every chapter in this book asks you to do things that you might not want to do — even things you are inclined to think are a waste of time. But, again, you do a lot of things you don't want to do. I'm willing to bet the behavior that helped you make progress in your life involved behavior that you didn't really want to do — behavior that might have been hard, unpleasant, and frustrating. Pride comes from overcoming obstacles.

Do it.

EXERCISE: BENEFITING FROM EXERCISE

Avoid becoming passive while you are between jobs by acting on the following points:

- Exercise is a great way to counteract poor health and the risk of depression.
- Your period of unemployment might lead you to become more passive—to exercise less. This will negatively affect your health.
- Do an honest evaluation of your current exercise program.
- In the past, when you did exercise, how did it affect your mood?
- What are the advantages—short term and long term—of exercising regularly?
- What are the excuses that you are telling yourself that keep you from exercising?
- How would you challenge these excuses?
- Try an experiment: exercise regularly for two months and evaluate how you feel.

SUMMARY

Because I realize the importance of a healthy lifestyle for people who are unemployed, I originally thought of making this chapter the first one in the book. I decided, however, to place it towards the end because a lot of the techniques that I discuss throughout the book are relevant to your health habits. These include the negative thoughts that you have: "It's too hard"; "I don't want to do it"; "It won't work"; or "I can do it some other time. "We have seen that your negative thoughts, passivity, helplessness and isolation contribute to feeling worse during this time between jobs.

Develop good habits You have a lot more time on your hands, and since this is a time when your health is at risk, it's essential to develop the best habits possible. In fact, if you develop bad habits now you are likely to continue them when you get back to work. The effects can haunt you. Poor health outcome is one of the major risks for the unemployed. **It's essential to get a handle on your drinking and smoking** If you are drinking more than 3 drinks a day if you are a man, or 2 drinks a day if you are a woman, you might have a drinking problem. Consider reducing or eliminating alcohol during this time. You don't need to abstain—unless your drinking is out of control—but keep in mind that there is no problem that drinking won't make worse. The same applies to smoking. This might be a good time to eliminate nicotine. And, it will save you money—and could save your life.

Nurture your body You might look at this time as a real opportunity to get into better physical shape and develop better health habits. I sometimes tell clients that I want them to become "Health Nuts" during this time, since aiming for the positive seems more productive than sinking into the negatives. Some clients have taken me up on this and really changed their habits; others have been less motivated.

It's not easy sticking with the best health habits, but you can think of this time between jobs as a time when the quality of your health has become a priority. You no longer have the excuses that you are working too hard and don't have the time to exercise. You don't have the excuse that you can't plan what you eat. You can. Making yourself a priority during this time can be the best change that you can make—it can actually be the one advantage of being unemployed: you have time to make yourself healthy. Here are some reminders:

- Make your health a priority.
- Get a good night's sleep.
- Develop healthy eating habits.
- Get regular exercise.

12

TAKING IT TO THE FUTURE

What if you decided to use everything you have learned in this book for the rest of your life? You've gone through lots of exercises, learned a lot of techniques, tried dozens of new ways of thinking, behaving, relating, and confronting the challenges in your life. It's been hard at times—perhaps it's still hard. But you have learned something. Why stop here?

I've been encouraging you to think about planning and taking a proactive and positive approach to this time between jobs, using as many techniques and strategies to empower yourself during one of the most difficult times in your life. I hope these ideas have been helpful to you. But aren't they good ideas at any time? Wouldn't this be a new way to approach living life every day?

In fact, when I have presented these ideas at talks I have given, or in speaking with journalists, or counseling patients, the response has been the same: "These are things that you should be doing for the rest of your life. This is good advice no matter what you are going through."

Right.

Keeping your head—a new way of life

You might look at this time between jobs as an opportunity to take your life back, to take control of your own destiny and make every day a day that you are empowered. In fact, it is a way of life. Perhaps the time between jobs was a wake-up call that you can think, behave, choose, and feel in different ways. Perhaps this has been a time when you had to overcome some of the most difficult obstacles you have had to face. We often can become stronger—and wiser—when we are challenged, when life makes it difficult for us. We can practice our power in life when our back is against the wall and there seems no way out. No way out—except *through* the difficulty, always moving forward. *You don't get past it unless you go through it.*

It may be that no one will ever really know or appreciate how difficult this time has been for you. But it also may be a time when you have surprised yourself with your ability to handle difficulties that you thought you would never have to face. This may have been a time when you were tested. And you learned. And you grew.

Using your new understanding as you move on

So how can you take this new-found knowledge forward? How can you use these ideas to make the rest of your life as good as it can be? Why stop now, why leave your training, your experience, and your growth behind you? Perhaps this time between jobs is a platform for propelling you to a better way of approaching all of the problems you will have to face. Perhaps this wasn't a setback, perhaps this was an opportunity. Perhaps this was a new beginning.

That will be up to you. It always is, by the way. You always have choices.

Richard is a case in point. I had known him a few years before, when he had gone through a break-up in a relationship. At that point, he was ruminating, dwelling on what it meant and why it had happened to him. He was isolating himself, depressed, self-critical, and indecisive. He had become passive and felt helpless and hopeless. But during that time—many years before—we worked on all of these self-limiting behaviors and thoughts, and he broke through it and overcame his depression. A few years later he found a new partner and married her; she was much better for him. They had two kids, and things seemed to be going well. Then he lost his job. He came back to see me for a "refresher" course of therapy. "Let's see if we can use all the ideas we used before to help you cope with this time between jobs," I said.

We used most of the ideas in this book. He did his homework and worked on himself every day. After a few months, he found a new job. The period between jobs was hard at times, but Richard took the "bait" of my challenge to use it as a time to grow, to take charge, to make every day better, to take action and to take his life back. Of course, there were many times when he worried about money, how he would take care of his family, and whether he would get a job again, but he got through it. He worked on his life when he wasn't working at his job.

As his friends and family watched him during this time, they recognized how hard he had been working, how much he stayed in his game. They said to him, "We've never seen you handle something as well as you handled this. It was amazing. You were the best you've ever been." In fact, his time between jobs brought him closer to his wife, strengthened his marriage, and made him realize how much he loved his kids. It also made him recognize that he wanted to get his values and priorities straight, and that what was most important to him were the relationships and commitments he had to people—and they to him.

Richard also realized that money was less important than he had thought. He knew time was valuable because you could use it wisely—like spending time with your kids and taking care of yourself—or you could waste it brooding, feeling self-critical, or complaining. He learned that he could lose his job but he would never lose himself, never lose his ability to make choices, and do the difficult things. "I learned that I was capable of doing things I never thought I would be able to do," he told me. Overcoming obstacles helped him overcome some things about himself. He was not defeated by the time between jobs. He learned that he had the power to make his life better.

Your future

So let's think now how to take this to your future. Perhaps you have a new job, so you think, "I'm glad that's over." That makes sense. You want to move on. But what will you take with you that you can use? How can this experience of living between jobs help you make a better life?

How can you keep your momentum, moving your life on the best course, keeping your mind on remembering everything that you have learned so far? You don't have to leave the time between jobs behind. You can take the lessons to the future.

Your right to your feelings

Let's start with your right to your feelings. In Chapter Two, I described how you have a right to feel sad, angry, anxious, confused—and even relieved. How can you validate your feelings in the future? You don't need to shove your feelings to the side, nor do you need to feel embarrassed about your feelings. Things may be better when you get a job—perhaps they are getting better now.

But there will be other experiences that will lead to quite a range of feelings: losses, disappointments, frustrations, and obstacles. No matter what you accomplish or how hard you work on things, you have a right to the way you feel. You will always be human, won't you? You will always have emotions, and always have needs.

The most useless and invalidating thing to say to someone is, "You shouldn't feel that way. Snap out of it." You feel what you feel. You are human. And you will continue to be human. But you may have learned from this book that, just as you can validate your feelings and be compassionate towards yourself when you are down, you also have the ability to think, choose, and act in ways that can change the way you feel. Your feelings are not your destiny. They are a marker of where you are at one moment in time. And the next moment is up to you.

You can take action

You've learned in Chapter Three that you can either remain passive and isolated, waiting for the world to change to suit you, or you can take action. There is always some way to improve the present moment. There is always something to do. As long as you are alive, you can set goals, choose to act differently, and test out your ideas by doing something. Life will not get better by waiting. During the time between jobs, you had a choice between doing nothing or doing something. Every day was a day when you could make choices. The same holds true for the rest of your life. When you take action, you change reality. And when reality changes, your thoughts and feelings may follow.

Don't wait for it to get better. Make it better.

You can continue to build your self-esteem

In Chapter Four we discussed how you can build your self-esteem by examining some of the negative, distorted thoughts that plague you. Using the techniques that you have been practicing, you can identify your negative thoughts, examine the kinds of distortions you are using (for example, discounting your positives, labeling yourself, and selectively focusing only on the negative), and give yourself credit for what you do.

You can ask yourself, "What advice would I give a friend?" You can think about putting yourself on your side, rather than putting yourself down. This has been very important for you during this time between jobs, but it will also be important for the rest of your life. The great thing about giving yourself credit is that you are always around to support yourself. You can always choose to be on your side. Carry that thought forward.

Leave rumination behind

You learned in Chapter Five that you can get stuck in your head, worrying about the future, ruminating and regretting the past. When you are spinning your wheels in your mind, you are not moving forward. You are going nowhere—and to make matters worse, you are miserable in the process. You've learned that just because you have a negative thought doesn't mean you have to spend the entire day and night brooding over it. You can treat repetitive negative thoughts as background noise that you hear with one ear but choose to ignore as you make choices about acting and relating in more productive ways.

During the time between jobs, you may have found yourself hijacked by the noise in your mind. If you used my ideas effectively, you have set your mind's noise aside, assigned worry time, considered whether brooding or worrying was going to be productive, and decided to focus on effective problem-solving and action, rather than digging a deeper hole with your thinking. And this is exactly the choice you will have in other areas of your life in the future. You can always ask what the productive options are, what actions make sense. And you can always learn to accept what you cannot control.

Avoid the victim trap

It's natural during the time between jobs to ask, "Why me?" In Chapter Six we saw how easy it is for any of us to get stuck in the victim trap. In fact, a lot of really unfair things happen in life—and unfair things will happen again. It's sometimes an unfair world, and some people may have bad luck at times— some more than others. But you have learned that you can spend a lot of time thinking of yourself as a victim, or you can spend less time. I am confident that no matter how hard you try to make things work in the future, something unfair and unpleasant will come your way. I wish it were otherwise. I wish the good guys finished first. But it's not set up that way. Dealing with unfairness will be a challenge for you in the future. Again, you have a choice as to whether you want to spend your time and energy fixing the blame, or commit to fixing the problem. The important piece of wisdom is to recognize that you have a choice.

Put money in its place

Money is important and it's nice to have. It's better than not having money. I know, I grew up poor; we were on welfare. I know what it is like to be hungry. That's why I pause before I eat, to give thanks, to realize that I am lucky, to know that it could be otherwise. But just as money is important, it's also important to put money in its place. In Chapter Seven we looked at how budgeting, planning, and being careful about money are almost always good ideas. But we also learned there are a lot of things that are free; wonderful things, human things; experiences and emotions that don't cost you anything.

Some people have told me that during their time between jobs, they learned there are people and experiences they need to pay closer attention to. In taking it forward, try remembering this every day—what is there in your life that is wonderful and free? I like to think that the fact I can walk, talk, think, laugh, cry, embrace, be embraced, love, listen to music, read, learn and grow—all are wonderful, all free. All mine. Take that thought forward. *Put money in its place and replace it with what is priceless.*

Seek support from your partner and family

In Chapter Eight we saw how unemployment can pull you apart or bring you together as a family. I recall when I got married, the minister commented that the ring symbolizes you are no longer one person, but two who complete each other. That can be the way both of you cope together with this time between jobs. But as we saw, you both have responsibilities: you, as the unemployed person, have the responsibility to make an earnest effort to look for a job, and your partner has a responsibility to support you when you are coping adaptively. Both of you need validation because it is likely that you will have feelings of anxiety, anger, confusion, and sadness. You are human, and this is a difficult time.

You will want to discuss the difficulties you face, but the style you use will make all the difference. Creating time and space for opening up, rephrasing what the other says, identifying the feelings behind the message, validating the point of view and the emotions that your partner has, and asking how you can help, are all part of effective communication and part of being a partner. It will be hard for both of you, and you may have tension. That's natural. If you use the ideas and techniques in this book to cope with that, you will have an opportunity to be better together during this time.

Live in the Now, not in the future

A comedian once said, "I live in the past. The rent was cheaper." That's the only reason to live in the past. You're not moving forward by looking into the rear-view mirror. In Chapter Nine, we saw how you can make your life better now, in the present moment, doing something that keeps you focused on today, where life is lived every day. During the time between jobs, it's natural that you would worry about the future, or dwell on what happened to you in the past. But every day is an opportunity to take charge of the present—and to let the future take care of itself. You can take this forward by treating every day as a new day, a new chance, a new plan. You can practice mindful breathing, focusing on your breath coming and going. Taking it in and letting it go. Even as you move forward and take it to the next stage in your life, you can remind yourself to stay in the Now of the present moment, notice what is around you and appreciate what is happening. You don't want to sleepwalk through life. What is happening now *is* life.

Help yourself through helping others

We are often so preoccupied with ourselves, but we were not meant to be alone. In Chapter Ten, I suggested you get outside yourself, connect with others, participate, network, take chances meeting people, reach out, use social networking, and volunteer. The more connections you have, the more potential sources of rewards are available. This has been especially important during your time between jobs, since losing your job may have led to a loss of personal connections that matter. But you can continue building your support network, even when you go back to work. You will always need friends, always need contacts, always need support. If you keep yourself connected and make people matter to you, you won't have to worry about being alone.

Care for yourself

Your health and your self-care habits are important—not only during the time between jobs but for every day of your life. In Chapter Eleven, I described how you can use this time to get into better physical—and, therefore, mental—shape, or you can allow things to fall apart. Exercising regularly, eating a heart-healthy, balanced, diet, and reducing or eliminating alcohol and tobacco are great ideas for your entire life. This is something I always emphasize for anyone between jobs, since the temptation to overeat, remain passive, and overdrink is so strong. But getting in shape is not the same thing as *staying* in shape. In taking it to the future, you can remind yourself that self-care is your responsibility. No one can do that except you. It's easy to let things fall apart and a lot harder to put them back together. In taking it to the future, you may want to remind yourself that feeling better depends on acting better. And exercise, diet, and health habits are part of that. But it's your actions that will determine this.

Pay it forward

I want to ask you to consider one more idea—one more way of taking it to the future. If you have used these ideas and helped yourself, then you are both wise and lucky. Lucky to be able to do it, wise to choose it. You've worked hard to help yourself. You've overcome your fear of discomfort, you've challenged and changed your thoughts, and you've acted in spite of the way you felt. You have taken the time between jobs to learn new things, practice new habits. That's good.

But what I would like you to think about is how you can help other people. No, I'm not suggesting that you become a therapist. But I am sure you may have friends and family who will have difficult times. Some of it may be related to their own experiences of being unemployed. Some of it may be due to setbacks, frustrations, or problems in their lives. There is always someone out there who is going to have a hard time.

There's a wonderful way of looking at paying it forward. If you have much, give your wealth; if you have little, give your heart.

You now have these techniques that you've used. You've helped yourself, you feel better. That's great.

Wouldn't it be great if you could *pass it on*? I've given you these skills, now it's your turn to give the skills to someone else. Help someone to help themself. Teach them what you have learned. You've made your world a better place, now make their world better.

Who was it that once said, "whoever saves a life, has saved an entire world"?

REFERENCES

1. Martikainen, P.T. and Valkonen, T. (1996), "Excess mortality of unemployed men and women during a period of rapidly increasing unemployment," Lancet, 348(9032), 909–12

2. Platt, S., "Unemployment and suicidal behavior: A review of the literature," Social Science & Medicine, 1984;19(2):93–115; Voss, M., Nylén, L. et al., "Unemployment and early cause-specific mortality: A study based on the Swedish Twin Registry," American Journal of Public Health 2004; 94(12):2155–61

3. R.B. Freeman and D.A. Wise (eds), The Youth Labor Market Problem: Its Nature, Causes and Consequences, Chicago: University of Chicago Press, 1982, pp. 349–390

4. Berth, H., Förster, P. and Brähler, E., "Unemployment, job insecurity and their consequences for health in a sample of young adults," Gesundheitswesen, 2003;65(10):555–60

5. Gregg, P., and Tominey, E., "The wage scar from male youth unemployment," Labour Economics, 2005;2(4):487–509

6. McKee-Ryan, F.M., Song, Z., Wanberg, C.R. and Kinicki, A.J., "Psychological and physical well-being during unemployment: A metaanalytic study," Journal of Applied Psychology, 2005;90(1):53–76

7. Mattiasson, I., Lindgarde, F., Nilsson, J.A., and Theorell, T., "Threat of unemployment and cardiovascular risk factors: Longitudinal study of quality of sleep and serum cholesterol concentrations in men threatened with redundancy," British Medical Journal, 1990;301:461–6

8. Peck, D.F., and Plant, M.A., "Unemployment and illegal drug use: Concordant evidence from a prospective study and national trends," British Medical Journal (Clinical Research Edition), 1986;93(6552):929–32

9. Pew Research Center (2009, November 24), "Recession brings many young people back to the nest: Home for the Holidays . . . and every other day," retrieved 10 October 2011,from http://pewsocialtrends.org/files/2010/10/home-for-the-holidays.pdf;

Morgan, P., "Farewell to the Family? Public Policy and Family Breakdown in Britain and the USA," Institute of Economic Affairs, London (1995); Vani K. Borooah, "Does unemployment make men less "marriage- able?" Applied Economics, 2002, 34:1571–82

10. Nolen-Hoeksema, S., "The role of rumination in depressive disorders and mixed anxiety/depressive symptoms," Journal of Abnormal Psychology, 2000;109:504–11

11. Papageorgiou, C., and Wells, A., "Metacognitive beliefs about rumination in major depression," Cognitive and Behavioral Practice, 2001;8:160–3

12. Jansen, J., "The civic and community engagement of religiously active Americans," retrieved 28 December, 2011, from http://www.pewinternet.org/~/media//Files/Reports/PIP_The _social_side_of_the_religious.pdf

13. Rasmussen Reports, "47% Pray Daily," Retrieved December 28, 2011 from http://legacy.rasmussenreports.com /2005/Prayer.htm 25 April 2005

14. Barling, J., Employment stress and family functioning, Wiley, Chichester (1990); Grant, S., Barling, J., "Linking unemployment experiences, depressive symptoms, and marital functioning: A mediational model" in Keita, G.P. (ed.), Hurrell, J. Jr (ed), Job Stress in a Changing Workforce: Investigating Gender, Diversity, and Family Issues, Washington: American Psychological Association (1994), pp. 311–27

15. Mattiasson, I., Lindgarde, F., Nilsson, J.A., and Theorell, T., "Threat of unemployment and cardiovascular risk factors: Longitudinal study of quality of sleep and serum cholesterol concentrations in men threatened with redundancy, British Medical Journal, 1990;301(6750):461–6

16. Strully, K.W., "Job loss and health in the U.S. Labor market," Demography, 2009;46(2):221–46

17. Roelfs, D.J., Shor, E., Davidson, K.W. and Schwartz, J.E., "Losing life and livelihood: A systematic review and meta-analysis of unemployment and all-cause mortality," Social Science and Medicine, 2011;72(6):840–54

18. Beland, F., Birch, S., and Stoddart, G., "Unemployment and health: Contextual-level influences on the production of health in populations," Social Science & Medicine, 2002;55:2033–52

19. Ray, D., Development Economics, Princeton: Princeton University Press (1998); Thomas, D., Frankenberg, E., et al., "Causal effect of health on labor market outcomes: Evidence from a random assignment iron supplementation intervention," Paper presented at the Population Association of America Annual Meetings, Boston, MA, April 2004

ABOUT THE AUTHOR

Robert L. Leahy (BA, MS, PhD, Yale University), Director of The American Institute for Cognitive Therapy (www.CognitiveTherapyNYC.com), completed a Postdoctoral Fellowship in the Department of Psychiatry, University of Pennsylvania Medical School under the direction of Dr. Aaron Beck, the founder of cognitive therapy. Dr. Leahy is the Past-President of the Association for Behavioral and Cognitive Therapies, Past-President of the International Association of Cognitive Psychotherapy, Past-President of the Academy of Cognitive Therapy, Director of the American Institute for Cognitive Therapy (NYC) and Clinical Professor of Psychology in Psychiatry at Weill-Cornell University Medical School. He is the Honorary Life-time President, New York City Cognitive Behavioral Therapy Association and a Distinguished Founding Fellow, Diplomate, of the Academy of Cognitive Therapy. He has received the Aaron T. Beck Award for outstanding contributions in cognitive therapy.

Dr. Leahy was Associate Editor of the *Journal of Cognitive Psychotherapy* (serving as Editor 1998–2003) and he is now Associate Editor of the *International Journal of Cognitive Therapy*. He serves on a number of scientific committees for international conferences on cognitive behavioral therapy and is a frequent keynote speaker and workshop leader at conferences and universities throughout the world.

Dr. Leahy is author and editor of 21 books, including *Treatment Plans and Interventions for Depression and Anxiety Disorders* (with Holland), *Overcoming Resistance in Cognitive Therapy*, *Bipolar Disorder: A Cognitive Therapy Approach* (with Newman, Beck, Reilly-Harrington, and Gyulai), *Cognitive Therapy Techniques*, *Roadblocks in Cognitive-Behavioral Therapy*, *Psychological Treatments of Bipolar Disorder* (ed. with Johnson), *Contemporary Cognitive Therapy*, *The Therapeutic Relationship in the Cognitive*

Behavioral Psychotherapies (ed. with Gilbert) and *The Worry Cure*, which received critical praise from the *New York Times* and has been selected by *Self* magazine as one of the top eight self-help books of all time. *The Worry Cure* has been translated into twelve languages and is a selection of the Book of the Month Club, Literary Guild and numerous other book clubs. Eleven of his clinical books have been book club selections. His two recent popular audience books are *Anxiety-Free: Unravel Your Fears before They Unravel You* and *Beat the Blues Before They Beat You: How to Overcome Depression*.

   Dr. Leahy's recent clinical books include *Emotion Regulation in Psychotherapy: A Practitioner's Guide* (with Tirch and Napolitano), *Treatment Plans and Interventions for Depression and Anxiety Disorders*, Second Edition (with Holland and McGinn), and *Treatment Plans and Interventions for Bulimia and Binge-Eating Disorder* (with Zweig). He is the general editor of a series of books to be published by Guilford Press: *Treatment Plans and Interventions for Evidence-Based Psychotherapy*. His books have been translated into 18 languages and are used throughout the world in training cognitive behavioral therapists.